D1823455

OXFORD STUDIES IN AFRICAN POLITICS AND INTERNATIONAL RELATIONS

General Editors

NIC CHEESEMAN AND
RICARDO SOARES DE OLIVEIRA

Oxford Studies in African Politics and International Relations is a series for scholars and students working on African politics and International Relations and related disciplines. Volumes concentrate on contemporary developments in African political science, political economy, and International Relations, such as electoral politics, democratization, decentralization, the political impact of natural resources, the dynamics and consequences of conflict, and the nature of the continent's engagement with the East and West. Comparative and mixed methods work is particularly encouraged. Case studies are welcomed but should demonstrate the broader theoretical and empirical implications of the study and its wider relevance to contemporary debates. The series focuses on sub-Saharan Africa, although proposals that explain how the region engages with North Africa and other parts of the world are of interest.

Rural Democracy

Elections and Development in Africa

ROBIN HARDING

OXFORD

UNIVERSITY PRESS

OXFORD
UNIVERSITY PRESS

Great Clarendon Street, Oxford, OX2 6DP,
United Kingdom

Oxford University Press is a department of the University of Oxford.
It furthers the University's objective of excellence in research, scholarship,
and education by publishing worldwide. Oxford is a registered trade mark of
Oxford University Press in the UK and in certain other countries

© Robin Harding 2020

The moral rights of the author have been asserted

First Edition published in 2020

Impression: 1

All rights reserved. No part of this publication may be reproduced, stored in
a retrieval system, or transmitted, in any form or by any means, without the
prior permission in writing of Oxford University Press, or as expressly permitted
by law, by licence or under terms agreed with the appropriate reprographics
rights organization. Enquiries concerning reproduction outside the scope of the
above should be sent to the Rights Department, Oxford University Press, at the
address above

You must not circulate this work in any other form
and you must impose this same condition on any acquirer

Published in the United States of America by Oxford University Press
198 Madison Avenue, New York, NY 10016, United States of America

British Library Cataloguing in Publication Data

Data available

Library of Congress Control Number: 2019947627

ISBN 978-0-19-885107-3

DOI: 10.1093/oso/9780198851073.001.0001

Printed and bound in Great Britain by
Clays Ltd, Elcograf S.p.A.

Links to third party websites are provided by Oxford in good faith and
for information only. Oxford disclaims any responsibility for the materials
contained in any third party website referenced in this work.

To Tiffany

Acknowledgments

Elections are a powerful thing, but they are not a panacea. Despite being a means to peacefully manage conflict, they remain inherently conflictual, creating winners and losers out of those with competing interests and ideals. In light of this recognition, this book is in part an attempt to understand who has benefited from democratic electoral competition in sub-Saharan Africa, and why. The extent to which it succeeds in this endeavor is a consequence of the efforts, assistance, and insights of countless people, of whom there are too many to note all individually. Any weaknesses remain entirely my responsibility.

The idea for this book germinated while I was a doctoral student at New York University, where I was fortunate to work with a dissertation committee of David Stasavage, Josh Tucker, and Leonard Wantchekon. David Stasavage's work was a particular inspiration, which led me to consider the nature of Africa's urban–rural divisions, and the political impact of urbanization, in new and important ways. From the first seeds of an idea for the dissertation project, and throughout the ensuing process that has led to this point, he has provided a consistent source of encouragement and sage advice. Likewise, Josh Tucker and Leonard Wantchekon have offered invaluable support and insights, through the ups and downs of graduate school, and through lengthy periods of fieldwork. As a committee they helped to shape me into the social scientist that I am today, and as such their influence runs like a watermark throughout this book.

Many others at NYU contributed to this work also, not least Alex Scacco and Oeindrila Dube, who very generously read my dissertation papers and provided detailed and insightful feedback. This helped to form and burnish the ideas and evidence that are presented in the book, as did the education, input and feedback I received from many members of the faculty at NYU, including Adam Przeworski, Kanchan Chandra, Shanker Satyanath, Neal Beck, Rebecca Morton, and Michael Laver, to name but a few. I feel incredibly lucky to have had the opportunity to study within such a wonderful community of scholars, and I hope this book does justice to that opportunity.

The community of scholars at NYU also extended to my colleagues on the PhD program, with so many of whom I discussed and refined the ideas and research that constitute the book. In particular, I am grateful to Liam von Thien, Mike Tiernay, Kristin Michelitch, and Simon Chauchard, and many others, for insights and support, and for their willingness to seek out and enjoy many wonderful and necessary distractions in New York City, which kept me sane. As a graduate student working on this project I also benefited hugely from the advice of Susan Stokes,

Macartan Humphreys, Brian Min, Kate Baldwin, Nahomi Ichino, and Kimuli Kasara.

Working on this project, both as a graduate student and subsequently, has involved substantial periods of fieldwork in Ghana, and later in Botswana. During this work I have been blessed by the kindness, generosity, and wisdom of so many people. On an early trip to Ghana, a shopkeeper in Accra noted to me that "the stranger has big eyes, but he does not always see." I carried this with me throughout the course of my fieldwork, testing my thoughts and ideas out on countless patient people to whom the context was more familiar. This book owes a great deal to all those who have helped me to "see."

In Ghana my research was made possible by the help and generosity of officials at the Electoral Commission of Ghana, not least Kwadwo Afari-Gyan, Sulley Amadu, and Hubert Akumiah, who supported my research in Accra. I am also greatly indebted to the many other officers at regional and district offices of the Electoral Commission throughout the country, who very generously assisted me in tracking down records of election results. Similarly, bureaucrats at numerous government ministries freely gave me their time, and helped me to access data. This was especially true of the Ministry of Roads and Highways, where John Acquah, Ako Nai-Kwade, Peter Dagadu, and Ernest Osei Bonsu all made huge contributions to the success of my research. I was also assisted greatly by De-Graft Afful and Frank Agbanator at the Department of Urban Roads, Sulemana Abubakari at the Ministry of Energy, and countless other officials at the Ministry of Roads and Highways, the Ministry of Energy, and the Ministry of Education. In addition, my work was aided by researchers at the Centre for Remote Sensing and Geographic Information Services, in particular Foster Mensah and Philip Mantey, and by invaluable conversations with academics at the University of Ghana, Legon, including Professor Felix Asante and Professor Emanuel Debrah.

Likewise in Botswana, the path of my fieldwork was smoothed by the kindness, generosity, and wisdom of numerous people. In particular, I am indebted to Basutli Ramontshonyana, Mary Kasule, and Professor David Sebudubudu at the University of Botswana, as well as the incredibly helpful staff at the National Archives and Records Services, and the Central Statistics Office. Throughout the course of my fieldwork to date, I have been immensely fortunate to have met many wonderful people, whose friendship and support helped to sustain me during long periods away from home. In particular, I owe a debt of thanks to Senam Gbeho, Mario Ariza, Jane Baldwin, Peter Gross, Jessica Gross, Sara Goldblatt, and Josanna Lewin, for all the laughter. I must also thank Emmanuel Gyimah-Boadi, for his wisdom and insights, and for his kindness when I was ill. And Sarah Weltman, for her good sense and friendship in Cotonou.

The process of developing my doctoral research into this book has not been short. Throughout that time I have had the enormous fortune of receiving excellent advice and input from numerous people while as a postdoctoral fellow at Nuffield

College, and during my subsequent appointments at the University of Rochester and the University of Oxford. This includes in particular Andy Harris, Daniel Stegmueller, Gretchen Helmke, Bonnie Meguid, G. Bingham Powell, Bethany Lacina, Adam Cohon, Avi Acharya, Nicolas van de Walle, Anne Pitcher, Ben Ansell, Elliott Green, and Joachim Wehner, among many others.

The research that informs this book has been facilitated by funding from a variety of sources, including a National Science Foundation Doctoral Dissertation Improvement Grant (Award Id: 1024363), a Robert Holmes Travel/Research Award for African Scholarship from NYU Africa House, a Henry M. MacCracken Doctoral Fellowship from NYU, and a Researcher Mobility Travel Grant from the University of Rochester.

Most importantly, this book exists because of my family. Without the support of my parents, Shāron and Alan Harding, I would not have pursued an academic career. They encouraged me to ask questions, and to do what I found interesting. In doing so they provided me with a rare freedom, and an excellent example for so many aspects of life. My brother Nick Harding, and sister Sophia Peiris, are anchors of love and support. My children, Maybelle, Thomas, and Rufus Harding, amaze and motivate me every single day. They provide perspective and purpose, and so much joy. And my wife, Tiffany Ko, makes everything possible. This book is dedicated to her. For her patience and understanding through the highs and lows, for her sensitivity and frankness, for her humor, and for all the ramen. I could not have done this without her.

Contents

List of Figures

List of Tables

1

Introduction

> No amount of glitter and prosperity in our urban centers should be
> regarded as national progress as long as the rural population continues
> to live the way it lives today.
>
> Seretse Khama, September 1974.[1]

Having seen his party's share of the vote fall by more than 12% in the previous election, Seretse Khama had learned the hard way. And while he had held on to power
in 1969, the first president of Botswana would not run the same risk again. Five
years on, almost 90% of Botswana's population still lived in the countryside, and in
such a context the political incentives created by electoral competition were clear.
They might have been clear in 1969 too, had Khama and his Botswana Democratic
Party (BDP) not still been riding the wave of independence. Nevertheless, in 1974
Khama knew what to do; if the BDP was to ensure electoral success, some of the
newfound glitter and prosperity of Botswana's towns needed to be seen in the
countryside.

Almost half a century later, more than 90% of African countries hold elections,
and the political systems of a majority of these countries are at least "partly
free."[2] At the same time, the average level of urbanization across the continent
remains around 40%, and almost three-quarters of African countries still have
rural majorities. Just as in Botswana in 1974, the political incentives generated
by democratic elections in these predominantly rural societies remain clear. The
implications of these incentives are the focus of this book.

Everywhere that they are held, elections make rulers nervous (Przeworski 2018).
Nervous that they will lose control of the process, or of the office, or that they will be
shut out of the system entirely. How rulers respond to this depends on a multitude
of factors, but wherever rulers are chosen by elections they must be able to point
to the support of some majority. Indeed, even where elections do not necessarily
determine the selection of rulers, the uncertainty created by the electoral process
means that rulers must pay some heed at least to the preferences of the voters.
Across sub-Saharan Africa, it remains the case that most people in most countries

---

[1] Botswana Daily News, September 20, 1974.
[2] The rating as "partly free" comes from Freedom House. For a useful summary of the status of
democracy in Africa see Cheeseman (2015).

Rural Democracy: Elections and Development in Africa. Robin Harding, Oxford University Press (2020).
© Robin Harding.
DOI: 10.1093/oso/9780198851073.001.0001

live in the countryside. The argument put forward in this book is that in such a demographic context, elections create incentives for rulers to court rural interests.

1.1 Elections and Rural Development in Africa

The story we hear about democracy in Africa is not a happy one. In both academic scholarship and the mainstream media, dismal tales of electoral fraud, corruption, and ethnic conflict abound.[3] This negativity is not unfounded, but the extent of it is misleading; the obsession with bad politics obscures the green shoots of democracy's promise in Africa. Wherever it is introduced, democratic accountability creates incentives for politicians to court voters by providing goods and services, whether this be through the implementation of programmatic policies or the delivery of pork. And Africa is no different. African rulers have sought to win electoral support, at least in part, through the provision of goods and services, from education and healthcare, through to water, electricity, and roads. This story therefore offers a very different answer to the question of how African rulers respond to electoral competition. Although the incidence of practices such as electoral fraud and corruption should not be discounted, nor their negative consequences underestimated, there is more to democracy in Africa than these negative tales imply. African governments are also responding to electoral competition by courting voters with goods and services. Acknowledging this is important, because it challenges the prevailing pessimism surrounding electoral politics in Africa.

But why should we care how rulers respond to electoral competition? It is widely acknowledged that making rulers accountable to the mass electorate induces them to distribute goods and services to a wider portion of the population in order to stay in office (Bueno de Mesquita et al. 2005). As a result, democracy has the potential to impact positively on development. However, although elections provide accountability structures that offer *opportunities* for development, the realization of these opportunities is not guaranteed. In particular, if elections are not used effectively to hold rulers accountable then the developmental benefits of democracy may be lost. Electoral practices that involve cheating, clientelism, and ethnic mobilization all reduce the extent to which rulers are held accountable through elections, albeit to varying degrees. Therefore it matters if rulers respond to elections by competing for votes through the provision of goods and services.

How they do so also matters, because it determines *who* benefits from democracy. Democracy provides arenas both for conflict and for representation, yet often too much emphasis is given to the former. Democratic rulers, to be rulers, must win elections. And whilst this process is inherently conflictual, it also induces

---

[3] For an excellent summary of scholarship on electoral politics in Africa, see Bleck & van de Walle (2018).

rulers to act in the interest of the public. But by its very nature democracy creates winners and losers, because only the interests of a winning majority need to be represented. This has important implications for how the benefits of democracy are distributed. In democracies everywhere, contextual factors shape electoral incentives, leading politicians to target particular *types* or *groups* of voters. Although it has not received much attention up to now, one particular contextual feature that prevails across much of Africa is the low level of urbanization. Stark variations in living conditions across urban and rural areas create constituencies with very different interests and concerns, which are likely to respond to public policies in very different ways. Large rural majorities in most African countries therefore create electoral incentives for African rulers to implement pro-rural policies, and as a result the benefits of democratic electoral competition have accrued primarily in terms of rural development.

In authoritarian regimes the more credible threat of opposition and unrest from urban areas can give rise to an urban bias in policy-making, even where the population is predominantly rural (Lipton 1977; Bates 1981). Rural areas struggle more with problems of illiteracy, communication, and coordination, creating greater obstacles to collective action than are faced in urban centers. These undermine the ability of citizens in rural areas to influence politics in systems where the primary threats to authoritarian governments come from protests, pressure, and ultimately coups. With the advent of competitive elections, however, the equalization of individual political power across urban and rural areas vastly reduces the disproportionate influence of urbanites in countries with rural majorities. Where government survival is determined at the ballot box, collective action is rendered less important, and rural voices become more audible. As governments have sought the support of an electoral majority, the greater power of what in most African countries tends to be a fairly small urban minority has diminished.

This is not to say that urbanites have suffered as a result of electoral competition, nor that they have been left powerless. But in the presence of a large rural majority, where elections can be won in the countryside rulers can pay less heed to urban demands. The consequence of this shift in incentives is that in countries with rural majorities, the introduction of elections should be more beneficial to rural than to urban interests. Of course, as the size of the rural majority decreases, so too will the extent of any such pro-rural impact resulting from elections. As the urban population increases, the feasibility of winning solely in the countryside will decrease, and the potential threat of urban unrest will rise, forcing incumbents to pay more attention to urban voters. Therefore while elections in predominantly rural countries should incentivize pro-rural policies, the degree of any such rural bias should reduce as the urban proportion of the population increases.

To reiterate, the argument here is not that African rulers have solely responded to electoral competition by courting rural as opposed to urban interests, nor even that this has necessarily been their primary response. More likely is that they have pursued mixed electoral strategies, and that voter choice as a result is influenced by a variety of factors. Strategies of clientelism, both individualized and at the group level, may be used to mobilize particular voters. At the same time, and in part as a result, parties may be able to rely to varying extents on the support of ethnically- or regionally-based constituencies. And undoubtedly, just as they do everywhere, politicians across Africa seek to manipulate elections to their own advantage. The claim herein is not that these strategies don't occur, but that they have been accompanied by efforts to court the votes of the rural majority, through policies designed primarily to benefit rural interests.

1.1.1 Development

What are these rural interests? Agriculture provides one obvious answer to this question, and it is no doubt important for many in rural areas, as a source of food, employment, and income. As a result of this, agricultural policy has been the primary focus of scholarly work on urban–rural dynamics in policy-making, in Africa and beyond.[4] But agricultural issues do not constitute the sum total of rural concerns. One of the important ways that this book builds on the existing literature is to broaden the focus beyond agriculture and consider other aspects of public policy that may impact upon rural interests. This is not to deny the importance of agricultural policy but simply to acknowledge that it is not the *only* thing that Africa's rural residents care about.

Nor is agriculture the *primary* concern of citizens in rural Africa. Of more than 28,000 rural respondents surveyed across thirty-one countries in sub-Saharan Africa in 2014–15, only 21% cited farming, agriculture, or agricultural marketing as being among the top three most important problems facing their country.[5] Beyond and even above agricultural policy, Africa's rural residents care about basic services, infrastructure, and jobs. In the same surveys from 2014–15, each of health, education, water supply, infrastructure and roads, and unemployment were highlighted as important problems by more rural residents than were agricultural issues. This reflects the state of development in Africa's countryside, which still lags far behind the rest of the world. It also reflects the fact that most of the people living in Africa's rural areas are not directly engaged in commercial agriculture.

Agricultural policy is an important tool that governments in Africa and elsewhere have frequently used to differentially benefit urban and rural constituencies. But it is neither the totality nor the pinnacle of rural interests. As Rubinoff notes with reference to Varshney's (1995) otherwise excellent study of democracy and

---

[4] See Lipton 1977, Bates 1981, Varshney 1995, and Bates and Block 2013.
[5] Data from http://www.afrobarometer.org.

rural development in India, the focus on agricultural issues pays insufficient attention to "the reality that a majority of India's villages have no clean drinking water, paved roads, or electricity" (Rubinoff 1997, 246). In contexts where access to basic services and infrastructure is so limited, extending and improving their provision is central to rural interests. For Africa's rural population, this is primarily what development means.

1.1.2 Democracy and elections

Questions about the consequences of democracy invariably raise definitional debates, leading to much wrangling over what does and doesn't constitute "the D-word." Such wrangling over definitions and concepts is valuable for refining the study of democracy (Collier and Levitsky 2009), and although this is not the central task at hand, it is important to acknowledge the essentially contested conceptual status of democracy. By focusing on elections the approach taken in this book, and following Przeworski (1999, 2018), is in essence a minimalist one. The intention here is not to argue that democracy is only about elections, nor that all elections are "democratic." But what this approach does do is acknowledge the central place that selection by competitive elections plays in all approaches to democracy, in the literature since the third wave of democratization at least.

What does it mean for elections to be competitive? Again following Przeworski (2018: 6), elections are competitive "if *ex ante* their results are uncertain, not when the margin of victory turned out to be small *ex post*." What matters is that the results are not pre-determined, rather than that they are close. Not all competitive elections are the same though, and the extent to which incumbents seek to use the tools of office to influence the outcome in their favor will vary, and with it the "quality" of democracy varies also.[6] Even where this quality is low, however, elections still generate incentives for incumbents to consider voters' preferences when making policy. But as is discussed further in Chapter 4, the extent to which elections create incentives for rulers to pursue more demanding electoral strategies likely diminishes below some level of quality. If a strategy of pro-rural development is relatively costly or difficult to implement, an incumbent who is prepared to rig or coerce their way to victory, and who is unconstrained in doing so, may instead choose manipulation as the path to victory.

Since by this conception the quality of elections is a function of both structure and agency, identifying it *ex ante* is not easy. In an effort to accommodate this,

---

[6] It is also worth noting that the certainty of electoral outcomes can vary even within a country, across presidential and legislative elections. As a result, even in competitive-authoritarian regimes where the presidency may be largely sewn up, the need to win seats to maintain a legislative majority may still create strong incentives to capture the rural vote.

the analysis of the impact of democratic electoral competition in Chapter 4 operationalizes the key explanatory variable in multiple ways. Theoretically though, the argument in this book focuses on the impact of competitive elections, as represented by a meaningful contestation for office, the outcome of which is not entirely pre-determined. The central theoretical claim is therefore that in countries with rural majorities, competitive elections create incentives for rulers to court rural votes via the implementation of pro-rural policies.

1.1.3 Alternative electoral strategies

Of course, this is not the only way that African rulers respond to electoral incentives; instead they choose from a range of alternatives, the first of which is to cheat. Electoral fraud and manipulation have been rife, and widely publicized, and as a result there is substantial variation in the competitiveness of African elections (Cheeseman and Klaas 2018). In extreme cases severe instances of electoral fraud can entirely pre-determine electoral outcomes, but rulers select from a wide menu of electoral manipulation, many items from which can coexist with varying degrees of electoral competitiveness. These can include, but are certainly not limited to, restrictions on who can register as candidates or voters, interference in campaign activities, a vast array of nefarious actions designed to prevent citizens casting their ballots, and efforts to falsify or otherwise influence the vote count (Schedler 2002).

A second possible response to electoral incentives has been to adopt or adapt strategies of clientelism, whereby the distribution of resources is made contingent on the provision of electoral support, such that votes are essentially bought. As with electoral fraud, clientelism is widely acknowledged to be a key aspect of electoral politics across Africa. And also akin to fraud, clientelism can take a wide variety of forms, from individualized vote buying transactions (Vicente 2014), to the contingent delivery of local development goods (Wantchekon 2003), and the use of state offices to provide resources to elite political clienteles (van de Walle 2003).

Thirdly, rulers in Africa have frequently relied upon, and sought to mobilize, the support of ethnic constituencies. The nature and extent of ethnically-based political competition have been much discussed,[7] and there is strong evidence to suggest that ethnicity very often plays a key role in African elections. Indeed, the same may be said for clientelism and fraud, both of which are viable and commonly-used electoral strategies. Again, my argument is not that these strategies are not used but rather that they are not the *only* strategies that are used. Instead, rulers have also sought to win the votes of the rural majority through policies designed to appeal primarily to rural interests.

---

[7] For examples see van de Walle (2003) and Posner (2005).

The incentives generated by meaningful electoral competition have led rulers across Africa to pursue mixed strategies, involving some combination of these approaches. My purpose in this book is to develop and investigate an argument about how one particular and understudied approach, the use of public policies to court the votes of a particular majority, might operate. Nevertheless, understanding how and why any particular mix of these strategies is chosen, how they interact, and when the different responses are given priority, are key questions that should demand the attention of future work. This work might consider, for example, that the extent of electoral fraud is likely to be a function of whether it is possible, whether it gets noticed, and the cost if it does. These three factors are themselves likely to be affected by, among other things, the independence and strength of the electoral commission, the presence and independence of election monitors, and the extent of domestic and international pressure, respectively. It may be reasonable to expect that rulers will cheat as much as they can get away with, or as much as is worth the cost. But it is also important to acknowledge that cheating is not always easy, and very rarely will it be costless. Therefore even when the level of cheating is high we should expect rulers to also seek votes through other means.

With regard to clientelism, the choice to engage in such strategies is likely to be at least in part a function of the types of resources being distributed; for some resources it is much harder to effectively exclude people from the benefits (this is certainly true, for example, of free schooling and healthcare). For others contingency may not be possible, because benefits cannot be taken away if support is withdrawn. This is likely to be true with regard to the extension of connectivity to water or electricity networks, for example, although network maintenance may be stopped, or supplies limited. Problems of monitoring can also render clientelistic strategies difficult to implement effectively, so the extent of clientelism may also depend in part on factors that overcome these problems, such as extensive party organizations, or influential traditional leaders (Koter 2016). Again then, even when clientelism occurs, we might also expect rulers to attempt to win votes through public policy choices.

Existing work on ethnic politics in Africa has highlighted how the salience of particular cleavages can depend on the nature of political institutions in place (Posner 2004, 2005). Nevertheless, within any given institutional framework the structure of ethnic cleavages places constraints on the nature of ethnic mobilization. The number and relative size of ethnic groups that have the potential to be politically relevant might alter rulers' incentives to pursue strategies of ethnic mobilization, as may the ethnic identities of rulers themselves. It is also useful to note that these various strategies are at the same time complements and substitutes. For example, while there are compelling reasons to think that ethnically-based competition can support strategies of political clientelism, other social structures (such as traditional authority) can potentially play a similar role, such that the two are not co-dependent (Koter 2016; Chandra 2004). In addition, the successful mobilization of co-ethnics often requires leaders to deliver, at the very least in terms of patronage or public services.

Understanding when and why rulers select any particular mix of electoral strategies is evidently an area that is ripe for further exploration. It is also one that is clearly beyond the scope of this book. Instead, what this book does do is highlight that fraud, clientelism, and ethnic mobilization are not the only available strategies. In addition, rulers across Africa can and do seek to win votes through the implementation of policies designed to appeal to particular interests. Specifically, they have sought to win the votes of the rural majority via the implementation of pro-rural policies.

1.2 Evaluating the Argument

The theoretical argument summarized above is developed more fully in Chapter 2. This argument is motivated by an empirical puzzle: despite the widespread acceptance that party competition in Africa is dominated by issues of ethnicity and clientelism, not by an urban–rural cleavage, urban residents across Africa are significantly less likely to support incumbents than their rural counterparts. This stark urban–rural electoral cleavage can be best explained by the argument that, given the urban–rural distribution of African populations, competitive elections tend to make African governments more responsive to rural interests. By acting on the electoral incentives to implement pro-rural policies, incumbents' policy choices generate dissatisfaction among urban voters. This argument implies a conditional effect whereby these electoral incentives should dissipate as the size of the rural majority decreases. As a consequence, the extent of urban–rural differences in development outcomes resulting from the introduction of competitive elections should be conditional on levels of urbanization, as should the degree of urban incumbent dissatisfaction. Finally, it is important to note that the argument rests on the assumption that voters in Africa condition their votes on the provision of public goods and services, at least in part. This assumption is crucial, because if it does not hold then there would be no reason to think that politicians should implement pro-rural policies in order to win rural votes.

The remainder of the book is devoted to evaluating this argument, and the strategy for doing so is threefold. First the central claim—that electoral competition in Africa has led to pro-rural development—is directly tested with cross-national analyses of public opinion data, and of objective individual level indicators of essential education and health outcomes. As well as enabling investigation of various indicators of pro-rural development, this also permits evaluation of the implied conditional effect, whereby the extent of urban–rural differences in development resulting from electoral competition should vary across countries according to levels of urbanization.

Leveraging data from twenty-eight countries across Africa, over multiple rounds of the Afrobarometer Survey Series, the analysis in Chapter 3 shows that support for incumbents is significantly higher amongst rural residents than it is among urbanites. The same is true, and to an even greater extent, for levels of satisfaction with democracy. Moreover, and crucially for the argument to hand, the extent of these urban–rural differences is conditional on urbanization. The extent to which rural residents are more likely than urbanites to support incumbents and express satisfaction with democracy is greater in countries with large rural majorities, and decreases with urbanization. These findings are important because the expectation that urban incumbent hostility should be conditional on urbanization is a unique observable implication of my argument. Although scholars have put forward a variety of reasons for why urbanites across Africa should be less likely than rural residents to support incumbents, none of these alternative explanations account for the observed conditional effects. As such, this evidence supports the theoretical claim that electoral competition leads African governments to pursue pro-rural development policies.

These attitudinal indicators offer powerful but indirect support for the claim that electoral competition has led African rulers to pursue pro-rural development policies. To bolster this, therefore, analyses of essential health and education outcomes across twenty-seven African countries provide further and more direct evidence of the link between elections and development outcomes. Through careful and rigorous investigation of individual level data on infant survival and primary schooling from the Demographic and Health Survey series, Chapter 4 presents evidence that the introduction of electoral competition significantly increases the probabilities that children in rural areas across Africa survive past the age of one, and that they ever go to school. At the same time, the introduction of electoral competition has no such effects for children in urban areas. Importantly, the extent of these urban–rural differences is again conditional on urbanization; the observed urban–rural difference in the effect of democratic elections on education and health outcomes decreases with urbanization. Taken together, the results from these cross-national analyses provide clear evidence of an emphasis on rural development resulting from the introduction of electoral competition across Africa.

While Chapters 3 and 4 provide strong empirical support for the book's central argument, Chapter 5 reinforces this by evaluating the core underlying assumption that voters in Africa engage in evaluative voting and condition their support on the provision of public goods and services. This assumption is crucial, because if it does not hold then there would be no reason to think that politicians should implement pro-rural policies in order to win rural votes. Moreover, it is not obvious that this assumption does hold, because existing work on the determinants of voter choice in African elections has tended to focus predominantly on issues of clientelism and ethnic voting.

The second stage of the empirical strategy is therefore to investigate whether voters in Africa use elections to hold governments accountable for their performance in office. In order to do so, the focus is narrowed to a single country— Ghana. This approach accounts for important contextual variations in how goods are provided, which influence the extent to which responsibility for this provision can be attributed to political action. The analysis in Chapter 5 uses data on two types of goods to evaluate whether Ghanaian voters are evaluative. Looking first at education, the investigation focuses on a range of inputs at the district level. Usefully, analysis of this data supports the idea that voters are more likely to condition their support on the provision of goods and services which can be attributed to political action than on those which cannot. However, since aggregation to the district level imposes limitations to inference, the focus then turns to roads. Analysis of an original panel dataset that combines actual electoral outcomes at the polling station level with precise, localized information on changes to road conditions throughout Ghana provides even more robust evidence that electoral support is affected by the provision of public goods.

The final stage of the book's empirical strategy is to dig deeper into the proposed theoretical mechanism by considering the historical case of Botswana in the decade immediately following independence. In doing so, it considers a potential counter to the central theoretical argument; it is possible that rather than resulting from electoral incentives, any urban–rural differences in development may be due instead to contemporaneous external forces, such as conditionalities in donor aid. For example, if foreign donors pushed African rulers into introducing both competitive elections and pro-rural policies, then the link between electoral competition and pro-rural development may be spurious. Chapter 6 addresses this possibility through an analysis of development in Botswana during the immediate post-independence period. This case is useful because, unusually in sub-Saharan Africa, Botswana has held competitive elections consistently since gaining independence from colonial rule in 1966. This makes it possible to explore the existence of a link between electoral competition and pro-rural development during a period when the international context was very different, and when no such external pressures to introduce competitive elections and rural development policies were likely to have been felt.

In contrast to the other empirical chapters, Chapter 6 makes use of qualitative evidence. Using archival resources such as minutes from government meetings, ministerial correspondence, and election manifestos, the ruling Botswana Democratic Party's (BDP) policy responses to electoral outcomes are traced through the early post-independence period. Despite its dominant position, the BDP responded strongly to losses of rural support with a major program of rural development policies. Interestingly, archival materials document an explicit policy of prioritizing rural development projects that were both highly visible and likely to be completed prior to the next election, suggesting a strong role for electoral incentives. Similarly, analysis of the ruling party's election manifestos highlight rhetorical changes in policy emphasis during this period. Taken together, the evidence from this historical case supports and illuminates the proposed theoretical mechanism, suggesting that electoral competition does indeed lead to rural development in Africa.

1.3 Looking Forward

This book is about elections and development in rural Africa. All of these things are dynamic, varied, and contextual. The nature and quality of elections differs widely from country to country, and within countries over time. Likewise, the demands of development fluctuate—voters have different needs and preferences, within countries and localities—such that, as is said in Ghana, "one man's meat is another man's poison." And "rural Africa" is neither static nor uniform. Urbanization is a process, by all accounts a rapid one in Africa. Bearing this in mind, the book concludes by attempting to situate the argument and findings in the context of a diverse and an ever-changing Africa. In a continent that has been experiencing historically unprecedented rates of urbanization, how should we expect political incentives, and subsequent policies, to evolve? How might pro-rural development affect the nature of urban–rural relations across Africa? How in turn might this influence the nature of electoral competition? And finally, how much reason do we have to be optimistic about democracy in Africa?

Taken together, the evidence provides a full and thorough evaluation of the central theoretical argument, in terms of its key empirical predictions, and of the core assumption and theoretical mechanism underpinning it. This means that there is some reason for optimism amongst the gloom; this book offers an important counterpoint to the scholarship on electoral politics in Africa which has focused predominantly on issues of fraud, clientelism, and ethnicity. While these things matter, they do not tell the whole story. The incentives created by democratic electoral competition have resulted in significant rural development across the continent, leading to real improvements in essential development outcomes such as infant mortality rates and access to primary education. This has happened because African governments are responding to the accountability structures imposed by electoral competition; in this sense at least, democracy in Africa is working.

2

Elections and Rural Development

2.1 Introduction

The argument about Africa's rural democracies is motivated by a puzzle: urbanites across Africa are significantly less likely to support incumbent governments than rural voters are. At first sight this may not seem all that puzzling to some; perhaps it simply reflects competition between urban and rural parties, with the latter achieving greater success. Yet it is widely accepted that African political parties mobilize ethnic or regional constituencies, not urban or rural ones. So why then should we see such a clear urban–rural cleavage in support for incumbents across Africa? This question is important because the urban–rual distinction is widespread; systematic evidence presented in this chapter shows a significant rural bias in incumbent support across the vast majority of countries for which relevant data is available.[1] Moreover, the evidence highlights substantial variation in the extent of this rural incumbent bias across countries.

Although seemingly puzzling, the urban–rural cleavage in support for incumbents can actually be seen as a fairly intuitive consequence of the electoral incentives created by the interaction between democracy and demography. Most simply stated, competitive elections make African governments more responsive to the demands of rural interests. In most African countries a majority of the population lives in rural areas, and as a result of this democracy creates political incentives for governments to court rural votes by implementing policies designed to benefit rural interests. While such policies are likely to appeal to rural voters, to the extent that they prioritize rural development over and above the interests of the urban minority, they are likely to generate dissatisfaction on the part of urbanites.

Of course, political behavior is always best understood as multi-causal, and it is likely that numerous factors explain the differences between urban and rural voters. Other possible explanations of urban–rural differences in incumbent support follow from the acknowledgment of socio-demographic differences between urban and rural residents, and of how differences between urban and rural contexts affect political competition and mobilization. While these alternative and complementary explanations have merit, they fail to adequately account for the observed variation in rural incumbent bias across countries. Usefully, a unique

---

[1] I use the terms *urban incumbent hostility* and *rural incumbent bias* interchangeably to refer to the lesser propensity of urban residents to support incumbents.

Rural Democracy: Elections and Development in Africa. Robin Harding, Oxford University Press (2020).
© Robin Harding.
DOI: 10.1093/oso/9780198851073.001.0001

implication of the argument offered herein is that the degree of urban incumbent hostility should reduce as the urban proportion of a country's population increases. This implication makes it observably distinct from alternative explanations, thereby enabling evaluation of the value added by this account. In Chapter 3 I undertake one such evaluation by investigating the relationship between urban incumbent hostility and the urban–rural distribution of the population across African countries. The primary purpose of the present chapter is to explain how an urban–rural cleavage in incumbent support results from the introduction of electoral incentives for African governments to pursue pro-rural policies.

2.2 Urban–Rural Cleavages in Incumbent Support

Before developing the explanation, however, it is worth establishing the puzzle more concretely, and highlighting the insufficiency of alternative explanations. In this section I present data from twenty-eight African countries to illustrate the extent of urban incumbent hostility across the continent. I then highlight why this phenomenon is so puzzling, before discussing possible explanations which focus on various socio-demographic and structural factors. As will be seen, although not without value, these cannot fully account for the cross-national variation in levels of urban incumbent hostility, thereby motivating the search for an alternative explanation.

2.2.1 Evidence for urban–rural cleavages

Across sub-Saharan Africa, urban residents are less likely to support incumbents than are their rural counterparts. Data on incumbent support from public opinion surveys carried out in twenty-eight countries between 2005 and 2015 show a stark divide between urbanites and rural residents.[2] In each of four separate survey rounds a significantly higher proportion of respondents in rural areas said that they would vote for the incumbent if an election were held the following day than did those in urban areas.[3] Averaged across all survey rounds, the proportion of

---

[2] The data come from the four most recent rounds of the Afrobarometer Survey Series, which undertakes standardized, nationally-representative public opinion polls across Africa. Data from Round 7 was not available at the time of writing. The surveys were carried out using face-to-face interviews in the language of the respondent's choice. The samples are representative of the voting-age population in each nation. Random selection is used at every stage of the sampling and the sample is stratified to ensure coverage of all major demographic segments. Data is available at http://www.afrobarometer.org.

[3] Incumbent support is operationalized as expressing an intention to vote for the incumbent party "if elections were held tomorrow." Across the four survey rounds the differences between the proportion of rural residents and urbanites expressing support for incumbents ranges from 5–10%, and is statistically significant at the 99% level in all rounds.

rural respondents expressing support for incumbents was almost 8% higher than that of urbanites. Regression analysis in Chapter 3 demonstrates that the greater propensity for rural residents to support incumbents holds at the individual level even when a host of potentially confounding factors are taken into account. But the data described here provides clear prima facie evidence of a rural–urban divide in incumbent support across Africa.

If it were simply the case that parties compete on urban or rural platforms, then this rural–urban divide might be somewhat intuitive. Given that a majority of Africans live in rural areas, we might expect to see "rural" parties in power across the continent, with urbanites supporting "urban" parties that are perennially in opposition. However, as analysts of African politics have consistently noted, political competition tends to take place predominantly along regional or ethnic lines, with party support traversing both rural and urban areas.[4] Yet despite this, there exists a clear tendency for rural voters to be more supportive of the incumbent party, whichever party this may be.

This point is illustrated nicely by data from Ghana. Table 2.1 presents vote shares from the six presidential elections in Ghana since the return to multiparty competition in 1992, for the two dominant political parties, the National Democratic Congress (NDC) and the New Patriotic Party (NPP).[5] The table compares each party's vote share nationally to its share in Greater Accra, the region containing the capital and largest city.[6] The NDC was the party formed by Jerry Rawlings, who came to power in a coup in 1981, and who then implemented the return to multiparty politics in 1992. It won the 1992 and 1996 elections, before losing power to the NPP in 2000, and then contesting (and losing) the 2004 elections as the major opposition party. Under the leadership of John Atta Mills the NDC returned to power in 2008.[7] The NDC retained power in 2012 under Mills' successor John Mahama, before losing to the NPP in 2016, with longtime NPP leader Nana Akufo-Addo winning the presidency.

The results shown in Table 2.1 make two points very clearly. First, neither the NDC nor the NPP can simply be labeled an urban or a rural party. Their vote shares are quite evenly balanced in Accra, which would not be so if either one

---

[4] See for example: Kasfir (1979); Glickman (1995); Mozaffar (1995); Chazan (1999); Omolo (2002); Mozaffar, Scarritt, and Galaich (2003); Salih (2003). One exception of a specifically rural party is the National Lima Party (NLP), which contested the 1996 elections in Zambia on an agricultural platform, and won no seats.

[5] Since no candidate won a majority of votes in the first rounds of the 2008 and 2016 Presidential elections, the data for these years are taken from the second rounds.

[6] Ideally national vote shares would be compared to those in all urban areas, but such data is not available, and therefore vote shares from Greater Accra are taken as a proxy for urban vote shares. The intention here is not to suggest that there is a specific "capital" or "largest city" effect in Ghana, or elsewhere in Africa. The analyses in Chapter 3 are all robust to the inclusion of controls for capital or largest city, demonstrating that the findings are not driven only by respondents in these types of urban locations.

[7] See Gyimah-Boadi (2001, 2009) for useful discussions of these elections.

Table 2.1 Ghanaian election results, 1992–2016

NDC Vote Share					
Election	Vote Share in Accra	Vote Share Nationwide	Difference	Incumbent?	% Urban
1992	53.4%	58.4%	−5%	Yes	37.9%
1996	54%	57.4%	−3.4%	Yes	40.9%
2000	40%	43%	−3%	Yes	43.9%
2004	46.3%	44.6%	+2.3%	No	46.6%
2008	54.5%	50.5%	+4%	No	49.4%
2012	52.3%	50.7%	+1.6%	Yes	52.1%
2016	46.7%	44.5%	+2.2%	Yes	54.7%

NPP Vote Share					
Election	Vote Share in Accra	Vote Share Nationwide	Difference	Incumbent?	% Urban
1992	37%	30.3%	+6.7%	No	37.9%
1996	43.3%	39.6%	+3.7%	No	40.9%
2000	60%	57%	+3%	No	43.9%
2004	51.9%	52.4%	−0.5%	Yes	46.6%
2008	45.5%	49.5%	−4%	Yes	49.4%
2012	46.9%	47.7%	−0.8%	No	52.1%
2016	52.4%	53.7%	−1.3%	No	54.7%

Note: The 2000 and 2008 elections went to a second round runoff between the NDC and NPP candidates. The results shown here are from the second round. All electoral data comes from the Electoral Commission of Ghana.

were effectively an urban party representing specifically urban interests. If the parties were divided between the cities and the countryside we would expect to see one party consistently outperforming the other in Accra, but that is not the case. This fits with the recognition that the two dominant political parties in Ghana are cleaved primarily along ethnic lines, with the NPP perceived to be a predominantly Asante party and the NDC an Ewe party (Fridy 2007).

The second point that comes out of this data, however, is that Accra votes differently to the rest of the country. Specifically, for the five elections prior to 2012 voters in Accra were consistently less likely to support the incumbent, whichever party was in power. When the NDC was in power, its vote share in Accra was lower than its vote share in the country as a whole. As the opposition party in 2004 and 2008, however, its vote share in the capital actually exceeded its share of the national vote. Likewise, as the major opposition party in 1992, 1996, and 2000, the NPP consistently performed better in Accra than it did nationally. After defeating the NDC in 2000, however, as the incumbent party it then fared worse in the capital than elsewhere in 2004, and again in 2008. This clear reversal in fortunes adds further weight to the view that neither the NDC nor the NPP is naturally an urban party. Rather, it seems that prior to 2012, no matter which party was in power, the incumbent party simply did worse in Accra than in the rest of the country. Interestingly, the 2012 elections bucked this trend. For the first time since the return to multiparty elections in 1992 the incumbent party actually performed better in Accra than in the country as a whole, a pattern that was repeated in 2016. If we bear in mind the level of urbanization in Ghana by this point in time, however, this apparent end to the rural bias in incumbent support fits neatly with the explanation developed in Section 2.3.

But Ghana is just one of many countries in Africa. Returning to the public opinion data noted above, it is clear that this pattern holds across Africa more generally. What is also clear is that countries exhibit substantial variation in the degree of rural incumbent bias. Fig. 2.1 shows the differences in incumbent support between rural and urban voters in 28 different African countries, averaged across Rounds 3 to 6 of the Afrobarometer Survey Series.[8] In the vast majority of cases, rural respondents are significantly more likely to express support for

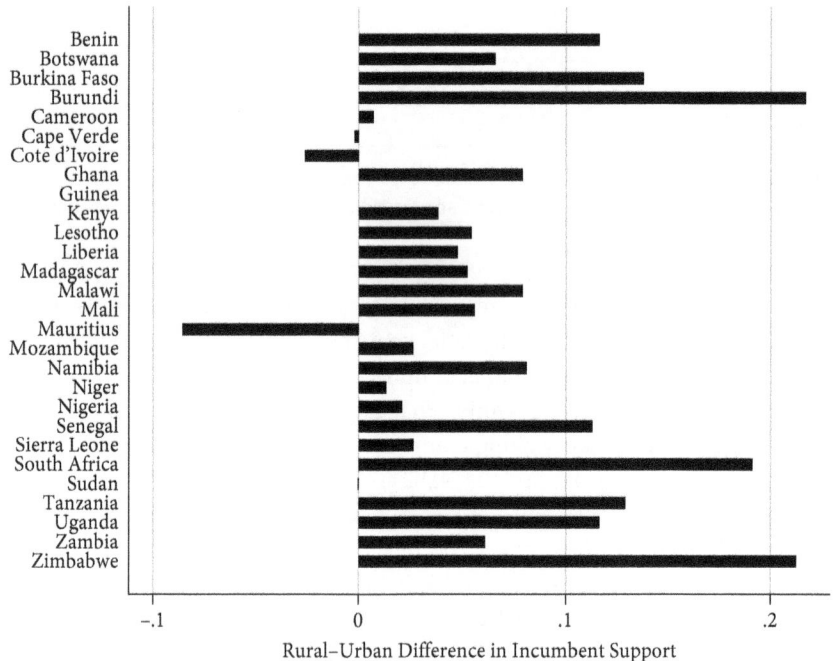

Fig. 2.1 Difference between incumbent support in rural and urban areas by country, Afrobarometer Rounds 3–6.

---

[8] The value of interest plotted in Fig. 2.1 is the proportion of rural respondents who would vote for the incumbent less the equivalent proportion of urban respondents, for each country. The number of countries included in the Afrobarometer has increased over time, meaning that some of the twenty-eight countries were not included in all four of the survey rounds considered here.

incumbents than are urbanites. Mauritius represents a notable exception, with urbanites therein fully 8.5% more likely to express support for the incumbent than rural residents. In addition, the proportion of urbanites expressing support for the incumbent is also greater than that of rural residents in Cote d'Ivoire, Cape Verde, and Sudan, although in these cases the differences are not statistically significant at standard levels. But the clear pattern across Africa is one of rural bias in incumbent support.

It is important to note the substantial variation in democratic quality across these countries, with Polity scores ranging from −4 to 10 over the country-years in the sample, and all three Freedom House categories represented (Free, Partly Free, and Not Free). The inclusion of data from illiberal contexts likely exacerbates problems of response bias that are common in public opinion data, since in a small number of countries we see almost uniform expressions of incumbent support. In Sudan, Niger, and Guinea more than 99% of survey respondents who answered the question about likely voting intention said that they would support the incumbent. This is likely to explain the very small differences in incumbent support between the proportions of urbanites and rural residents in these countries. It is also worth noting, however, that in all of these countries opposition candidates have won sizable vote shares in presidential elections during the period covered by the data. This suggests that citizens are prepared to express dissatisfaction at the ballot box, and incumbents are prepared to allow them to do so. The regression analysis in Chapter 3 controls for potentially confounding contextual factors with country fixed effects and control variables at the individual level. The key thing to note here is the general pattern of rural bias in incumbent support, and the extent of variation in the degree of this urban–rural cleavage across countries.

In twenty-three of the twenty-eight countries represented in the data, the proportion of urbanites expressing support for the incumbent was less than the corresponding rural proportion, and in almost all of these the difference is statistically significant at standard levels. The results of regression analysis presented in Chapter 3 show that this urban incumbent hostility is robust to the inclusion of numerous control variables. But even from this raw data the general pattern is clear—urbanites across Africa are less likely than rural residents to support the incumbent. What is also clear though is that there is a significant amount of variation in the extent of this difference across countries. While in cases such as Nigeria and Sierra Leone the difference is less than 3%, in more than a quarter of cases the proportion of rural residents expressing support for the governing party was over 10% higher than that of urban respondents.

This raises two important questions: Why are urbanites less likely than rural residents to support incumbents? And why does the magnitude of this difference vary across countries? After considering a number of possible explanations for urban incumbent hostility, in Section 2.3 I propose an additional argument, that given the demographic structure of African populations, electoral competition creates incentives for incumbents to focus resources on pro-rural policies while largely ignoring the demands of urban voters. Before doing so, however, it is worth returning briefly to the question of why evidence for such a clear urban–rural distinction in incumbent support is so puzzling.

2.2.2   Why is an urban–rural cleavage puzzling?

At first glance the lower propensity of urbanites to support incumbents may not seem all that puzzling; it could simply reflect competition between urban and rural parties, with the latter achieving greater success due to low levels of urbanization across the continent. But such an explanation jars sharply with standard accounts of African politics. Political competition in Africa is frequently deemed to run along ethno-regional lines, with parties mobilizing voters according to their communal identities, and elections being subsequently reduced to ethnic censuses. Indeed, for countries across Africa, analyses of patterns in voting behavior at the individual level, and of the aggregate distributions of party vote shares, have shown that divisions of political competition tend to be ethnically or regionally based.[9]

Explanations for the predominance of ethnically-based politics often draw on Horowitz (2000)'s claim that there is a reciprocal relationship between ethnic conflict and political parties in many African states, whereby deep ethnic cleavages give rise to ethnic parties, which in turn exacerbate ethnic divisions. Although most scholars acknowledge that political competition in Africa is also influenced by other factors alongside ethnicity, the importance of ethnic divisions remains central to many accounts.[10] If political competition is ethnically based, it seems highly unlikely that parties would represent distinctly urban or rural constituencies, as this would require urban–rural cleavages to map neatly on to ethnic divisions.

Although ethnicity has been shown to matter significantly for political competition across Africa, its importance is often likely overstated. As Bleck and van de Walle (2018) note, the literature on African politics "has demonstrated a predeliction for the darker or more exotic dimensions of African elections," chief among them being a focus on ethnic politics. But in recent years scholars have begun to acknowledge this, and to widen the focus. Cheeseman (2015) argues that a variety of mobilization strategies have been employed by parties across Africa, including appeals to ideological traditions and nationalist sentiments, and that where voting does take place along ethnic lines this rarely reflects a reductionist ethnic census model. Similarly, Elischer (2013) argues strongly that

---

[9] See for example: Marae (1993); Fox (1996); Throup and Hornsby (1998); Oucho (2002); Norris and Mattes (2003); Ferree (2004); Ishiyama and Fox (2006).

[10] See for example, Salih (2003), Posner (2005), Ishiyama and Fox (2006), and Arriola (2013).

the political salience of ethnicity is much exaggerated, and that a variety of non-ethnic party types exist and compete across Africa alongside ethnic parties. These include catch-all parties that promote national unity, as well as programmatic and personalistic parties.

While this broadening of the debate over the bases of political competition in Africa is useful, discussion of parties mobilizing along urban or rural lines remains notably absent. One exception is the case of Zambia, where in the early 1990s opposition leaders utilized trade union networks to mobilize organized labor in urban areas (Cheeseman 2015, 188), and where the NLP contested the 1996 elections on an agricultural platform, winning no seats.[11] This exception does not therefore support a generalized vision of competition between urban and rural parties. Why, then, should urban residents across Africa be less supportive of incumbents?

2.2.3 Socio-demographic and structural explanations

Although very little attention has been paid to the existence of an urban–rural cleavage in African electoral politics, the scholarship on a range of other aspects of African political economy and political competition offers a number of possible explanations for this puzzling phenomenon.

The first of these relates to the skewed impact of economic Structural Adjustment Programs (SAPs) that imposed conditionalities on loan packages received by many African countries in the 1980s. While SAPs certainly created winners and losers in both urban and rural areas, it has been argued that most of the negative impact was borne by urban residents (Bawumia 1998; Nugent 1999). This was due in large part to job losses resulting from public sector retrenchment, but was also in some cases exacerbated by the more effective system of urban taxation that resulted from the reforms. In contrast, the most visible benefits resulting from SAPs tended to be more heavily skewed towards rural areas, where increased investment in basic public services such as pipe-borne water, electricity, and roads had a much more noticeable impact. Furthermore, the removal of price distortions often meant that agricultural producers in the countryside received vastly improved prices for their crops. Focusing specifically on Ghana, both Bawumia (1998) and Nugent (1999) argue that urban hostility towards the incumbent party in the 1992 and

---

[11] In a study of economic voting in Zambia's 1996 elections, Posner and Simon (2002) include urban–rural location as a control variable, and find that voters in urban areas were more likely to support the incumbent than were rural voters. While this makes sense given the context of Zambian politics in the early 1990s, as Fig. 2.1 shows this trend has since reversed, with the proportion of urban residents expressing support for the incumbent on average 6% lower than the equivalent proportion of rural respondents.

1996 elections was in part a reaction to these effects of the SAP that had been pursued by President Jerry Rawlings since 1983.[12]

A second possible explanation follows from acknowledgment of the constraints facing opposition parties across Africa. Due to limited resources, opposition parties lack the capacity to campaign as extensively as incumbents in remote rural areas, and to communicate effectively with rural voters. This constrains their ability to mobilize rural residents, who due to lower literacy levels and limited exposure to independent media often lack awareness of opposition parties (Nugent 1999; Resnick 2012). The obstacles to mobilization generated by this lack of awareness are compounded by the fact that the benefits of holding office give the campaign promises of incumbent parties greater credibility in rural areas (Resnick 2014). Taken together, these factors may make it more difficult for opposition parties to mobilize strong bases of support in rural areas, leading them instead to focus their attention on the cities.

A third potential explanation is suggested by work on clientelism. In addition to differences in the impact of SAPs, and in the reach of opposition party campaigning, it has been argued that rural residents are more likely than urbanites to be engaged in clientelistic relationships, in which political support is exchanged for private benefits (Hicken 2007; Conry-Krutz 2009). One reason for this is that lower incomes and resource scarcity make rural votes cheaper than those in cities, thereby rendering vote-buying efforts more cost-effective in rural areas (Kuenzi and Lambright 2007). In addition, it has been argued that urbanization breaks patron–client linkages whilst at the same time generating greater demand for public rather than private goods (Hicken 2007). Since incumbents across Africa likely have a comparative advantage in clientelism, given their access to state resources, higher levels of voter bribery in rural areas could explain why rural voters are more likely than urbanites to support incumbents. It is worth noting, however, that both Kramon (2013) and Jensen and Justesen (2013) find no significant relationship between urban–rural residence and vote-buying.

A fourth possibility stems from literature that focuses on the continued and developing role of traditional authority in African politics. In contrast to claims about vote buying being more prevalent in rural areas, others have argued that hierarchical ties keep rural villagers deferential to traditional leaders, whereas it is urbanites who are free to exchange their political support for jobs, cash, or consumption goods (Scott 1969; Lehoucq 2007). The perseverance of such hierarchical ties may enable traditional leaders to act as brokers, delivering rural

---

[12] In a study of economic voting in Ghana using survey data from 1999, Youde (2005) demonstrates a significant negative relationship between urban location and incumbent support. Here however, the urban–rural variable is simply included as a control variable, and no attempt is made to explain the relationship.

votes to incumbents. Along these lines, Koter (2016) argues that where local authority figures—such as chiefs, royals, or religious leaders—are sufficiently powerful, politicians will engage them as intermediaries to deliver votes.[13] Given that brokers have a material interest in working with the politicians who are most able to provide resources, the benefits of office should give incumbents a comparative advantage in this type of brokered vote mobilization.[14] Therefore if hierarchical ties render rural voters less autonomous in their voting decisions than urbanites, this dynamic could thus explain the observed rural bias in incumbent support.[15]

An important alternative view of the role of traditional chiefs is offered by Baldwin (2016), who argues that they serve not as *vote* brokers but as *development* brokers. By this account, the ability of traditional chiefs to deliver votes to politicians is limited. Instead, through their connections with politicians chiefs can serve to facilitate the delivery of development projects in the context of Africa's weak states. Since the ability of chiefs to fulfill this developmental role is influenced by the closeness of their relationship with politicians, by this account rural voters condition their electoral support on the connections between candidates and chiefs. What then does this mean for rural bias? To the extent that incumbency establishes and/or strengthens connections with chiefs, this alternative view of chiefs could also underpin an explanation for rural bias that focuses on the role of traditional authority. But unlike the vote broker account, where incumbency clearly furnishes incumbent politicians with a comparative advantage, such an advantage is less clear in the development broker model; high transaction costs resulting from poor quality relationships between chiefs and politicians may not simply be bought off with the spoils of office.

To summarize the arguments discussed so far, urban–rural variations in incumbent support may result from socio-demographic differences between urban and rural residents, and from structural differences between urban and rural contexts that affect the nature of political competition and mobilization. More specifically, urban residents may be less likely to support incumbents because: (1) they have suffered more from SAPs; (2) they are more exposed to opposition party campaigning; (3) they are less likely to have their votes bought by incumbents (and less likely to sell them, and to do so cheaply); and (4) they are more autonomous

---

[13] On the ability of chiefs to influence political support, see also Lemarchand (1972) and Boone (2014).

[14] See also de Kadt and Larreguy (2018) on the links between traditional leaders and incumbents in Africa.

[15] The question of how and why the authority of traditional leaders varies across countries in Africa is an interesting one, and may suggest further factors that could explain variation in the relative significance of different mobilization strategies. For example, it is certainly possible that the authority of traditional leaders, and their resulting influence over voter choice, is lower in Ghana as a result of Kwame Nkrumah's decision to take on the chiefs. A similar claim might be made about Botswana, where Seretse Khama's renunciation of his chieftaincy claim to create a tribal council effectively formalized democratic constraints on the chiefs prior to independence.

in their voting decisions. These explanations all have value, though they are not without their limitations. Moreover, they leave open two nagging questions: Why would incumbents risk the development of hostility in major urban centers? And why should the level of urban incumbent hostility vary so widely across countries?

2.3 Elections and Pro-Rural Policies

Electoral competition across Africa generates incentives for incumbents to implement pro-rural policies, in order to court the votes of what in most countries is a rural majority. This greater propensity for African governments to favor rural interests through policy-making gives rise to a rural bias in support for incumbents. When retention of power depends on winning an electoral majority, and most voters live in the countryside, a degree of urban dissatisfaction can be tolerated. The extent to which this holds true varies across countries with the level of urbanization; as the size of the rural majority decreases, so too should the focus on pro-rural policies, and with it the degree of urban incumbent hostility.

This parsimonious argument depends on a particular assumption about voter choice, namely that voters condition their support on the government's performance in providing desired goods and services. Beyond this, however, the argument asks very little but offers a great deal by way of observable implications. In what remains of this chapter I flesh out the bones of this argument, before highlighting these implications.

2.3.1 Why do elections in Africa lead to pro-rural policies?

Urban bias

Most famously expounded by Lipton (1977) and Bates (1981), the urban bias argument posits that authoritarian regimes in developing countries have incentives to favor urban over rural interests, because urban groups present a more credible threat of political opposition and unrest that could potentially destabilize the regime. As a result, resources are pumped out of the countryside through distortionary price policies, which reduce the cost of living for urban residents while returning lower profits to rural producers. This model was widely accepted as a powerful explanatory tool for understanding urban–rural relations in authoritarian developing countries, not least because it recognized the political calculations underlying policies that affect the distribution of resources between different sectors of society. Of particular importance to the question at hand, however, is the expectation that this urban bias should dissipate with the onset of democracy. As Robert Bates hypothesized in 1993, "[in] nations with competitive party systems, political competition for votes leads to a shift in policy in favor of rural interests" (Bates 1993, 225).[16]

This hypothesis about the impact of electoral competition is reflected in the work of Varshney (1995), who argued that elections had precisely this effect in India, where the countryside was empowered by the introduction and persistence of democracy prior to an industrial revolution, resulting in the pursuance of policies that were beneficial to rural interests.[17] More recently, Stasavage (2005a) has related this logic to Africa, by addressing the link between democracy and public education spending. Recognizing that competitive elections force governments to seek a majority of votes, and that a majority of electors in almost all African countries live in rural areas, Stasavage argued that in democratic systems public policy decisions should reflect a greater responsiveness to the preferences of rural voters. Consequently, he claimed that electoral competition should lead to increased spending on primary education, on which rural voters place a higher premium than secondary and tertiary education spending. Bates and Block (2013) make a similar claim with regard to agricultural policy, arguing that with electoral competition and a large rural share of the population, politicians face strong incentives to prioritize the interests of farmers. This simple yet powerful idea, that democracy in Africa leads governments to shift their focus towards rural interests in order to secure a majority of votes, offers a complementary and explicitly political account for the puzzle of why rural residents across Africa are more likely than urbanites to support incumbents.

Electoral Incentives

Most simply stated, rural residents are more likely to support incumbents because African governments have an electoral incentive to implement policies that primarily benefit rural interests. Under authoritarian regimes, urbanites have much greater potential political power than do rural residents, for whom issues such as illiteracy and geographic dispersion exacerbate coordination problems. The more credible threat of urban as opposed to rural opposition and unrest leads regimes to bias resources towards urban interests. With the advent of competitive elections, however, this incentive to discriminate in favor of urban interests dissipates. The equalization of individual political power via the ballot box removes, or

[16] Recent work by Rabinowitz (2018) has questioned the ubiquity of urban bias across post-colonial Africa, arguing that regimes pursued a mix of what she terms "urban" as opposed to "rural political strategies." By this account, strategies of urban bias were tempered by more inclusive ethno-regional patronage-based ("rural") approaches, with the extent to which this was done dependent on the choices of leaders. Focusing primarily on non-democratic regimes, Rabinowitz says little about the operation or impact of these political strategies under democracy. However, much like Bates (1993), she suggests that if anything democracy should be expected to increase the influence of rural interests (Rabinowitz 2018, 30).

[17] Similarly, Min (2015) argues that high levels of poverty in rural areas has led democratically-elected politicians in India to seek the votes of the rural poor.

at least vastly reduces, the disproportionate influence of what in most African countries has (at least until recently) tended to be quite a small urban minority, as governments become dependent on the support of an electoral majority. Therefore in countries where a majority of voters live in rural areas, elections generate incentives for governments to implement policies that benefit rural interests, while paying less attention to the demands of urban residents.[18,19]

This is not to say that elections resolve rural collective action problems; lower population densities and obstacles to communication mean that coordination remains more difficult in rural than in urban areas. Rather, elections institutionalize political competition, regularizing conflict over power through periodic battles at the ballot box. By accepting the rules of electoral competition urbanites effectively agree to a reduction of their influence relative to rural voters, because the urban bias that resulted from their comparative advantage in terms of coordination in an authoritarian system is undermined by democratic politics, under which government survival is determined much more by electoral support than by urban protest. The primary threat to an authoritarian government is a coup, which requires coordination, and which is therefore much more likely to generate in urban than rural areas. The point of democracy is that ballots are used as "paper stones," such that elections provide an alternative means to manage conflict without recourse to violence (Przeworski 1999). Thus the primary threat to democratic governments is electoral defeat, which is a priori no more likely to stem from urban than rural areas.

In the presence of a large rural majority, incumbents who can win in the countryside can afford to ignore urban voters, and risk generating a certain degree of urban dissatisfaction, so long as doing so does not lead to urban unrest that may destabilize the regime.[20] Therefore where a majority of the population is rural, incumbents should distribute sufficient resources to buy off urban unrest, but

---

[18] Such pro-rural policies may also be expected to be more electorally efficient than pro-urban policies, because rural votes may be less expensive per capita. For example, it may be cheaper to supply primary education to 100 rural villagers than to provide university places to the same number of urban residents.

[19] It has also been noted that democracy can advantage rural areas due to electoral malapportionment, since population size tends to be greater in urban as opposed to rural electoral districts (G. Bingham Powell and Vanberg 2000; Samuels and Snyder 2001; Chen and Rodden 2013; Min 2015). Applying this argument to the African context, Boone and Wahman (2015) provide evidence from five African countries that malapportionment leads to rural overrepresentation. As such, it is worth acknowledging the possibility that this may have some bearing on policy outcomes, not least in the small number of parliamentary systems, and countries with meaningful constituency development funds. But in general the relative strength of executives and the marginalization of legislatures across the continent mean that this is unlikely to be the key driver of any rural bias in either policy outcomes or in subsequent incumbent support.

[20] Stasavage (2005a) effectively captures the logic underlying this argument, but applied specifically to education spending, in a simple game-theoretic model. Assuming that the threat of unrest posed by urbanites is constant across authoritarian and democratic regimes, and that a majority of voters are rural, he shows that the advent of democracy should lead incumbents to cater to the demands of rural interests by increasing spending on primary education, while the level of spending on university education desired by urbanites should remain constant.

without needing to ensure that they win urban votes. Any such urban unrest may certainly bring with it the risk of instability, and where this risk is heightened rulers will act to offset it.[21] This was seen clearly by the response to large-scale urban riots in Cameroon in early 2008, in which at least twenty-four people were killed and over 1,600 were arrested. Faced with such a heightened risk of instability, the President of Cameroon, Paul Biya, responded with an array of measures including reductions in fuel costs, increases to civil service and military salaries, and the slashing of customs duties on basic foodstuffs, which effectively bought off the urban unrest.

Where popular rulers enjoy widespread electoral support they may be more willing to accommodate urban demands, and thereby more comfortably offset the potential instability posed by urban dissatisfaction, at the risk of suffering some loss of rural votes. Moreover, where the urban population is smaller, urban unrest should have less potential to destabilize the regime, which will therefore be able to accommodate a higher level of urban dissatisfaction, or buy it off more feasibly. As the urban population increases, however, not only will the feasibility of winning solely in the countryside decrease but the potential threat of urban unrest will rise, forcing incumbents to pay more attention to urban voters. Therefore this demographic factor—the distribution of the population between urban and rural areas—should alter the political calculations of the incumbent. Specifically, increasing the urban proportion of the population should induce the government to implement policies that benefit urban as well as rural voters, which in turn should increase the level of support that it receives from urban voters.

By this reasoning, the greater propensity for rural residents to support incumbents results from governments pursuing pro-rural policies in order to ensure electoral support from the rural majority. The logical implication of this argument is that the degree of any such rural bias towards incumbents should reduce as the urban proportion of the population increases, because governments have an incentive to more evenly balance pro-rural and pro-urban policies. Before proceeding, it is worth restating that party competition in Africa does not take place primarily along an urban–rural cleavage. Instead, the widespread perception is that party support tends to be based on ethnic or regional constituencies, with groups linked to parties through clientelistic ties. This state of the world is consistent with the argument that a predominantly rural population induces incumbents to implement policies that favor rural interests.

It is also important to be clear that the argument being made here concerns *interests*, not *identities*. It is not the intention to claim that voters *identify* as either

---

[21] The downside risk of being deposed may be greater if loss of office results from a coup as opposed to an election, because coups are more likely to lead to death or exile of the former ruler. Since rulers want to stay in office, we should expect that they will act to carefully balance the risks posed by urban and rural dissatisfaction.

rural or urban, nor is it to deny that they could. Rather, the argument is that rural voters are likely to share a variety of common interests, for example in primary education, essential health services, rural roads, rural electrification, or agricultural prices, which may differentiate them from urban voters. As a result, politicians can court rural voters not by appealing to a voter's rural identity but by implementing (or promising) policies that serve these particular rural interests.

Voter choice, like all other political phenomena, is multi-causal. Thus while ethnicity may be a more or less powerful predictor of voting behavior in different countries across Africa, nowhere is it likely to be a perfect one. Parties may in general be able to rely on the support of "their" ethnic groups, especially due to clientelistic links, and to the influence of traditional and religious leaders. But for some of the voters some of the time these ethnic links may not be enough, because circumstances may make particular interests a more powerful determinant of voter choice than ethnic identities. For example, a rural resident may value the public services provided by an out-group incumbent party sufficiently for her to support that party, irrespective of ethnicity.[22] Alternatively, an urban resident might be so frustrated by high food prices that she will vote against an in-group incumbent. Moreover, many voters do not have an in-group party to vote for. As noted above, in Ghana the NPP is perceived to be an Asante party, and the NDC an Ewe party. These are the only two viable parties, and between them they have won over 93% of the votes in each of the last four elections. And yet, more than 40% of the population belongs to ethnic groups other than the Asante and the Ewe. Therefore for at least 40% of Ghanaian voters, it may be far less clear which one is "their" ethnic party.

Although ethnic or regional identities may impact powerfully on voting behavior, they are not the only determinant factors. Furthermore, although governments may engage in clientelistic distribution along ethnic lines, certain policies may not be amenable to such group-specific targeting. For example, distortionary food prices are likely to affect members of all ethnic groups.[23] At the same time, other policies may tend to distinguish more naturally between urban and rural interests, rather than between ethnic or regional groups. In setting such policies, it makes sense that with electoral competition and a rural majority, governments should cater primarily to rural interests. It is worth considering some of the policy tools with which governments might distinguish between rural and urban interests in this way.

---

[22] Ichino and Nathan (2013) provide compelling evidence of cross-ethnic voting in Ghana, which they argue stems from voters' calculations about likely benefits from locally non-excludable goods.

[23] Kasara (2007) shows that certain agricultural taxes can be used to target specific ethnic groups, and that actually governments in Africa have tended to extract more from their *own* ethnic groups. This finding is based on data that covers predominantly authoritarian regimes, and therefore it would be interesting to see whether this pattern holds as strongly under democracy.

2.3.2   What types of policy areas might be affected?

Agriculture

Agricultural policy is perhaps the most obvious tool with which incumbents can differentiate between urban and rural interests. As noted above, the urban bias literature posited that authoritarian regimes benefit urban at the expense of rural interests by introducing discriminatory price and resource flows. In particular, they use agricultural policies as a tool to reduce the cost of living for urban dwellers, primarily by distorting the cost of food (Bates 1981, 33). Just as agricultural policy can be used to discriminate against the rural sector, so it can also be turned to the producer's benefit. Despite the introduction of SAPs across Africa, which prescribed the liberalization and deregulation of prices, governments retained a great deal of control over these areas. Nicholas van de Walle has highlighted the fact that implementation of SAPs was far from complete, and that the degree of implementation of reforms to food markets and export agriculture in particular was mediocre (van de Walle 2001, 90).

Despite liberalizing economic reforms, African governments retained significant leverage over policies that enable them to appease, or discriminate between, rural and urban interests. van de Walle (2001) also noted that consumer prices were liberalized more than producer prices, a fact that lends intuitive support to the argument that democracy gives African governments greater incentives to appease rural rather than urban interests. Intervening in producer prices but leaving consumer prices to the vagaries of the market fits perfectly with the aforementioned expectation that incumbents should be happy to ignore urban demands while being more responsive to the rural sector.[24]

An interesting example of this is provided by price liberalization policies in Kenya. Market liberalizations implemented by the Kenyan government in 1992 resulted in a dramatic drop in the input/output ratio of prices for producers of maize, Kenya's key food crop. This drop was greatly beneficial to the maize producers, and coincided nicely with the multiparty elections in December of that year (De Groote et al. 2005). Rather than ceding power over electorally useful policy levers the Kenyan government retained control of maize seed prices through the state-owned Kenya Seed Company (KSC), and continued to manipulate maize prices via the National Cereals and Produce Board (De Groote et al. 2005; Jayne, Myers, and Nyoroc 2007).

While Kenyan maize output prices fluctuated somewhat following the significant increase in 1992, they rose dramatically again in 1997, following the introduction of fixed prices and tariffs on imports. This sharp increase again greatly

---

[24] African governments are still prepared to intervene in consumer prices when the political need arises, however, as the aforementioned action by President Paul Biya's government in Cameroon in 2008 illustrates.

benefited maize producers just prior to the elections that occurred at the end of that year (van de Walle 2001). At the same time, however, urban consumers were faced with higher food prices as a result. Although only suggestive, this pattern fits neatly with the idea that electoral incentives motivate policies that favor rural over urban interests. More systematic evidence of this effect is provided by Bates and Block (2013), who analyze the impact of electoral competition and rural population shares on trade policies that support agriculture across Africa. Specifically, they find that where rural population shares are high, nominal rates of assistance to agricultural importables increase with electoral competition.

Basic Services

Although the livelihoods of many rural residents are affected by agricultural policies, such policies are unlikely to be the only or even the primary means by which politicians in Africa seek rural votes. According to public opinion surveys carried out across eighteen countries in 2005, of those rural residents who cited farming as their primary occupation (just a little over 43%), more than 44% were engaged in subsistence farming, producing food solely for domestic consumption.[25] For these farmers, the impact of food subsidies and price distortions is likely to be more muted than for those engaged in commercial farming. Therefore although certainly important for many rural residents, the benefits of pro-rural agricultural policies are unlikely to have sufficiently broad appeal for such policies alone to win an electoral majority. Beyond agricultural policies though, African governments have control over a wide range of policy tools, including those that affect the provision of a variety of goods and services.[26]

Levels of basic service provision in Africa's rural areas remain the lowest in the world. In 2017 infant mortality rates in sub-Saharan Africa were almost twice as high as the global average, and net primary school enrollment was 12 percentage points lower.[27] Within Africa, rural residents fare much worse than urbanites. Since 1980, children in rural areas have been 15% less likely to receive any schooling than those living in urban locations, and infant mortality rates have

---

[25] Data from http://www.afrobarometer.org. Data cited is from Round 3 of the Afrobarometer Series. Not all Afrobarometer survey rounds disaggregate occupation sufficiently to examine these differences, but these numbers are closely reflected by the data from Round 2, carried out in sixteen countries between 2002 and 2004.

[26] It is worth noting here the distinction between public and quasi-public or club goods. While in a strict sense public goods are non-excludable and non-rivalrous, many things that are commonly viewed as public goods, such as roads or aspects of education provision, may actually be better classified as quasi-public or club goods (Harding 2015). This follows from the fact that certain citizens may be excluded from accessing them by location. Private goods, of course, are both excludable and rivalrous. The policy tools that I consider here affect the provision of goods and services that vary in the degree to which they may be excludable by location. Weghorst and Lindberg (2011) find that voters in Ghana place greatest value on the provision of collective development goods, which would fit here under the classification of quasi-public or club goods.

[27] Data from the World Bank's World Development Indicators, accessed at https://databank.worldbank.org/data/source/world-development-indicators on April 8, 2019.

been 20 percentage points higher. As a result, policies designed to improve access to basic education and health services are likely to generate widespread support from rural voters across Africa.

Various policy tools can be used to influence the provision of education and health services, the effects of which may be felt differently by urban and rural voters. One of these is education spending. Stasavage (2005a) notes that rural dwellers prefer that a greater proportion of the education budget is spent on primary schooling, whereas urbanites prefer increases in secondary and university education spending. Of course, the education budget need not be fixed, and the amount allocated to both sectors could be increased, but the point is that education spending is a policy over which urban and rural voters might be expected to have divergent preferences. Although the government could subsidize both sectors, if the electoral process allows it to ignore urban demands and accumulate rents instead, this would seem an attractive option.[28]

A nice example of the use of education spending in this way is provided by Stasavage (2005b), who presents evidence that the policy of Universal Primary Education (UPE) in Uganda was adopted by President Museveni in order to win rural votes during the 1996 presidential election. Stasavage also notes a similar link between electoral incentives and education policy in Malawi, where UPE was implemented in September 1994, after having been a key policy on the basis of which the new government was elected in May of that year. The two cases of Uganda and Malawi highlighted by Stasavage are not isolated examples. Just as in Malawi, the provision of free primary education was a key electoral issue on which new governments came to power in Lesotho and Kenya in 1998 and 2002, respectively (Avenstrup, Liang, and Nellemann 2004).

Looking at all cases of primary school fee abolitions in Africa since the early 1990s, Harding and Stasavage (2014) provide strong evidence of a causal link between competitive elections and the abolition of primary school fees across Africa. Assuming that rural voters do indeed have stronger preferences for increased access to primary school than their urban counterparts, this evidence further supports the idea that elections create incentives for governments to pursue policies that benefit the rural majority. Data from Round 3 of the Afrobarometer Series lends support to this assumption: when asked to evaluate the trade-off between abolishing school fees and raising educational standards, rural respondents were 11% more likely than urbanites to prefer free schooling even if the quality of education was low.[29]

---

[28] It is also worth noting that education spending might be amenable to targeting towards specific regions or groups, in order to appease a party's core constituency, and that this might be even more so for spending in the primary sector, where schools are smaller and more numerous, than in the secondary or tertiary education sectors.

[29] Data from http://www.afrobarometer.org.

That being said, rather than being driven by electoral incentives, one might argue that the prevalence of UPE policies over the last two decades has simply been a consequence of prevailing temporal trends, perhaps resulting from donor pressures. One way to address this claim is to look at the case of Botswana, which presents an interesting counterfactual. Unlike most African countries, Botswana has held multiparty elections consistently since independence in 1966. As a result, if it is correct that electoral incentives result in policies designed to benefit the rural majority, then we should expect primary education to have been expanded much earlier in Botswana than elsewhere. As discussed in far greater detail in Chapter 6, this is exactly what happened; after suffering a drop in rural support in the 1969 elections, the ruling Botswana Democratic Party (BDP) set in motion a program of rapid primary school expansion. This was extremely popular with rural voters, and proved key to the BDP's subsequent electoral successes (Al-Samarrai 2005).

As with education, policies affecting the provision of and access to healthcare services can also be used by African governments to prioritize rural over urban interests. The obvious way to do this is simply to divert healthcare resources to rural areas. While healthcare policies can present opportunities such as these for governments to engage in explicit rural bias, this can also be done more subtly. The Ghanaian National Health Insurance Scheme (NHIS), conceived in 2000, provides a useful example of a programmatic policy whose benefits accrue differentially across urban and rural areas in this way.

By design, the Ghanaian NHIS offers programmatic benefits to all citizens, and since these benefits are non-excludable and non-rivalrous the scheme can arguably be viewed as a public good. However, the nature of the resources provided by the policy (essentially a health insurance subsidy) means that rural residents are likely to benefit more than urbanites, because they are more likely to lack the financial resources required to purchase essential health services in the absence of the NHIS.[30] Moreover, because of the progressive nature of the policy, and because rural residents are on average poorer than urbanites, those in rural areas are likely to pay lower premiums (on average) than their urban counterparts. This likely rural bias in the distribution of benefits received under the Ghanaian NHIS is evidenced by the fact that in 2009 the lowest levels of enrollment in the scheme were in Greater Accra, the most urbanized region of the country, which Amporfu (2013) argues was due to the higher level of private health insurance coverage through formal sector employment in Accra, compared to the rest of the country.

---

[30] Ross (2006) highlights the inelasticity of demand for essential health services, in that mortality-averting goods and services will always be purchased where possible. One thing this means is that the NHIS can be seen as subsidizing healthcare for those who could afford to purchase it anyway. In addition, however, reducing barriers to access is likely to make mortality-averting health services accessible to those who would otherwise not have been able to access them. As a result, the impact on basic health outcomes is likely to be felt most intensely for poorer citizens, of whom there are more in rural areas.

Infrastructure

As well as basic health and education services, it is also possible to court voters with infrastructure policies. The rapid expansion of access to primary education rolled out in Botswana in the early 1970s was only one of numerous rural development policies implemented by the BDP to garner electoral support from Botswana's rural majority. Having learned from its electoral failures in rural areas in 1969, the BDP instigated the Accelerated Rural Development Program (ARDP) shortly before the 1974 election, which was designed specifically to win votes from the rural population (Colclough and McCarthy 1980). Most of the ARDP consisted of public works projects such as roads, schools, and village wells. Not only were these goods central to the interests of rural voters, they were also highly visible, and therefore likely to produce the desired short-term electoral pay-offs for the incumbent BDP government. That such a significant package of pro-rural policies was implemented just prior to the 1974 election strongly suggests that they were driven by electoral incentives, as competitive elections give rural majorities the political power to demand recognition of their interests.

As the Botswanan case highlights, in addition to education and health services, infrastructure such as roads, electricity, and water provision are all central to the interests of rural populations. That is not to say that urbanites have no interest in the provision of these types of basic infrastructure. But it is important to recognize differences in both the likely level of demand for these things across urban and rural areas, as well as in the nature of their provision. As Carlitz (2017) notes with reference to Tanzania, for example, the proportion of rural residents lacking access to clean water is substantially higher than that of urbanites (56% compared to 22%), and the proportion with access to piped water into their homes is substantially lower (4% compared to 23%).

A similar pattern can be seen in access to electricity. In Ghana for example, in the mid 2000s less than 21% of the rural population had access to electricity compared to 77% of urbanites, rising to 34% and 84%, respectively, by the late 2000s (Foster and Pushak 2011). While these proportions make Ghana fairly representative of middle-income countries in Africa, the urban–rural gap in electricity access was notably larger for low-income countries. For these, by the mid 2000s only 12% of the rural population had access to electricity, compared to 71% of urbanites. Clearly then, the proportion of voters likely to benefit from improved access to basic infrastructure is greater within rural as opposed to urban electorates.

The provision of basic infrastructure is an area where governments can differentially benefit urban and rural voters quite easily, since money and effort can be directed towards the provision of rural as opposed to urban infrastructure projects. Focusing on post-apartheid South Africa, Kroth, Larcinese, and Wehner (2016) demonstrate the extent to which access to electricity can be targeted by identifying the politically-motivated distribution of electrification projects. Similarly, Min (2015) highlights the efforts of Indian governments to expand electricity provision to the poor, a population which in India is predominantly rural. And in providing evidence for significant increases in access to rural as opposed to urban infrastructure—including water, roads and power—since the re-introduction of multiparty competition in Ghana, Foster and Pushak (2011) highlight the existence of distinct resources for these two sectors.

2.3.3 Implications for development and incumbent support

Between agricultural subsidies, infrastructure, and basic service provision, governments in Africa have a variety of potential policy tools with which they can court rural voters. As noted above, aside perhaps from certain agricultural policies there is nothing about these policy tools that makes them necessarily zero-sum, and therefore governments could direct resources to both urban and rural areas. However, under the reasonable assumption of a budget constraint, it is not possible to please all of the voters all of the time. Incumbents must therefore make decisions about how to allocate public funds, and if they can ignore urban voters and accumulate rents instead, they might well be expected to do so. The central argument here is that electoral competition and the urban–rural distribution of their populations provide governments with incentives to design and implement policies that primarily benefit rural voters. As a result, rural residents should be more supportive of incumbent governments than are those in urban areas.

This is not to deny the value of the accounts noted in Section 2.2.3. The differential impact of SAPs, along with differences in the nature of political competition and mobilization, no doubt affect the voting behavior of urban and rural residents. But in recognizing the political calculations resulting from the interaction between democracy and demography, the account proposed herein offers an answer to why incumbents might risk generating dissatisfaction in urban centers. By rendering governments reliant on the support of an electoral majority, democracy reduces the often disproportionate influence of urbanites across Africa, where in most countries a majority of voters still live in rural areas. As a result, incumbents can afford to risk a certain amount of urban dissatisfaction, so long as they can win elections in the countryside. This account also offers an explanation for why the magnitude of urban incumbent hostility varies across countries: what matters is the distribution of a country's population between rural and urban areas. As the urban population increases, the feasibility of winning solely in the countryside decreases, forcing incumbents to seek urban as well as rural support. As a result, the extent of urban incumbent hostility should be conditional on the urban proportion of the population.

This conditional relationship is a unique observable implication of the explanation for urban incumbent hostility offered herein, making it possible to assess its validity independent of other accounts. As noted above, the level of urban incumbent hostility should be inversely related to the urban proportion of the population, because as the rural majority decreases the government can less comfortably tolerate dissatisfaction on the part of urban voters. Whatever other factors may lead to differences in the political attitudes and voting behavior of urban and rural residents, none obviously account for this hypothesized conditional effect.

2.3.4 Microfoundations

The argument about rural democracy rests on a key assumption: that voters in Africa condition their votes (at least in part) on evaluations of the incumbent's performance with regard to the provision of public goods and services. This assumption is crucial, because if it does not hold then there would be no reason to think that politicians should implement pro-rural policies in order to win rural votes. If voters do not engage in some form of evaluative voting by conditioning their support on politicians' performance in office rather than communal ties or *quid pro quo* arrangements, then politicians will not use policies to court their votes. Instead, politicians would invest their time, effort, and resources in cultivating communal links, or building and maintaining clientelist relations. Moreover, it is not obvious from the existing literature that this assumption does hold, given that work on the determinants of voter choice in African elections has tended to focus predominantly on issues of clientelism and ethnic voting.[31]

At the same time, there are reasons to think that this assumption may not be fanciful. Alongside the work on ethnicity and clientelism, a growing body of research has noted other possible determinants of voting behavior in Africa, such as economic factors (Nugent 1999; Posner 2005; Kimenyi and Romero 2008). In addition, researchers have begun to consider whether votes may also be affected by evaluations of incumbent performance (Lindberg and Morrison 2005; Lindberg 2010; Bratton, Bhavnani, and Chen 2012; Young 2009b). Chapter 5 builds on this work by providing robust evidence from Ghana that voters do indeed condition their support on the outcomes of programmatic policies. This evidence therefore suggests that evaluative voting does influence the electoral choices of citizens in Africa.

2.4 Conclusion

Where people have divergent interests, which they do everywhere, simple majority elections have the strong virtue of minimizing collective dissatisfaction with political outcomes (Przeworski 2018). Since people vote on multiple issues there may be many possible majorities, thereby increasing the uncertainty of elections.

---

[31] On clientelism see for example, Lemarchand (1988), Lewis (1998), van de Walle (2003), Bratton (2008), and Kramon (2009). See also Koter (2016) on the role of traditional chiefs and other local authority figures as clientelistic vote brokers. And on ethnicity see for example, Posner (2005), van de Walle (2007), and Ishiyama (2012).

But unlike dictators, rulers selected through competitive elections must have the support of some majority. Across many countries in Africa, one clear majority can be found in the interests of those living in the countryside. Nowhere is this the *only* possible majority, nor is it a uniform phenomenon—the substance of rural interests varies within as well as across countries. But the demographic importance of the countryside, and the distinctiveness of many rural as opposed to urban interests, motivates this book's claim about Africa's rural democracies.

Most simply stated, in countries with rural majorities meaningful electoral competition creates incentives for governments to design and implement pro-rural policies. This has two major implications. First, all else equal, rural residents should be more likely to support incumbents and more satisfied with democracy than those in urban areas. While the current chapter provides suggestive evidence of this phenomenon, in Chapter 3 I assess this much more rigorously, and investigate a unique observable implication of the argument: that the extent of urban incumbent hostility is conditional on and decreasing in urbanization. The second implication relates to the argument's underlying mechanism, that electoral competition in countries with rural majorities leads to the implementation of pro-rural policies. Chapter 4 addresses this mechanism empirically, looking at the impact of democracy on basic education and health outcomes across Africa. If the argument is valid we should see a rural bias in this impact, the extent of which should be conditional on urbanization. Taken together, evidence of these things suggests that the introduction of electoral competition across Africa has given rise to rural democracies.

3
Urban Incumbent Hostility

3.1 Introduction

Urbanites across Africa are disgruntled. As was highlighted in the previous chapter, they are more likely to vote against incumbents, and less likely to be satisfied with democracy than their rural counterparts. There are of course many potential reasons for this, such as differences in levels of education and access to information across urban and rural areas, some or all of which may matter to varying extents. But acknowledging these factors still only offers a partial explanation for the lack of incumbent support and democratic satisfaction, because they fail to consider the impact of pro-rural policies pursued by African governments seeking re-election. In this chapter I use public opinion data to demonstrate that urban–rural differences in incumbent support and satisfaction with democracy transcend structural differences across urban and rural locations, and appear to follow at least in part from the strategic actions of governments that are faced with electoral incentives. In particular, I demonstrate that urbanites are significantly and substantially less likely to express support for incumbents and satisfaction with democracy, even when a range of other potential explanations are taken into account. I then show that the extent of urban hostility and dissatisfaction is conditional on (and decreasing in) levels of urbanization. This supports a unique observable implication of the argument, that elections in largely rural countries incentivize the pursuance of pro-rural policies.

3.2 Estimating Incumbent Support

To some extent, urban hostility towards governments in Africa is plain to see. From the numerous food price riots of 2007–08 in countries such as Guinea, Mauritania, and Senegal, to Uganda's "Walk to Work" protests of 2011, to the demonstrations that broke out in cities across Sudan in 2018, urban dissatisfaction in Africa is widespread. But while these intense, coordinated protest moments are highly visible, they are not particularly useful as measures of urban dissatisfaction at the micro-level. For the same reason that revolutions seem impossible to predict ex ante, the occurrence (or not) of protests is a bad measure of opposition at the micro-level because individuals engage in preference falsification. Protesting

Rural Democracy: Elections and Development in Africa. Robin Harding, Oxford University Press (2020).
© Robin Harding.
DOI: 10.1093/oso/9780198851073.001.0001

against the government is dangerous, or time-consuming, or otherwise costly in some way or another, such that an individual's willingness to participate is not truly indicative of her feelings about the incumbent. While there is no perfect solution to overcoming the discrepancy between private and revealed public preferences, we can go some way with the use of public opinion data, coupled with an awareness of its limitations.

3.2.1 Public opinion data

The public opinion data introduced in the previous chapter provides a powerful tool for evaluating the correlates of political support and satisfaction with democracy. This type of data goes a long way to alleviating the problem of preference falsification. This is because the threshold for individuals to express dissatisfaction with democracy, or a preference for the opposition, to an interviewer during a survey is likely to be far lower than that for them to participate in a protest, whether it be peaceful or not. That being said, problems of response bias in surveys are well known, and we should certainly not assume that all survey responses reflect sincere private preferences. This is especially true when asking sensitive questions about issues such as political support, about which individuals may feel unwilling to respond honestly. What this means is that it is important to be aware of any potential sources of bias, to attempt to correct for them where possible, and to condition our conclusions where necessary.

As in Chapter 2, for the following analysis I use data from four rounds of the Afrobarometer Series, which provide individual-level data from twenty-eight African countries. Fig. 3.1 shows the countries included in the sample (see Table 3.3 in the Appendix for a list of the countries and survey rounds included in the analysis). As well as asking respondents who they would support in a future election, and how satisfied they are with democracy, the Afrobarometer surveys also gather information on a wide array of factors that could plausibly influence responses to these questions, such as age, gender, level of education, and access to media. This is useful because it allows me to investigate the potential causes of urban hostility and dissatisfaction across Africa very rigorously.

Dependent variables
Of primary interest here is support for the incumbent president's party.[1] This is operationalized using a question from the Afrobarometer surveys that asks,

---

[1] All of the countries included in the analysis have presidential systems except for Lesotho, which is a parliamentary constitutional monarchy. For Lesotho incumbent is taken as the Prime Minister's party.

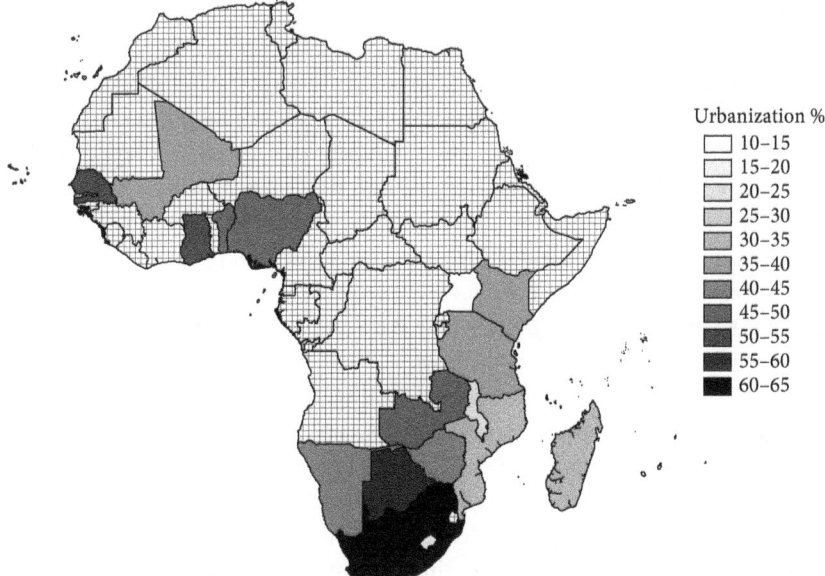

Fig. 3.1 Map of countries in sample

Note: Map shows countries in the sample, shaded by levels of urbanization (mean over sample period), where darker shading reflects higher levels of urbanization. Countries with gridded lines are not included in the sample.

"If a [presidential] election were held tomorrow, which party's candidate would you vote for?" A dummy variable for incumbent support is therefore coded 1 if the respondent names the incumbent party, and 0 otherwise. This question provides the most direct measure of incumbent support, but as noted above it is important to acknowledge that asking questions about sensitive topics such as voting intentions has the potential to introduce bias into responses.[2] Therefore I also analyze a related measure, which is whether the respondent is satisfied with democracy in their country. Although this is certainly a less direct measure of incumbent support, asking about satisfaction with democracy is potentially far less sensitive than asking about voting intentions (as illustrated by the fact that the former elicits a much higher response rate than the latter), and therefore may be less prone to bias.[3]

---

[2] For a discussion of how the sensitivity of survey topics affects the validity of responses see Clausen (1968).

[3] There is some ambiguity as to whether questions about satisfaction with democracy measure support for incumbents or support for regimes. However, analysis of survey responses suggests that although it may be in part a measure of both of these things, there is evidence that it is strongly correlated with incumbent support (Canache, Mondak, and Seligson, 2001). Therefore, while it is a less direct measure, it is a useful alternative.

Explanatory variables

The main explanatory variable of interest at the individual level is whether the respondent lives in an urban or a rural location. The Afrobarometer data include a binary urban–rural indicator drawn from each country's official census classification of enumeration areas, which the Afrobarometer uses as primary sampling units. This is used to construct an *Urban* dummy (rural = 0, urban = 1), with the expectation that it will be negatively related to incumbent support. However, given the argument that urban–rural differences in incumbent support and democratic satisfaction result from the pursuance of pro-rural policies, it is important to control for other structural differences that exist across urban and rural contexts, and which may influence these outcomes.

One such difference that has been suggested to account for the divergent levels of incumbent support between urban and rural voters is exposure to campaigning by opposition parties. Accepting that this is a very difficult thing to measure, I attempt to proxy for the degree of exposure by including an index of media access calculated from questions about how frequently the respondent gets news from various different media, with the expectation being that it should be negatively related to incumbent support.[4] Another possibility is that the socio-demographic profile of rural residents makes them less demanding and less autonomous in their voting behavior, which in turn may render them more likely to support the incumbent. To investigate this I include measures of age, education, and gender.

One concern with the conclusions about urban incumbent hostility drawn from aggregate data is that this data fails to distinguish between a general *urban* effect and a more specific *capital city* effect. As a result, I check that the results are robust to the inclusion of an indicator for whether the respondent lives in the country's capital city, in an effort to control for the possibility that any significant urban effect is driven solely by respondents in these locations.[5] As noted above, party competition in Africa tends to take place along ethnic lines. If this is the case, we should expect ethnicity to be a powerful predictor of voting behavior, and a decent model of incumbent support will need to incorporate this.[6] Specifically, we should expect respondents to be more inclined to support the incumbent president's party if they share the same ethnicity as the president. Unfortunately, information on ethnicity is not garnered for all survey rounds in all countries. In those for which it is I construct a dummy variable for *Coethnic*, coded 1 if the respondent is from

---

[4] The survey question asks, *"How often do you get news from the following sources? Radio; Television; Newspapers".* Every day; A few times a week; A few times a month; Less than once a month; Never; Don't Know.

[5] The results are no different if the analysis includes an indicator for largest instead of capital city, which is not always the same thing.

[6] For existing evidence of the link between ethnicity and voter behavior see Norris and Mattes (2003), and; Bratton, Bhavnani, and Chen (2012).

the same ethnic group as the president, and 0 otherwise.[7] For breadth of coverage I do not include this variable in the baseline specification, but check the results for robustness to its inclusion.

It is also important to recognize the possible bias in individuals' responses resulting from their perceptions of who is responsible for the survey. Public opinion surveys are still fairly uncommon in Africa, and many people assume that any such survey is being carried out on behalf of the government, despite assurances to the contrary by the interviewer. Someone who believes that the interviewer is an agent of the state may feel compelled to express support for the governing party, whatever her true vote intention. Fortunately the final question on the Afrobarometer survey asks respondents who they think sent the interviewers out into the field. Therefore I include a dummy variable indicating whether or not the respondent thought that the government was responsible for the survey.

In addition to these individual level factors, it is also possible that variation at the national level might affect individual attitudes towards incumbents and/or democracy. One fairly obvious factor is economic development, and therefore I include a measure of per capita GDP taken from the World Bank Development Indicators, on the basis that objective economic development at the national level may affect incumbent support. I also include a measure of regime type taken from the Polity IV dataset in an effort to capture the quality of democracy. Finally, I include a measure of the level of urbanization in each country over time, also taken from the World Bank Development Indicators, in order to evaluate whether the negative effect of being an urban resident on a respondent's propensity to support the incumbent party, or express satisfaction with democracy, varies systematically across countries, according to the proportion of the countries' population residing in urban areas.

3.2.2 Are urbanites hostile to incumbents?

Given this data, I pursue two complementary approaches to estimating the determinants of incumbent support and satisfaction with democracy. The first is to pool the data across all countries and survey rounds, accounting for country-level factors through the inclusion of both time-varying factors at the country level and country fixed effects. The latter control for any time-invariant features of particular countries, such as historical or geographic characteristics, and the former account for potential confounding factors at the country level that vary over time, such as levels of economic growth, or regime type. The second approach is to cut the data by country, in order to generate country-specific estimates of urban–rural differences in support for incumbents.

---

[7] Again, because Lesotho is a parliamentary constitutional monarchy this variable will be based on the Prime Minister's identity.

Table 3.1 presents results from pooled OLS regressions of incumbent support and satisfaction with democracy. For ease of interpretation I present estimates from linear probability models, but the results are robust to a variety of alternative specifications. For each outcome I estimate a range of models, all of which include country and survey round fixed effects as well as a control for whether the respondent believed the survey was being undertaken by the government. In all estimates robust standard errors are clustered by survey. I begin with a very basic specification, looking only at the key explanatory variable, urban location. To this I then add a set of individual level controls, and then a set of time-varying country-level factors.

What is very clear from these results is that compared to rural residents, urbanites across Africa are less likely to support incumbents, and less likely to express satisfaction with democracy. The coefficient on the urban variable is negative and significant across the full range of specifications for both outcomes of interest. Substantively, these results imply that urbanites are, on average, at least 5 percentage points less likely to say both that they would vote for the incumbent's party, and that they are satisfied or very satisfied with the way democracy works in their country. Moreover, this is true even after alternative explanations for urban hostility and dissatisfaction have been taken into account.

As discussed in Chapter 2, urban hostility towards incumbents across Africa may have a number of potential causes, both at the individual and the country levels. In line with explanations that have been suggested elsewhere, these results demonstrate that women express less hostility and dissatisfaction, as do older respondents, while those with at least a primary school education express more. Intriguingly, respondents with greater access to information appear to be less likely to express support for incumbents, but more likely to be satisfied with democracy (perhaps because they are more informed about the alternatives in both regards?). And at the country level, higher quality of democracy (as measured by the Polity IV index) correlates with an increase in both incumbent support and democratic satisfaction.

These factors do seem to explain part of the difference in incumbent support between urbanites and rural residents, as suggested by the fact that the *Urban* coefficient reduces in magnitude by about 25% when they are included in the model (though there is no reduction in the magnitude of the coefficient for the estimates of democratic satisfaction). But they do not explain all of it; even controlling for these things, urbanites remain both significantly and substantially less likely to express support for incumbents and satisfaction with democracy. This is true on average across the eighty-nine surveys included in the sample, controlling for both fixed and time-variant factors at the country level. As one might expect, however, the extent and significance of urban hostility and dissatisfaction varies substantially across countries and over time.

Table 3.1 Determinants of incumbent support and democratic satisfaction

	(1)	(2)	(3)	(4)	(5)	(6)
	Intend to vote for incumbent			Satisfied with democracy		
Urban	-0.0734***	-0.0551***	-0.0571***	-0.0524***	-0.0539***	-0.0547***
	(0.0091)	(0.0082)	(0.0081)	(0.0077)	(0.0068)	(0.0068)
Age		0.0014***	0.0013***		0.0010***	0.0009***
		(0.0004)	(0.0004)		(0.0002)	(0.0002)
Female		0.0303***	0.0305***		-0.0005	-0.0003
		(0.0062)	(0.0062)		(0.0041)	(0.0041)
Primary Education		-0.0174*	-0.0179*		-0.0337***	-0.0344***
		(0.0101)	(0.0101)		(0.0079)	(0.0078)
News Access		-0.0132***	-0.0136***		0.0122***	0.0121***
		(0.0040)	(0.0040)		(0.0030)	(0.0030)
GDP Growth (lag)			0.0034			-0.0019
			(0.0033)			(0.0015)
Polity IV			0.0681***			0.0375***
			(0.0201)			(0.0114)
Urbanization			0.0051			-0.0083
			(0.0164)			(0.0129)
Observations	83854	82957	82957	114722	113579	113579
Number of countries	28	28	28	28	28	28

Note: Linear probability models with country fixed effects, survey-clustered standard errors in parentheses. $^*p<.1$, $^{**}p<.05$, $^{***}p<.01$.

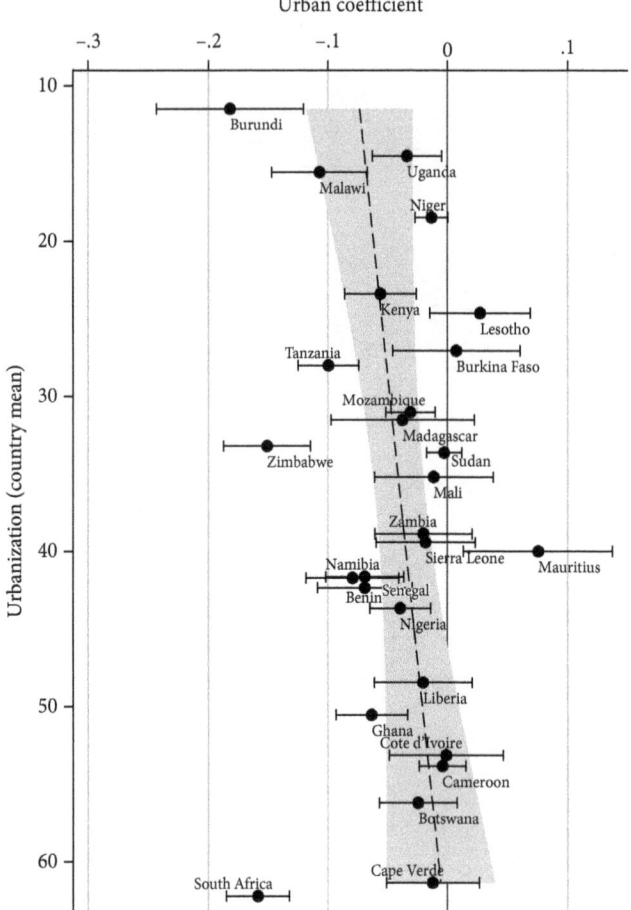

Fig. 3.2 Estimates of urban on incumbent support by country

Figs. 3.2 and 3.3 present country-specific point estimates for the impact of *Urban* location on incumbent support and satisfaction with democracy, respectively. The estimates are from individual-level regressions that pool data across all surveys in the sample for each of the twenty-eight countries. For all countries this means pooling data across at least two survey rounds, and for some it uses data from as many as four surveys. As with the estimates in columns 2 and 5 of Table 3.1, the regressions include controls for age, gender, education, access to news, and whether the respondent thought the survey was being carried out on behalf of the government. The dark gray dots represent point estimates and the protruding bars represent 95% confidence intervals.

The point estimates in Figs. 3.2 and 3.3 highlight the substantial variation across countries in the extent to which, compared to rural residents, urbanites express

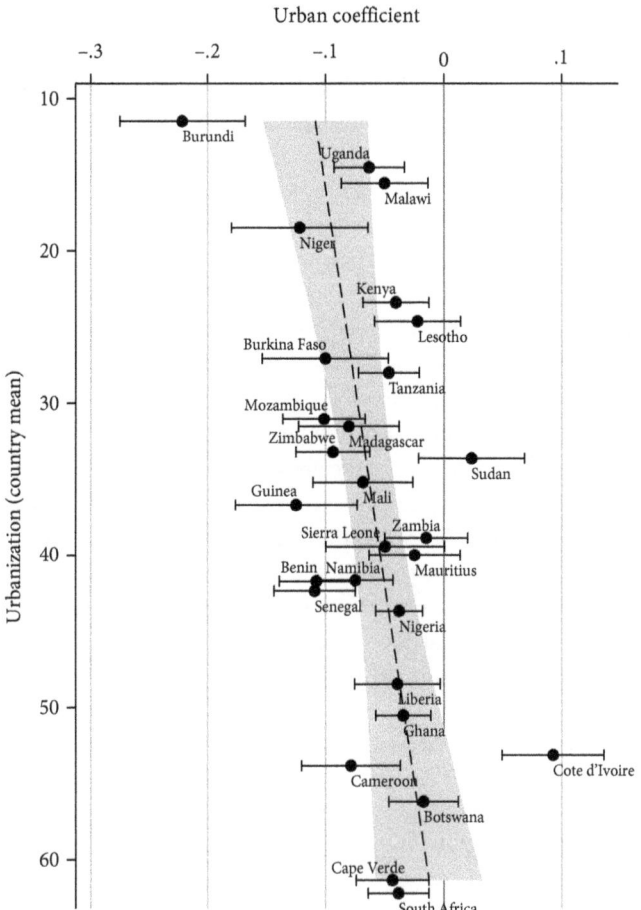

Fig. 3.3 Estimates of urban on satisfaction with democracy by country

support for incumbents and satisfaction with democracy. As was demonstrated earlier, on average urbanites take a consistently more negative view than those living in rural areas. But despite this clear trend, there are fairly stark differences in the extent to which this is expressed. In Burundi, for example, urbanites are fully 18 percentage points less likely to support incumbents, and 22 percentage points more likely to be dissatisfied with democracy than their rural counterparts. By contrast, in Botswana and Zambia there are no significant differences between urbanites and rural residents in terms of incumbent support or satisfaction with democracy.

There may of course be many potential explanations for this variation, and country- and/or time-specific factors should not be dismissed here. South Africa, for instance, is a notable outlier; while South African urbanites are only marginally (less than 4 percentage points) more likely than rural residents to express dissatisfaction with democracy, they are almost 16 percentage points less likely to express support for the incumbent African National Congress (ANC) government. This discrepancy bears consideration, suggesting as it does some country-specific issue pitting urbanites against the incumbent there. In the South African case, this is due in part to the racial distribution of both the population and political support, and to the growing urban support for Julius Malema's leftist Economic Freedom Fighters party during the period under examination. It may also be a result of the ANC's near-uncontested dominance of South African politics since 1994, which is likely to have reduced the impact of electoral incentives on the strategic distribution of public goods and services.

But while acknowledging country-specific factors may be necessary to achieve a rich and detailed understanding of any particular case, one of the many values of comparative research stems from the ability to look across cases for systematic differences that may explain the observed variation in a generalizable way. The explanation that I offer in this book is that this cross-national variation in levels of urban hostility results from variation in the extent to which African governments face electoral incentives to favor rural voters through the implementation of policies that promote pro-rural development. Since the strength of these incentives should vary with urbanization, so too should the extent of urban incumbent hostility.

The country-specific point estimates in Figs. 3.2 and 3.3 are ordered by average levels of urbanization in each country over the period covered by the surveys, with the most rural countries at the top. Eyeballing the estimates in this way provides an intuitive albeit informal way of evaluating the effects of cross-level interactions in hierarchical data.[8] Looking at the figures, it is possible to discern a broad but distinct pattern: compared to rural residents, urbanites appear most hostile to incumbents, and most dissatisfied with democracy, in countries with the lowest levels of urbanization. Moving down the figures, the negative point estimates for the *Urban* variable decrease in size, on average. What this suggests then, at least informally, is that urban hostility and dissatisfaction may indeed be conditional on urbanization.

It is important not to overstate the case here; Burundi is doing a lot of work, and much like the famous Magic Eye autostereograms, some may see nothing more than a random array of dots no matter how long or hard they stare at the plots. Statistically though, there is a relationship here. For both outcomes of interest a simple bivariate estimate of the coefficients for the *Urban* variable returns a positive coefficient on the level of urbanization, as depicted by the dashed gray lines in Figs. 3.2 and 3.3. For the estimates of satisfaction with democracy

---

[8] See Gelman and Hill (2007) for a useful discussion of this.

this coefficient is significant at the 5% level, and if we omit South Africa then for the estimates of incumbent support it is significant at the 10% level. Bear in mind the very limited number of cases and it becomes apparent that there is indeed something here. As such, though not conclusive by any means, these plots certainly indicate a conditional relationship between urban hostility and the level of urbanization. In Section 3.3 I evaluate the existence of such conditional effects more robustly.[9]

3.3 Estimating Conditional Effects

The results presented thus far demonstrate that urbanites across Africa are significantly less likely to support incumbents and express satisfaction with democracy. Moreover, they suggest that this urban hostility and dissatisfaction results from more than just structural differences across urban and rural contexts. Urbanites are not more hostile and dissatisfied simply because they know more about the alternatives, or because their demographic profile makes them more autonomous in their attitudes and behavior. Instead, there appear to be systematic differences in the political attitudes and preferences of urban and rural residents, which transcend these structural differences. I argue that at least part of the explanation for this stems from the strategic behavior of incumbent governments who, in countries with large rural majorities, face strong electoral incentives to pursue pro-rural policies. If this is indeed the case, then the extent of these urban–rural differences in incumbent support and satisfaction with democracy should be conditional on the level of urbanization, because as the size of the rural majority decreases so too should incentives to pander to the rural vote. Figs. 3.2 and 3.3 provided suggestive evidence for this, but in this section I evaluate it with far greater rigor.

3.3.1 Are the effects conditional on urbanization?

One of the many benefits of leveraging data from multiple rounds of the Afrobarometer Series is that it generates significant variation in levels of urbanization both over time and across countries. Fig. 3.4 presents the proportion

---

[9] It is worth noting a further benefit of Figs. 3.2 and 3.3, which is to highlight that the results are not being driven by countries at any particular level of development. If rural areas were most neglected in Africa's poorest countries, it might be the case that the ease of and gains from paying even a little more attention to the countryside are likely to be much greater in these cases. This could give rise to a possible concern that the broad theoretical argument does not travel across levels of development but instead is limited to only the poorest countries. The results here suggest that this is not the case, because point estimates for richer countries such as Botswana, Nigeria, and Kenya fit the expected pattern just as well as those for poorer countries such as Malawi, Mozambique, and Liberia.

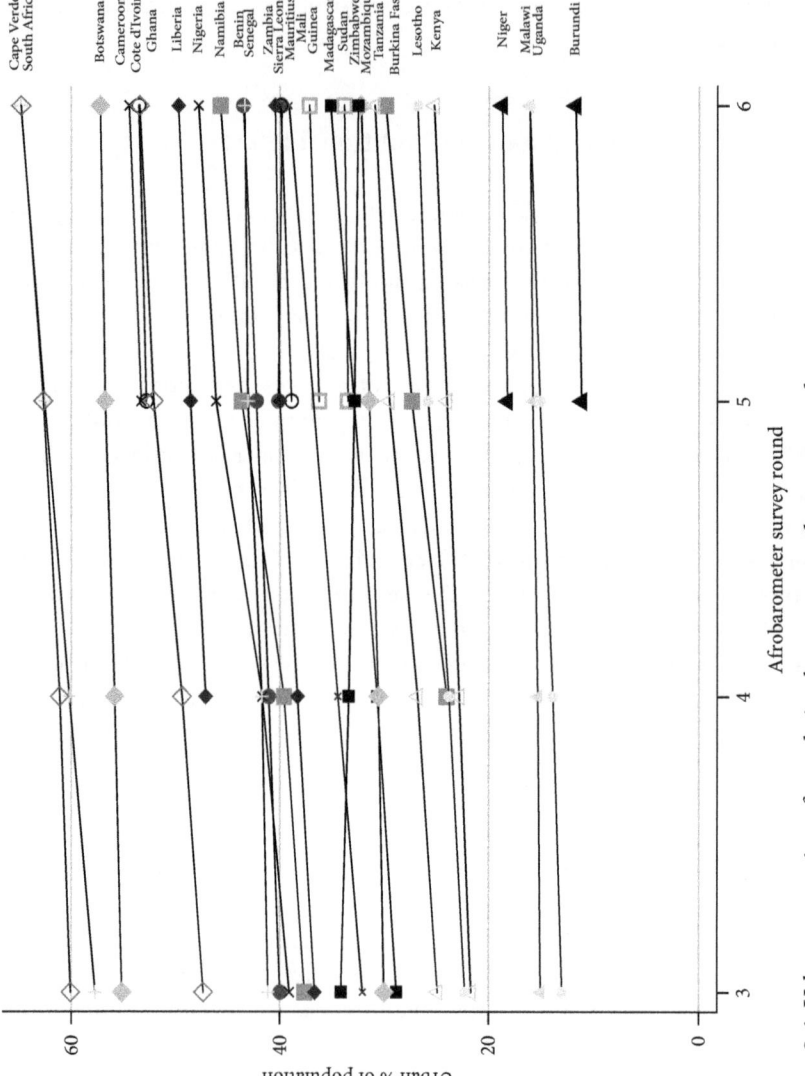

Fig. 3.4 Urban proportion of population by country and survey round

of each of the twenty-eight countries' populations that reside in urban areas for the years in which each survey round was carried out. This proportion ranges from a little over 11% in Burundi to almost 65% in Cape Verde. In only six countries was there an urban majority (Botswana, Cameroon, Cape Verde, Cote d'Ivoire, Ghana, and South Africa), at least in some survey years, reflecting the low level of urbanization across sub-Saharan Africa. Importantly though, there is substantial variation in levels of urbanization both across and within the countries in the sample. Also worth noting here is that in general, although not uniformly, urbanization has increased over time; the only countries in which urbanization has decreased are Mauritius and Zimbabwe.

If the argument that electoral incentives lead politicians to deliberately pursue policies of rural bias is correct, this variation should be significantly and inversely related to the degree of urban incumbent hostility. On the other hand, finding no systematic effect would suggest that urban incumbent hostility is not related to the deliberate strategic calculations of political actors, at least not in the way that I suggest. To evaluate whether urban–rural differences in incumbent support and satisfaction with democracy decrease as the proportion of the population living in urban areas increases, I interact the *Urban* variable with the time-varying measure of urbanization in each country. I then re-estimate the models discussed in Section 3.2.2, this time including the interaction between *Urban* and the level of urbanization. As demonstrated by Fig. 3.2, South Africa is a fairly extreme outlier in terms of urban–rural differences in incumbent support. As such, I omit it from the conditional effects estimates of incumbent support, though not from the estimates of satisfaction with democracy.[10] The results are presented in Table 3.2.

The key outcome of interest here is the presence of a significant inverse relationship between the urban proportion of the population and the effect of urban location on an individual's propensity to support the incumbent. If the argument is correct, the negative effect of urban location should reduce in magnitude as urbanization increases. Such a relationship would provide strong support for the argument that political calculations, driven by electoral incentives, underlie urban incumbent hostility in Africa. As before, all models in Table 3.2 include country and survey-round fixed effects, with robust standard errors clustered by survey. The dependent variable in the first three columns is intention to vote for the incumbent, and in the fourth, fifth, and sixth it is satisfaction with democracy. Models 1 and 4 contain just the *Urban* indicator, the *Urbanization* measure, and the interaction between these two variables. Models 2 and 5 also include the additional individual-level control variables, and Models 3 and 6 include time-varying country-level factors.

---

[10] The directions of all the coefficients remain unchanged when it is included, but the coefficient on the interaction term is no longer significant at standard levels.

Table 3.2 Conditional effects of urbanization on incumbent support and democratic satisfaction

	(1)	(2)	(3)	(4)	(5)	(6)
	Intend to vote for incumbent			Satisfied with democracy		
Urban	-0.1239***	-0.0975***	-0.1013***	-0.1173***	-0.1209***	-0.1229***
	(0.0238)	(0.0233)	(0.0231)	(0.0219)	(0.0205)	(0.0205)
Urbanization	-0.0269**	-0.0268**	0.0043	-0.0169*	-0.0169*	-0.0091
	(0.0135)	(0.0135)	(0.0165)	(0.0100)	(0.0099)	(0.0129)
Urban × Urbanization	0.0016**	0.0013**	0.0014**	0.0017***	0.0017***	0.0017***
	(0.0006)	(0.0006)	(0.0006)	(0.0005)	(0.0005)	(0.0005)
Age		0.0017***	0.0017***		0.0010***	0.0009***
		(0.0003)	(0.0003)		(0.0002)	(0.0002)
Female		0.0343***	0.0343***		-0.0002	0.0000
		(0.0063)	(0.0062)		(0.0041)	(0.0041)
Primary Education		-0.0149	-0.0145		-0.0341***	-0.0344***
		(0.0101)	(0.0102)		(0.0078)	(0.0078)
News Access		-0.0119***	-0.0124***		0.0131***	0.0130***
		(0.0042)	(0.0041)		(0.0030)	(0.0029)
GDP Growth (lag)			0.0035			-0.0019
			(0.0033)			(0.0015)
Polity IV			0.0676***			0.0377***
			(0.0203)			(0.0115)
Observations	79037	78188	78188	114722	113579	113579
Number of countries	27	27	27	28	28	28

Note: Linear probability models with country fixed effects, survey-clustered standard errors in parentheses. *p<.1, **p<.05, ***p<.01.

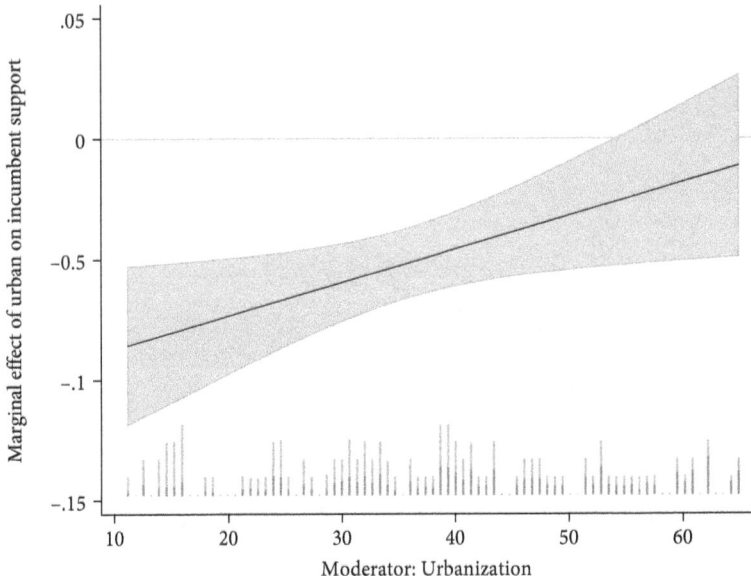

Fig. 3.5 Effect of urban location on incumbent support by urban % of population

Note: The marginal effect of being an urban resident on the probability of supporting the incumbent, as the urban % of the population increases from 11 to 65 (the sample range). The solid line is the marginal effect, the shaded area demarks 95% confidence intervals. The stacked histogram above the x-axis shows common support across observed values of the mediating variable.

The coefficients on the control variables are largely unchanged from those reported in section 3.2.2. All else being equal, female respondents, and older respondents are more likely to express support for incumbents and satisfaction with democracy, while educated respondents and those with more news access are less likely to do so. More important for the argument at hand, however, is that urban residents are significantly less likely to support incumbents than are their rural counterparts. Moreover, the positive coefficients on the interaction terms (*Urban* × *Urbanization*) demonstrate that the negative effect of being an urban resident is indeed mitigated by an increase in the urban share of the population.

This conditional effect can be seen much more clearly in Fig. 3.5, which plots the marginal effect of being an urban resident on the probability of expressing support for the incumbent, as the urban proportion of the population in the respondent's country increases. The sloped line represents the marginal effect, and the shaded area reflects 95% confidence intervals. The x-axis is constrained to reflect the range of urbanization levels observed in the sample.

What the figure shows is that if only 11% of the population live in urban areas (the lowest level of urbanization for which we have data, from Burundi in 2012), the implied effect of living in an urban location is to reduce ones probability of supporting the incumbent by 8.5 percentage points, all else equal. As the rural

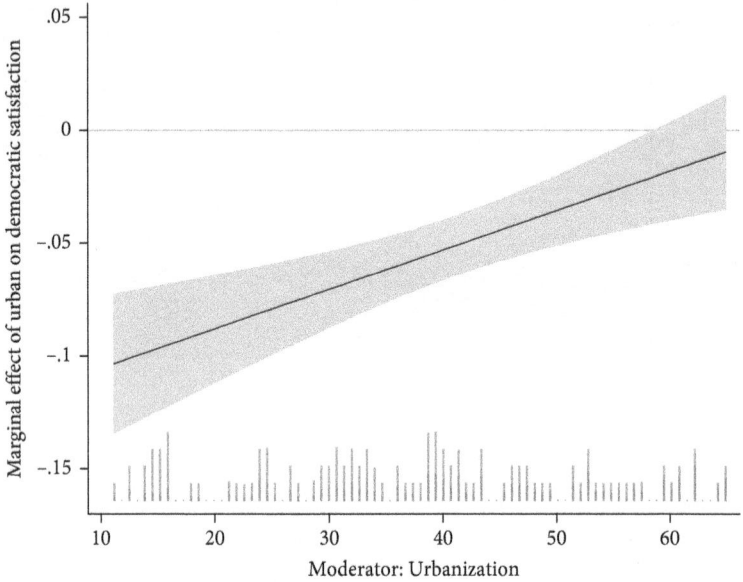

Fig. 3.6 Effect of urban location on satisfaction with democracy by urban % of population

Note: The marginal effect of being an urban resident on the probability of being satisfied with democracy, as the urban % of the population increases from 11 to 65 (the sample range). The solid line is the marginal effect, the shaded area demarks 95% confidence intervals. The stacked histogram above the x-axis shows common support across observed values of the mediating variable.

proportion of the population decreases, however, so does the implied effect, such that when roughly 54% of the population live in urban areas the likelihood of an urbanite expressing support for the incumbent is no longer significantly different from that of a rural resident.[11]

This effect is mirrored by the results for the estimates of satisfaction with democracy, which are plotted in Fig. 3.6. The effect here comes through even more starkly than with incumbent support. Again, what we can see is that urban residents are significantly less likely to express satisfaction with democracy, but only in contexts where they are part of an urban minority. At the lowest level of urbanization observed in the sample, urbanites are fully 10.3 percentage points less likely to express satisfaction with democracy than their rural counterparts. As the urban share of the population increases though, so the effect of urban location diminishes, and once the urban share of the population is more than 58% the

---

[11] As highlighted by Hainmueller, Mummolo, and Xu (2016), linear interaction models of this type assume common support across the observed values of the mediating variable, which is demonstrated by the stacked histogram overlaid above the x-axis. They also assume linear interaction effects, for which support is provided by marginal effects from a binning estimator, which demonstrate statistically different effects of urban location at typical low and high values of urbanization, but are omitted for clarity of presentation.

difference between urbanites and rural residents is no longer significant. As noted above, although satisfaction with democracy is a somewhat less direct measure of incumbent support, it is also a less sensitive topic and therefore less prone to social desirability bias. It also elicits a higher response rate, thereby alleviating concerns about non-response bias.

It is important to acknowledge here that the estimated marginal effects are just estimates. While they give a strong sense of the relationships that exist in the data, the precise point estimates are a function of the data in our sample, errors and all, and of the form with which we specify the estimation. It would be a mistake to conclude, for example, that in *all* African countries the difference in incumbent support between urbanites and rural residents will disappear when urbanization hits the magical 54% level. That being said, these results follow from robust estimates of a large sample of high-quality data, using what is a fairly conservative fixed effects specification. Therefore we can be confident that the observed trend is not a spurious one.

The nature of that trend seems quite clear: urban incumbent hostility is conditional on the proportion of the population living in urban areas. All else equal, where this proportion is higher, urbanites are less likely to reject the incumbent, and more likely to be satisfied with democracy. Evidence of this relationship is consistent with a unique observable implication of the claim that in predominantly rural countries, elections generate incentives for politicians to implement policies that benefit rural interests, while ignoring the demands of the urban minority. Focusing on electoral incentives in this way makes it possible to understand why incumbents would risk generating hostility in urban areas. Moreover, this account complements others by offering a plausible explanation for the important question of why the extent of urban incumbent hostility varies so widely across countries.

3.4 Perceptions of Policy Performance

The public opinion data used in the foregoing analysis provides a very useful means by which to measure opposition to (and support for) regimes and incumbents. Survey data has its limitations of course, not least in terms of the possibilities of response bias. But the Afrobarometer Series' consistency of questions over both space and time, and the size and variety of the available sample, make it possible to undertake a very rigorous micro-level analysis of urban–rural differences in attitudes and preferences across Africa. The evidence resulting from this analysis—that urbanites across Africa are both less supportive of incumbents and less satisfied with democracy, and that these differences are decreasing in urbanization—strongly supports the implication of the central argument that I make in this book, that electoral competition in countries with rural majorities creates incentives for governments to pursue pro-rural policy agendas.

What this evidence does not do is pin down the intermediate step in the causal mechanism; while the public opinion data used in this chapter focuses on an observable implication of the argument, it does not investigate the policy choices and outcomes that I argue are the cause of differential levels of incumbent hostility and democratic satisfaction. Chapter 4 addresses this directly by investigating variations in key health and education outcomes. Before doing so, however, it is possible to get some leverage over this issue using the Afrobarometer data to hand. If it is correct that elections provide incentives for incumbents to favor rural residents with pro-rural policies, then urbanites should on average be less satisfied with the government's performance on salient policy issues. The Afrobarometer surveys ask respondents about their perceptions of government performance across a number of policy areas, thereby enabling an investigation of this further implication.[12]

Before analyzing urban–rural differences in perceptions of government performance, a first necessary step is to decide which policy areas to focus on. Usefully, the Afrobarometer surveys ask respondents to state the most important problems facing the country that they think the government should address.[13] Unsurprisingly, across Africa urbanites and rural residents care about a wide array of different policy issues. But out of this heterogeneity of concerns two key areas emerge as being particularly salient: unemployment and poverty. This is true over time, and across both urban and rural respondents alike.

Pooling the data across all of the countries surveyed, in all four survey rounds that I analyze unemployment and poverty/destitution were cited as two of the top three most important problems. This is the case when aggregating across all respondents, and when rural and urban respondents are considered separately. In fact, across all four survey rounds and for both urbanites and rural residents, unemployment is always cited as the single most important problem facing the country. When urbanites and rural residents are taken together, poverty/destitution is the second most important problem in all four survey rounds. This is true for rural residents in Rounds four and six, while in Rounds three and five poverty/destitution is the third most important problem behind food shortage/famine (Round three) and water supply (Round five). For urbanites poverty/destitution is the second most important problem in Round three, and third behind management of the economy in the other three survey rounds.

---

[12] The question asks *Now let's speak about the performance of the present government of this country. How well or badly would you say the current government is handling the following matters, or haven't you heard enough to say? Very badly, Fairly badly, Fairly well, Very well, DK/Haven't heard enough.* A wide range of issues are asked about, but for the purposes of this analysis I focus on: "Creating jobs" and "Improving the living standards of the poor."

[13] Respondents are able to list three problems in order. I focus here just on their first responses, which I take to be indicative of what they feel is the most important problem facing the country.

The bottom line is that across Africa, citizens are concerned about unemployment and poverty. Therefore if it is indeed the case that goverments are working harder to please rural residents, we should see higher approval of government performance in these areas among rural residents. To investigate this I adopt the same strategy pursued in Section 3.3.1. Using linear probability models I estimate the extent of urban–rural differences in the likelihood of respondents approving of their government's performance in addressing these two salient issues, and I look at whether these differences are conditional on urbanization. If the argument is correct we should expect lower approval on the part of urbanites, with this difference decreasing in urbanization.

3.4.1 Unemployment

Fig. 3.7 plots the marginal effect of being an urbanite on the likelihood that one approves of the government's performance in dealing with unemployment. Full results from the regression estimates are presented in Table 3.4 in the Appendix. Just as with incumbent support and satisfaction with democracy, Fig. 3.7 shows clearly that urbanites are significantly less likely than rural residents to approve of their government's job creation efforts. At the lowest level of urbanization in the sample, the implied effect of being urban is to decrease the likelihood of approval by more than 6 percentage points. Again though, the magnitude of this urban–rural difference is decreasing in urbanization. Since the sample is limited at the higher end of the urbanization range, it may be too much to conclude firmly that this difference ever loses significance entirely. But the conditionality is clear, and as such these results lend further support to the idea that urban hostility results from African governments pursuing pro-rural policies to court the electoral support of their rural majorities.

3.4.2 Poverty

Similarly, Fig. 3.8 plots the marginal effect of being an urbanite on the likelihood that one approves of the government's performance in improving the living standards of the poor. Again, full results from the regression estimates are presented in Table 3.4 in the Appendix. What those full results show is that while urbanites are significantly less likely to approve of the government's performance in this area, the coefficient on the interaction term between *Urban* and *Urbanization* is not significant at standard levels. This is true even when South Africa is omitted from the analysis, but in this case the coefficient comes much closer to standard levels of significance ($p = 0.131$).

Fig. 3.8 plots the marginal effects from model 6 in Table 3.4, and from this we can see that there does appear to be a conditional relationship. At the lowest level

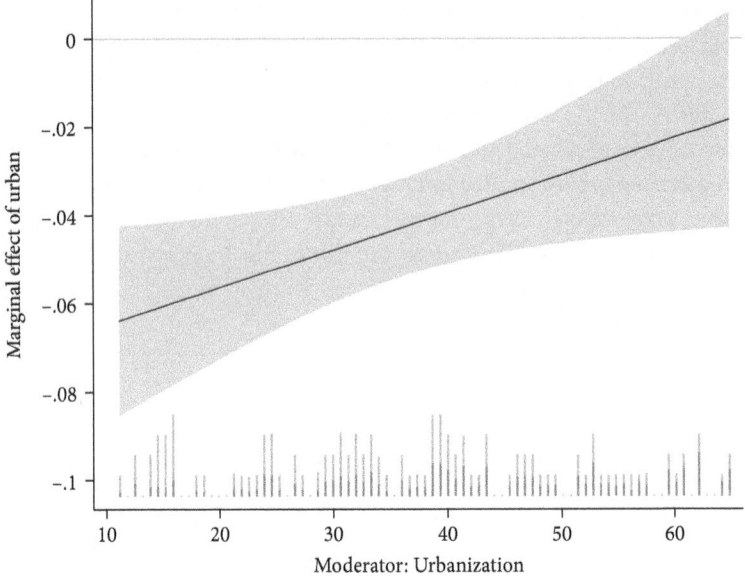

Fig. 3.7 Effect of urban location on perception of performance in creating jobs by urban % of population

Note: The marginal effect of being an urban resident on the perception of incumbent performance in creating jobs, as the urban % of the population increases from 11 to 65 (the sample range). The solid line is the marginal effect, the shaded area demarks 95% confidence intervals. The stacked histogram above the x-axis shows common support across observed values of the mediating variable.

of urbanization in the sample the implied effect of being urban is to reduce the likelihood of approval by roughly 5 percentage points. This effect is decreasing in urbanization, and loses significance when urbanization passes 52%. Again then, these results provide support for the claim that urban incumbent hostility and dissatisfaction results at least in part from governments' policy choices, which I argue are themselves the result of the electoral incentives faced by governments in rural democracies.

3.5 Conclusions

Urbanites across Africa are unhappy with their governments. Evidence from public opinion data demonstrates this clearly; urbanites are significantly and substantially less likely to support incumbents, and more likely to express dissatisfaction with democracy itself. While there are likely multiple facets to any explanation for this situation, it is not merely the result of structural factors, because these differences transcend demographic variations, and differential access to information. My argument in this book is that the large residual differences, those unexplained

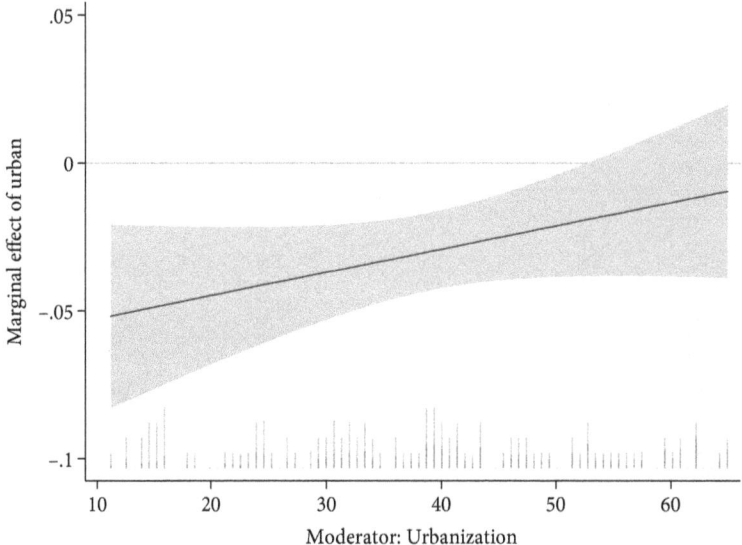

Fig. 3.8 Effect of urban location on perception of performance in improving living standards of the poor by urban % of population

Note: The marginal effect of being an urban resident on the perception of incumbent performance in improving living standards, as the urban % of the population increases from 11 to 65 (the sample range). The solid line is the marginal effect, the shaded area demarks 95% confidence intervals. The stacked histogram above the x-axis shows common support across observed values of the mediating variable.

by structural factors, result from the differential experiences of urban and rural residents with regard to government policy choices. Put simply, urbanites sense that they are getting a raw deal.

This is not unexpected. Faced with electoral constraints, African governments have incentives to pursue policies that primarily benefit their rural majorities. Of course, as urbanization increases so these incentives should dissipate, taking urban hostility and dissatisfaction with them. This is precisely what the evidence suggests. Across a range of indicators, the extent to which urbanites throughout Africa are unhappy with their governments appears to be conditional on the level of urbanization, decreasing as countries urbanize.

What we can't learn from this data is whether this unhappiness is justified. The expectation here is that urbanites are unhappy because electoral competition drives governments to pursue pro-rural policy agendas, but this data tells us nothing about actual policy outcomes. It is to this issue that I turn in Chapter 4, looking at urban–rural differences in the impact of electoral competition on basic health and education outcomes. The data analyzed in this chapter do, however, lend considerable weight to the book's central claim; the opinions and attitudes of ordinary citizens suggest that Africa's rural democracies are primarily benefiting their rural residents.

APPENDIX

Table 3.3 Country rounds in Afrobarometer sample

Country	Afrobarometer Round			
	Round 3 Year	Round 4 Year	Round 5 Year	Round 6 Year
Benin	2005	2008	2011	2014
Botswana	2005	2008	2012	2014
Burkina Faso		2008	2012	2015
Burundi			2012	2014
Cameroon			2013	2015
Cape Verde	2005	2008	2011	2014
Cote d'Ivoire			2013	2014
Ghana	2005	2008	2012	2014
Guinea			2013	2015
Kenya	2005	2008	2011	2014
Lesotho	2005	2008	2012	2014
Liberia		2008	2012	2015
Madagascar	2005	2008		2015
Malawi	2005	2008	2012	2014
Mali	2005	2008		2014
Mauritius			2012	2014
Mozambique	2005	2008	2012	2015
Namibia	2006	2008	2012	2014
Niger			2013	2015
Nigeria	2005	2008	2013	2015
Senegal	2005	2008	2013	2014
Sierra Leone			2012	2015
South Africa	2006	2008	2011	2015
Sudan			2013	2015
Tanzania	2005	2008	2012	2014
Uganda	2005	2008	2012	2015
Zambia	2005	2009	2013	2014
Zimbabwe	2005	2009	2012	2014

Table 3.4 Conditional effects of urbanization on approval of government policy performance

	(1)	(2)	(3)	(4)	(5)	(6)
	Job creation			Living standards of the poor		
Urban	-0.0404***	-0.0754***	-0.0813***	-0.0329***	-0.0460**	-0.0605***
	(0.0057)	(0.0147)	(0.0155)	(0.0066)	(0.0210)	(0.0211)
Age	0.0000	0.0000	0.0001	0.0001	0.0001	0.0002
	(0.0001)	(0.0001)	(0.0002)	(0.0002)	(0.0002)	(0.0002)
Female	0.0013	0.0014	0.0020	-0.0110***	-0.0109***	-0.0097***
	(0.0036)	(0.0036)	(0.0038)	(0.0040)	(0.0040)	(0.0040)
Primary Education	0.0022	0.0022	0.0020	0.0033	0.0033	0.0045
	(0.0059)	(0.0059)	(0.0061)	(0.0070)	(0.0070)	(0.0072)
News Access	0.0180***	0.0184***	0.0182***	0.0215***	0.0216***	0.0222***
	(0.0027)	(0.0028)	(0.0029)	(0.0028)	(0.0029)	(0.0030)
GDP Growth (lag)	-0.0061***	-0.0061***	-0.0063***	-0.0076***	-0.0076***	-0.0079***
	(0.0017)	(0.0017)	(0.0018)	(0.0025)	(0.0025)	(0.0026)
Polity IV	0.0255*	0.0256*	0.0256*	-0.0100	-0.0100	-0.0103
	(0.0139)	(0.0139)	(0.0140)	(0.0226)	(0.0226)	(0.0228)
Urbanization	-0.0141	-0.0145	-0.0150	0.0073	0.0071	0.0057
	(0.0105)	(0.0105)	(0.0108)	(0.0139)	(0.0139)	(0.0144)
Urban × Urbanization		0.0008**	0.0011***		0.0003	0.0008
		(0.0004)	(0.0004)		(0.0005)	(0.0005)
Observations	120441	120441	113393	97342	97342	92668
Number of countries	28	28	27	28	28	27

Note: Linear probability models with country fixed effects, survey-clustered standard errors in parentheses. Estimates in columns 3 and 6 omit South Africa. * p<.1, ** p<.05, *** p<.01.

4

Democracy's Rural Dividend

4.1 Introduction

For the time being at least, a majority of Africans live in the countryside. As a result, the introduction of democratic electoral competition across much of Africa has led governments to pursue pro-rural agendas in basic service provision. When the votes are in the countryside, you go to the countryside to look for votes. This is not undemocratic, however frustrating it may be for urbanites. But it is important to acknowledge, especially if we are to fully understand the impact of democracy on basic service provision. It is also important to demonstrate this fact if we are to be convinced by the explanation offered in this book, for why urbanites across Africa are more hostile towards incumbents, and more dissatisfied with democracy, relative to rural residents. If urban dissatisfaction is the result of governments' pursuing pro-rural policy agendas to win elections, it should be the case that the introduction of electoral competition is more beneficial for rural residents than for those in cities. Furthermore, if such pro-rural development does result from electoral incentives, then its extent should be conditional on the level of urbanization.

In this chapter I provide evidence that this is indeed the case.[1] Using individual-level data across twenty-seven African countries from the Demographic and Health Survey (DHS) series, I focus on the impact of democracy on the most basic health and education outcomes: primary education and infant mortality rates. The analysis demonstrates a substantial pro-rural effect of democratic elections on access to primary education and on infant survival. Moreover, it shows that the extent of these urban–rural differences is conditional on and decreasing in the level of urbanization. When it comes to essential health and education services then, it is the people in the countryside who appear to be the primary beneficiaries of Africa's rural democracies.

4.2 Who Benefits from Democracy in Africa?

There is a growing consensus that democracy increases the provision of public goods and services. While a number of studies have provided evidence of this broad relationship at the national level, with ever-increasing sophistication and

---

[1] Some of the evidence presented in this chapter is contained in Harding (2020). ©2019 by the Southern Political Science Association. Reprinted with permission.

Rural Democracy: Elections and Development in Africa. Robin Harding, Oxford University Press (2020).
© Robin Harding.
DOI: 10.1093/oso/9780198851073.001.0001

rigor, for the most part the effects of democracy have not been disaggregated across different groups.[2] This matters in a broad sense, because by focusing on average effects we can lose sight of important nuances related to the heterogeneous impact of democracy. Moreover, theoretically there are good reasons to think that the effects of democracy will not be uniform across all individuals.

Following from the theoretical discussion in Chapter 2, my argument in this book is that any increase in basic service provision resulting from democracy will primarily benefit rural residents, because competitive elections create incentives for African governments to implement policies that favor the interests of the rural majority. Central to this argument is the role of accountability; democracy increases public goods provision because competitive elections render politicians accountable to the mass electorate. In order to win elections governments must capture the support of a majority of voters. Since the large numbers of voters involved in popular elections make it prohibitively expensive and impractical to mobilize an electoral majority with private goods, a cheaper and more feasible alternative is to implement policies that increase the provision of public goods and services. Consequently, the introduction of democratic electoral competition should imply an increase in the overall level of basic service provision.

What the introduction of democratic elections does not imply, however, is that all citizens will benefit equally from any such increase in basic service provision. In Africa's rural democracies, electoral competition creates incentives for governments to target the support of rural voters, to the extent that they represent an electoral majority. As noted in Chapter 2, my expectation is that democracy in Africa leads to pro-rural development because African governments engage in both programmatic and targeted forms of distribution. For example, democracy leads governments to implement ostensibly universal policies such as the abolition of school fees or the creation of health insurance schemes that happen to benefit rural residents more than urbanites. At the same time, these governments are likely to target resources such as schools and clinics to rural areas rather than urban centers.

If we are to evaluate this expectation, what outcomes should we investigate? This choice is hugely important, and can entirely determine the conclusions we might draw about the relationship between democracy and distributive politics. A first-order consideration should be that the outcomes under investigation are consequential to the voters themselves; voters are unlikely to respond positively to things that they neither want nor need. Therefore if electoral competition drives African governments to court the rural majority, we should expect these

---

[2] Studies have investigated the impact of democracy on healthcare and education spending, and on outcomes such as infant mortality rates, literacy levels, and electrification. Examples include Stasavage (2005a), Ross (2006), and Besley and Kudamatsu (2006). A small number of studies do consider heterogeneous effects, such as the research by Brown and Mobarak (2009), Min (2015), and Kroth, Larcinese, and Wehner (2016).

governments to pursue policies that appeal broadly to rural voters. Such policies are likely to include those which increase access to basic services.

At the most basic levels, rural development in Africa lags far behind the rest of the world. Data from the World Bank's World Development Indicators show that in 2017 infant mortality rates in sub-Saharan Africa were almost twice as high as the global average, and net primary school enrollment was 12 percentage points lower. Moreover, urban–rural differences within Africa are substantial; since 1980 children in rural areas have been 15% less likely to receive any schooling than those living in urban locations, and infant mortality rates have been 20 percentage points higher. In this context, it seems reasonable to expect widespread support for policies that increase access to basic education and health services, especially in rural areas.

This is borne out by public opinion data from the Afrobarometer Series. For example, data from the third round of surveys carried out between 2005 and 2006 show that 22% of respondents saw education as one of the top three most important problems facing the country, with 21% saying the same about health. While the proportion concerned with education was roughly equivalent across urban and rural respondents, those in rural areas were 5 percentage points more likely to view health as a major concern compared with urbanites. Given the weight placed by voters on health and education, democratic elections are likely to create incentives for governments to implement pro-rural development policies that improve basic health and education outcomes for people living in the countryside.

Furthermore, if pro-rural policies are driven by incentives to court the rural majority, then as the size of this majority decreases so too will these incentives. As a result, the extent of any urban–rural differences in the impact of democracy on basic health and education outcomes will be conditional on national levels of urbanization. Taken together, this argument has three observable implications: (1) democratic electoral competition will have a positive effect on basic education and health outcomes; (2) these positive effects will be greater in rural areas; (3) the extent of this pro-rural difference will be conditional on, and decreasing in, the level of urbanization. My goal in this chapter is to rigorously evaluate these three implications.

4.3 The Effect of Democracy on Education and Health

4.3.1 Measuring democracy

There is no single accepted definition of democracy, and debates over what constitutes "the D-word" have run over countless pages. But while these debates are both important and interesting, they have led to a proliferation of definitions that is not conducive to the rigorous analysis of democracy's effects. Confronted with this array of definitions, we must therefore make a choice. The theoretical argument laid out in Chapter 2 emphasizes the impact of incentives created by meaningful democratic elections. Facing what are often large rural majorities, it is these incentives that lead many African governments to pursue pro-rural policy agendas in order to retain political power. Therefore, although scholars have adopted various approaches to defining and measuring democracy, the choice of approach herein is informed by this theoretical argument.

The first consideration is whether to adopt a purely procedural approach, focusing solely on observable formal institutions, or a more subjective measure such as Polity or Freedom House that relies on the judgments of individual coders. Given the theoretical focus on electoral institutions, I opt for the greater objectivity of an *ex ante* measure of formal institutions. The second question is whether multiparty elections are sufficient, or whether the set of democracies should be limited to those countries in which the electoral playing field is more level. Harding and Stasavage (2014) take the more inclusive approach, and demonstrate that, irrespective of quality, the presence of multiparty elections alone has been sufficient to encourage the abolition of primary school fees in many countries, which has led to significant increases in primary school enrollment across Africa.

By contrast, in his analysis of the impact of democracy on infant mortality rates across Africa, Kudamatsu (2012) follows Cheibub and Przeworski (1999) in requiring elections that have led to the replacement in power of the chief executive. The addition of this replacement requirement brings with it the virtue of prudence. As Cheibub and Przeworski (1999) note, the problem with classifying regimes as democratic purely on the basis of formal institutional criteria is that in some cases these criteria are met and yet the incumbent always wins. This matters because in cases such as these it is impossible to know both whether the incumbent would have held elections if they were not certain of victory, and whether they would have ceded power if they had actually lost. One option is to classify such cases as democracies, but this runs the risk of inducing type I errors, or false positives. The more prudent alternative is to opt for type II errors, or false negatives, classifying these cases as not democratic when in fact they might have been. While this may be upsetting to supporters of Botswanan democracy, it is prudent in a general sense because it reduces the risk of falsely concluding that democracy is the cause of any observed effect, if in fact it is not.

This may seem to some like an exercise in pedantry, since globally this question may bite in only a very small proportion of cases. But it is a pertinent issue when classifying regime types in Africa, because in many cases the rapid introduction of multiparty elections in the 1990s did not immediately lead to the replacement of authoritarian incumbents. Table 4.1 lists the countries that are included in the analysis in this chapter, along with the years in which they would be coded as democratic under either the replacement rule (in the *Democracy Years* column) as opposed to the more inclusive alternative (in the *Multiparty Years* column). What

Table 4.1 Countries included in analysis, with years democratic

Country	Survey Year	Democracy Years	Multiparty Years
Benin	2011	1992–	1992–
Burkina Faso	2010		1980, 2006–
Cameroon	2011		1993–
Chad	2004		1997–
Comoros	2012	1991–1999, 2002–	1991–
Cote d'Ivoire	2011	2001–	1991–
Ethiopia	2011		1996–
Gabon	2012		1994–
Ghana	2008	1980, 2001–	1980—1981, 1993–
Guinea	2012	2012–	1994–2008
Kenya	2008	2003–	1993–
Lesotho	2009	1994–	1994–
Madagascar	2008	1994–2009	1983–2009
Malawi	2010	1995–	1995–
Mali	2012	1993–	1993–
Mozambique	2011		1995–
Namibia	2013	1991–	1991–
Niger	2012	1994–	1994–2009, 2012–
Nigeria	2013	1980–1983, 2000–	1980–1983, 2000–
Rwanda	2010		2004–
Senegal	2010	2001–	1980–
South Africa	1998	1995–	1980–
Tanzania	2010		1996–
Togo	2013		1995–
Uganda	2011	1981–1985	1981–1985, 1997–
Zambia	2007	1992–	1992–
Zimbabwe	2010	1981–	1981–

Note: Democracy years updated from Kudamatsu (2012). Multiparty years from the Database of Political Institutions. Years cover full years under specific regime type. For example, Benin became democratic in 1991, so 1992 was the first *full* year under democracy. Table covers period from 1980 to survey year.

this demonstrates is that the former is significantly more restrictive, resulting in nine of the twenty-seven countries being coded as never having democratized during the period under analysis (1980 to the present).

One way to think about the replacement criterion is as an objective indicator of democratic quality, albeit a rather blunt one. By adding this criterion to the coding rule, what we are doing then is effectively restricting the set of democracies to cases where we can be certain that multiparty elections impose a meaningful constraint on the executive. Given the theoretical emphasis on meaningful electoral competition, this addition seems reasonable. This is not to say that elections of lesser "quality" have no impact; as Harding and Stasavage (2014) have shown, policy change can result from the introduction of elections which do not pass this higher democratic bar. But it is possible that the incentives required for incumbents to pursue more costly policy changes, and/or more demanding electoral strategies, may not kick in until the electoral playing field is somewhat more level.

Rulers everywhere pursue a variety of strategies to win elections, including some that seem downright undemocratic. Even when the electoral playing field is unlevel, rulers may choose to implement fairly costless policies that maximize vote share—such as abolishing school fees—in order to offset the costs of electoral manipulation. But where electoral constraints are weaker, rulers may be unwilling to pay the costs of designing and implementing policies in order to more carefully construct an electoral majority. To an incumbent who is prepared to rig or coerce their way to victory, the costs of carefully targeted resource provision may seem unreasonably high. If this is the case, then we should not expect such weaker electoral constraints to induce a strategy of pro-rural development. And as such, a measure of democracy that omits the replacement rule, or that imposes no similar "quality" criterion, will fail to provide an adequate test of the theoretical claim.

Therefore in line with the theoretical argument, I adopt a measure of democracy that includes the replacement criterion, updating the coding provided by Kudamatsu (2012) to cover the additional country-years in my sample. Alongside this, however, I evaluate the impact of the replacement requirement by also employing a less restrictive *Multiparty* measure, using data from the Database of Political Institutions (Beck et al. 2001) to determine whether a country's chief executive was elected in multiparty competition.

4.3.2 Measuring education and health outcomes

In order to evaluate the effect of democracy on basic service provision I need data on education and health outcomes across countries, before and after the introduction of competitive elections. Futhermore, in order to differentiate the effects for rural as opposed to urban residents the data must be disaggregated below the national level. Various international and inter-governmental organizations provide data on education and health outcomes over time. For example, UNESCO collects official education statistics by country, and UNICEF and the World Bank provide country-level data on a variety of health indicators. But for all of these sources the data is aggregated at the national level, which prevents investigation of potential urban–rural differences.

Instead then, I use household survey data taken from the Demographic and Health Surveys (DHS) Program. The DHS provides high-quality individual-level data on a variety of development indicators, including education attainment and child health, for over ninety countries around the world. I use data from the most recent surveys at the time of writing, from the twenty-seven African countries listed in Table 4.1.[3] The DHS are carried out at household level, and the data contain information on years of schooling completed for all individuals in each household. In addition, a survey of women collects birth histories for all mothers surveyed, providing information on infant mortality.[4]

Using these data, I am able to estimate the impact of democracy on infant mortality and access to primary schooling. For the infant mortality estimates I have a total sample of 879,856 children, born to 231,784 mothers. For each child I construct the variable *Infant Death*, coded 1 if the child died before her first birthday, and 0 otherwise. To measure the impact of democracy on infant mortality I code the variables *Multiparty* and *Democracy* as 1 if the child was born in a country that was democratic by the relevant measure throughout the year in which she was born, and 0 otherwise.

For the education estimates I have a total sample of 578,695 individuals, from 267,383 households. For each individual I construct the dummy variable *Any Schooling*, coded 1 if an individual has ever attended primary school and 0 otherwise. To measure the impact of democracy on primary schooling I code the variables *Multiparty* and *Democracy* to capture the proportion of an individual's primary school-age years spent in a context of democracy, again by the relevant measure.[5] These variables take a value of 1 for all cases in which an individual reached the official age of school entry subsequent to the introduction of democracy. If an individual reached the normal school leaving age prior to competitive elections being introduced, the variables take a value of zero. Finally, in cases where an individual reached the normal age of school entry before competitive elections were introduced, but elections were subsequently introduced before the individual reached normal school leaving age, the variables take a value between 0 and 1 equal to the proportion of their school age years spent under democracy.

4.3.3   Evaluating the impact of democracy

With these data it is possible to very rigorously evaluate the impact of democracy on infant mortality rates and access to primary education, and to separate the effects across urban and rural areas. In order to do so I estimate linear probability

---

[3] This includes all of the countries analyzed by Kudamatsu (2012) apart from Mauritania, for which data access is restricted.

[4] I restrict all of the analyses to children born since 1980 in order to limit bias resulting from the effects of education on life expectancy. This is done because educated people tend to live longer (Cutler and Lleras-Muney 2006), and therefore if all individuals born since independence were included then we would be less likely to observe individuals who were of primary school age prior to the introduction of democracy but who did not go to school than those who did. Any such bias should only be expected to impact the estimates of education, and for the infant mortality estimates doing so has no substantive effect on the results.

[5] Official primary school ages vary by country, and are available from UNESCO.

models where the outcome of interest is either infant mortality or access to primary education. Given that many additional factors might also affect basic health and education outcomes, I pursue a range of strategies to better identify the impact of democracy. First, all of the estimates include year-of-birth fixed effects and country-specific linear time trends, which control for any country-level changes in education and health that are unrelated to electoral competition. I also include dummy variables for birth order and gender, and the estimates of infant mortality include a dummy variable for multiple births (i.e. twins, triplets, or quadruplets).[6] Moreover, since *Democracy* does not vary across individuals born in the same country in a given year, I cluster standard errors by country-year-of-birth.

To increase robustness further I include mother fixed effects in the estimates of infant mortality, and household fixed effects when the outcome of interest is access to primary education. Including household fixed effects is useful for the education analysis because it means we are only estimating the effect of democracy for households in which there were children of primary school age both before and after democratization. This controls for any potentially confounding household level characteristics that may vary systematically over time within a country, and which might affect both the chances of democratization and access to primary education. Similarly, including mother fixed effects for the estimates of infant mortality exploits within-mother variation in infant survival, thereby ensuring that any estimated effect of democracy is robust to the possibility that broader demographic changes might affect both regime type and infant survival rates.

If democratic elections in Africa reduce infant mortality rates, what we should find is that the estimated coefficient for the *Democracy* variable should be negative; if democratic elections increase primary school attendance, the coefficient should be positive. The second observable implication of the theoretical argument is that any positive effects of democracy on education and health will be greater in rural areas. The simplest way to evaluate this is to split the sample based on whether respondents live in urban or rural locations.[7] Therefore as well as estimating the impact of democracy on education and health outcomes for the full sample, I also estimate all of the models separately for urban and rural households. If the theoretical argument is correct, the effect of democracy will be greater for rural residents than for urbanites.[8]

The third implication of the theoretical argument is that the extent of any pro-rural difference in the effect of democracy will be conditional on urbanization

---

[6] This follows the approach taken by Kudamatsu (2012).

[7] This information is coded into the DHS data at the household level based on national census files.

[8] An alternative approach is to include an interaction term between the *Democracy* variable and the rural location dummy in the estimates using the full sample. Doing so yields almost identical results (which are included in the Appendix). For ease of interpretation I split the sample between urban and rural residents, but it is worth highlighting that the estimates using the interaction term demonstrate that the urban–rural differences in the effect of democracy are statistically significant at standard levels.

at the national-level. I evaluate this by interacting the *Democracy* variable with a national-level measure of urbanization taken from the World Bank's World Development Indicators. For the infant mortality estimates this measure reflects the level of urbanization in the child's year of birth, and for the education estimates it reflects the level of urbanization in the year that the child reaches primary school age. If the theoretical argument is correct, this term should be positive and significant in the estimates of infant mortality for rural residents, and significantly negative in the education estimates for rural residents. There is no reason to expect it to be significant in the estimates for urban residents.

4.4 Results

Table 4.2 contains results from OLS estimates of infant mortality and access to primary education, for the full sample as well as the urban and rural subsamples. The outcome of interest in panel (a) is whether a child died before her first birthday, and in panel (b) it is whether a child ever attended primary school. Coefficients for the control variables noted in section 4.3.3 are omitted for clarity of presentation, but these variables are included in all of the regression models.

4.4.1   Average effects of democracy

Does democracy in Africa improve basic education and health outcomes? We can answer this question by looking at the first column of Table 4.2, which contains the results from models (1) and (7). These represent the average effect of democracy on infant mortality and access to primary education, respectively, for all individuals across the twenty-seven countries in the sample. The answer given by these results is clearly positive; the introduction of democracy in Africa has led to a reduction in infant mortality rates, and an increase in access to primary education. For both outcomes these average effects are statistically significant at or close to the 0.05 level.[9] Perhaps more importantly, these effects are also substantial.

The *Democracy* coefficient in model (1) implies that if a child is born in a democracy as opposed to a non-democratic regime, the probability of her dying before her first birthday is reduced by just under one-third of a percentage point. In more concrete terms, this implies that the introduction of democracy has led to 3.2 fewer infants dying before reaching one year of age, for every 1,000 live births. As far as education is concerned, the results imply that if a child spends all her primary school age years in a democracy as opposed to a non-democracy, the probability of her ever attending school increases by 1.3 percentage points.

---

[9] For the infant mortality estimate $p=0.064$, and for the education estimate $p=0.021$.

Table 4.2 The effects of democracy on basic service provision

	All		Urban		Rural	
	(1)	(2)	(3)	(4)	(5)	(6)
(a) DV = Infant Death						
Democracy	-0.0032*		-0.0016		-0.0041**	
	(0.0017)		(0.0023)		(0.0021)	
Multiparty		-0.0068***		-0.0023		-0.0083***
		(0.0015)		(0.0022)		(0.0017)
Number of countries	27		27		27	
Number of mothers	231784		75408		156376	
Observations	879856		240690		639166	
	(7)	(8)	(9)	(10)	(11)	(12)
(b) DV = Any Schooling						
Democracy	0.0133**		0.0036		0.0205***	
	(0.0058)		(0.0067)		(0.0074)	
Multiparty		0.0157***		0.0203***		0.0121*
		(0.0058)		(0.0054)		(0.0072)
Number of countries	27		27		27	
Number of households	267383		91826		175557	
Observations	578695		206204		372491	

Note: Estimates from linear probability models of the effect of democracy on: (a) infant mortality rates; (b) access to primary education. All estimates include gender and birth order dummies, year-of-birth fixed effects, country-specific linear time trends, and either (a) mother fixed effects or (b) household fixed effects. Estimates of infant mortality also include a dummy for multiple births. Estimates of primary education also include dummies for relationship to household head. Standard errors in parentheses, clustered by country-year-of-birth. * $p<.1$, ** $p<.05$, *** $p<.01$.

For the most part, it appears that these average effects are not dependent on multiparty elections being of any sufficiently high level of quality. From the coefficient in model (8) we can see that when the *Multiparty* variable is used instead, the average effect on access to primary education is very similar. Interestingly, the *Multiparty* coefficient in model (2) demonstrates that the implied effect on infant mortality is almost twice the size of that of the more restrictive *Democracy* measure. One possible explanation for this is that major gains in infant health may have followed the introduction of multiparty elections, irrespective of whether these elections led to incumbent turnover.

Given the robustness of the estimation strategy, these results provide convincing evidence that the introduction of democratic elections in Africa has had a positive impact on basic health and education outcomes. On average, children born in democracies are more likely to survive past their first birthdays. And when they do, the chances of them going to school increase as they spend more of their primary school years under democratic rule. Interestingly, the results from the estimates that use the *Multiparty* measure imply that even where the playing field is uneven, multiparty electoral competition generates incentives for incumbents to pursue vote-maximizing policies that improve basic health and education outcomes.

Up to this point, the results are in line with the theoretical argument; democracy apears to generate electoral incentives for governments to improve basic service provision. But as was argued in Chapter 2, electoral success does not require winning all the votes, only a majority. And since most African countries have rural majorities, the benefits of democracy are likely to be felt primarily by rural residents.

4.4.2   Differential urban–rural effects

To investigate whether the benefits of democracy are indeed felt more strongly in the countryside, I estimate the impact of democracy on infant mortality and access to primary education separately for urban and rural households. The results from models (3) and (5) in Table 4.2 show the effect of democracy on infant mortality for urban and rural residents, respectively, and those from models (9) and (11) do the same for access to primary education. The differences here are fairly stark; across Africa, the impact of democracy on basic education and health outcomes is primarily a rural phenomenon. When the analysis is restricted to urbanites, democracy has no significant effect on either infant mortality or access to primary education. Moreover, the coefficients on the *Democracy* variable are less than half the size of those estimated using the full sample.

Instead, for both education and health, the significant average effects of democracy are being driven by democracy's impact in rural areas. For infant mortality, when estimated on just the rural subsample the effect of democracy is greater than the estimated average effect, and remains significant at the 0.05 level. In rural areas, the probability of dying before the age of one is reduced by almost half a percentage point if a child is born into a democracy. For every 1,000 live births in rural areas, democracy means that 4.1 more infants celebrate their first birthdays. The differential effect of democracy on access to primary education is similarly clear. For the rural subsample the impact of democracy is more than 50% larger than the average estimated effect, and this is significant at the 0.01 level. In the countryside, spending all their primary school age years in a democracy increases the probability of children going to school by 2 percentage points.

For both education and health outcomes the positive effects of democracy are primarily pro-rural; in its impact on basic service provision, democracy is good for Africa's rural residents. It is worth noting here that pooling the data across urban and rural residents and including an interaction term between the *Democracy* variable and a dummy for rural location yields almost identical results, and demonstrates that the urban–rural differences in the effects of democracy on access to primary education and infant mortality rates are statistically significant at the 0.05 level (results are presented in the Appendix, in Table 4.9).

A similar pattern can be seen when the *Multiparty* measure is used, although here there is weaker evidence for rural bias in the impact of electoral competition on education. Even when the electoral playing field may not be level, the introduction of multiparty elections has a substantially smaller effect on infant mortality for urbanites than for rural residents, and one that is only statistically significant for the latter group. For education the estimated effect is larger for urbanites, although again pooling the data and including an interaction term between the *Multiparty* variable and a dummy for rural location demonstrates that the effects of elections on access to primary education and infant mortality rates are significantly larger for rural residents.

4.4.3   Are the effects conditional on urbanization?

These results therefore highlight a clear pro-rural accent to the impact of democracy on basic education and health outcomes. This is strongly supportive of the argument that democratic elections create incentives for governments to prioritize pro-rural policies, but we can go further still. If these outcomes really do result from the strategic actions of incumbents seeking to mobilize the rural majority, then the extent of the pro-rural differences that have been illuminated should be conditional on urbanization. If governments implement pro-rural policies in order to court the votes of the rural majority, it follows that the extent to which this strategy is pursued will depend upon the size of that rural majority. To evaluate this, I interact the *Democracy* and *Multiparty* variables with a measure of urbanization at the national level. The results are presented in Tables 4.3 and 4.4. Table 4.3 shows results when the outcome of interest is infant mortality, and in Table 4.4 the outcome is access to primary education.

Looking first at the infant mortality estimates in Table 4.3, the results from model (1) show that when the entire sample is used there is indeed a significant interaction between democracy and urbanization, in the expected direction. As noted above, democracy reduces infant mortality rates, but what we can see now is that this effect decreases as the level of urbanization increases. Again though, of greater interest is the difference in the conditional effect of democracy across urban and rural residents. As before, I investigate this by splitting the sample and re-estimating the conditional effects separately for urban and rural residents. The coefficients from model (3) show that there is no significant effect of democracy for urban residents nor is there a significant interaction between democracy and urbanization. Instead, the average conditional effects are driven by the conditional effects of democracy on infant mortality for rural residents. When estimated only for rural residents, the coefficient on the *Democracy* variable in model (5) is slightly larger than that estimated for the entire sample, and remains statistically significant. Moreover, the coefficient on the interaction term between *Democracy* and *Urbanization* is also statistically significant when estimated for the rural subsample.

The magnitude of these conditional effects can be seen far more clearly in the graphs presented in Fig. 4.1. In each graph the sloped line represents the predicted marginal effects of democracy on infant mortality at all levels of urbanization included in the sample, with the gray area around it showing the 95% confidence interval.[10] Panel (a) shows the marginal effects for urban residents and panel (b) shows the same for rural residents. What these graphs demonstrate is that for urbanites democracy has no statistically significant effect on infant mortality at any level of urbanization. By contrast, for rural residents democracy has a negative and statistically significant effect on infant mortality up to a level of urbanization of 29%.

A majority of the children in the infant mortality sample were born in countries where the level of urbanization was less than 30% (full summary statistics are included in Table 4.8 in the Appendix). Taking into consideration the distribution of urbanization for the rural subsample, the marginal effects presented in panel (b) of Fig. 4.1 imply that the effect of democracy on infant mortality is significant

---

[10] These graphs were created using the code provided by Hainmueller, Mummolo, and Xu (2016). The stacked histograms at the bottom of each panel show the distribution of urbanization in the sample, with the dark and light portions of the histogram bars showing the distribution of democracy to non-democracy, respectively. These demonstrate that the estimates of conditional effects have common support, and do not rely on excessive extrapolation. Marginal effects from a binning estimator support the assumption of linear interaction effects for the rural subsample, and demonstrate statistically different effects of democracy at typical low and high values of urbanization, but are omitted for clarity of presentation.

Table 4.3 Conditional effects of democracy on infant mortality

DV = *Infant Death*	All		Urban		Rural	
	(1)	(2)	(3)	(4)	(5)	(6)
Democracy	-0.0128**		-0.0069		-0.0143**	
	(0.0054)		(0.0074)		(0.0061)	
Urbanization	-0.0023***	-0.0019***	-0.0019***	-0.0018***	-0.0025***	-0.0020***
	(0.0006)	(0.0006)	(0.0008)	(0.0008)	(0.0008)	(0.0008)
Democracy × Urbanization	0.0003**		0.0002		0.0004**	
	(0.0002)		(0.0002)		(0.0002)	
Multiparty		-0.0068**		-0.0044		-0.0070*
		(0.0033)		(0.0044)		(0.0041)
Multiparty × Urbanization		0.0000		0.0001		-0.0000
		(0.0001)		(0.0001)		(0.0001)
Number of countries	27		27		27	
Number of mothers	231784		75408		156376	
Observations	879856		240690		639166	

Note: Estimates from linear probability models of the effect of democracy on infant mortality. All estimates include gender and birth order dummies, year-of-birth fixed effects, country-specific linear time trends, a dummy for multiple births, and mother fixed effects. Standard errors in parentheses, clustered by country-year-of-birth.
*p<.1, **p<.05, ***p<.01.

Table 4.4 Conditional effects of democracy on access to primary education

DV = *Any Schooling*	All		Urban		Rural	
	(1)	(2)	(3)	(4)	(5)	(6)
Democracy	0.0428**		0.0231		0.0489**	
	(0.0171)		(0.0201)		(0.0206)	
Urbanization	0.0110***	0.0119***	0.0048***	0.0048***	0.0153***	0.0169***
	(0.0020)	(0.0020)	(0.0017)	(0.0017)	(0.0029)	(0.0029)
Democracy × Urbanization	−0.0012*		−0.0007		−0.0013*	
	(0.0006)		(0.0007)		(0.0008)	
Multiparty		0.0468***		0.0421***		0.0562***
		(0.0109)		(0.0104)		(0.0139)
Multiparty × Urbanization		−0.0014***		−0.0008***		−0.0021***
		(0.0003)		(0.0003)		(0.0005)
Number of countries	27		27		27	
Number of households	267383		91826		175557	
Observations	578695		206204		372491	

Note: Estimates from linear probability models of the effect of democracy on access to primary education. All estimates include gender and birth order dummies, year-of-birth fixed effects, country-specific linear time trends, dummies for relationship to household head, and household fixed effects. Standard errors in parentheses, clustered by country-year-of-birth. *p<.1, **p<.05, ***p<.01.

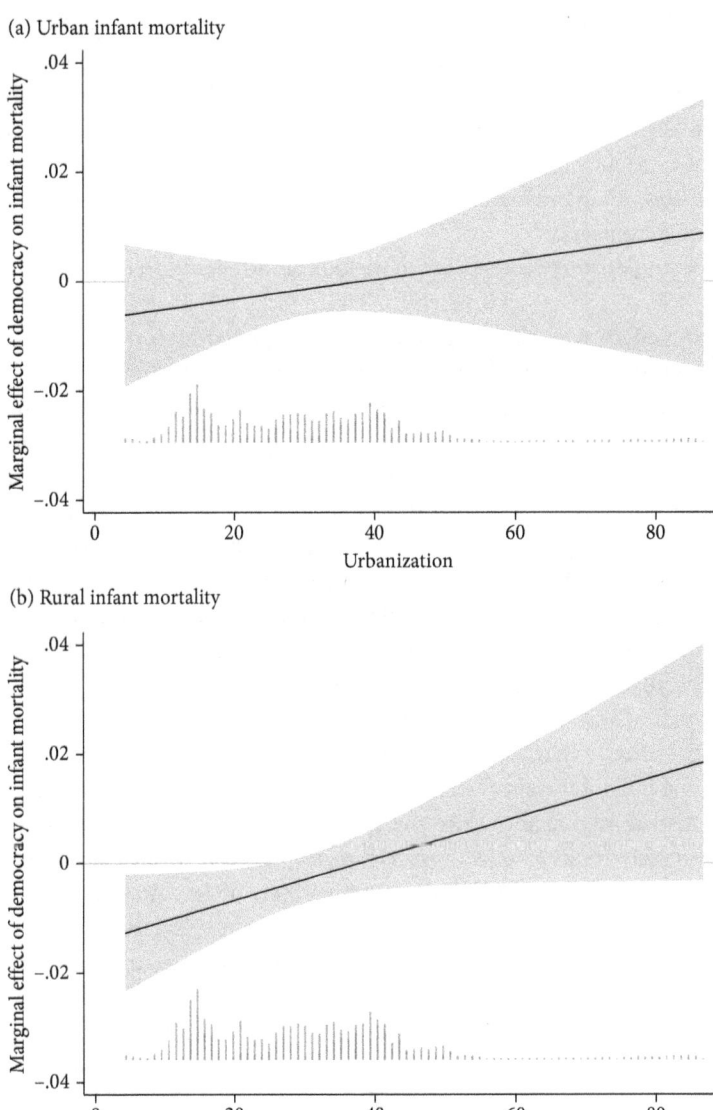

Fig. 4.1 Marginal effects of democracy on infant mortality

Note: Sloped lines show marginal effects of democracy on the probability of a child dying before reaching her first birthday. Gray areas are 95% confidence intervals. (a) shows effects for urban residents and (b) shows effects for rural residents. Stacked histograms show the distribution of urbanization, with the dark and light portions of the bars showing the distribution of democracy to non-democracy, respectively.

for half of the sampled rural residents. Most importantly, these graphs show that in countries with large rural majorities (where those living in rural areas make up more than 70% of the population), the effects of democracy are clearly pro-rural. In such contexts, democracy leads to a statistically significant reduction in infant mortality for rural residents, but has no statistically significant effect for urbanites. As urbanization increases beyond 29%, however, this urban–rural difference disappears.

A very similar story emerges when we look at the education estimates. Looking at Table 4.4, we can see that when the entire sample is analyzed there is a clear interaction effect, whereby the positive effect of democracy on access to primary education is decreasing in the level of urbanization. As with infant mortality this fits the theoretical expectations, but again the average effects obscure important differences across urban and rural areas. Model (3) in Table 4.4 again shows that there is no statistically significant conditional effect for urbanites, whereas the results from model (5) show that for rural residents the positive effect of democracy on access to primary school is significantly decreasing in urbanization.

Figure 4.2 presents the magnitudes of these conditional effects. For the urban subsample, panel (a) demonstrates that while it may be decreasing in urbanization, the effect of democracy on access to primary education never reaches standard levels of statistical significance, at any level of urbanization. For rural residents though, panel (b) shows that in countries with big rural majorities democracy has a large, statistically significant, and positive effect on access to primary education. As with the infant mortality estimates this effect decreases with urbanization, and loses statistical significance once the proportion of urbanites in the population becomes greater than 28%. Almost 48% of respondents in the education sample were living in countries with urbanization levels of less than 28% when they reached primary school age, and a majority of the rural subsample reached primary school age in contexts where democracy is estimated to have a significant effect on their likelihood of going to school.

Again though, what is most important here is that in countries with large rural majorities the effect of democracy on access to basic education is much greater for children in rural areas. Where the rural share of the population was greater than 71%, democracy has a significantly positive effect on access to primary education for rural residents, but not urbanites. As the level of urbanization increases, this urban–rural difference reduces as the incentives to target rural voters dissipate. These clear conditional effects bolster the claim that democracy in Africa creates incentives for governments to increase the provision of basic services to rural residents in order to court the votes of the rural majority.

It is worth noting here the difference in the conditional effects when the *Multiparty* variable is used in place of the *Democracy* measure. For the estimates of infant mortality in Table 4.3 there is no significant interaction between multiparty elections and urbanization, whether estimated for the full sample or separately

(a) Urban primary education

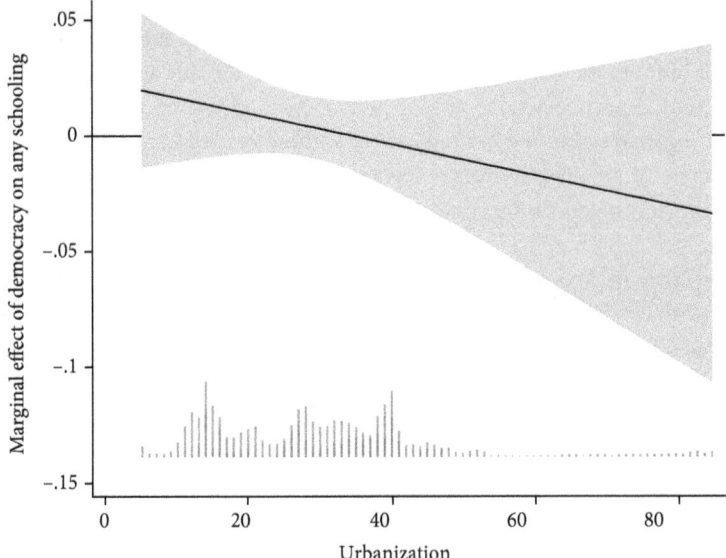

(b) Rural primary education

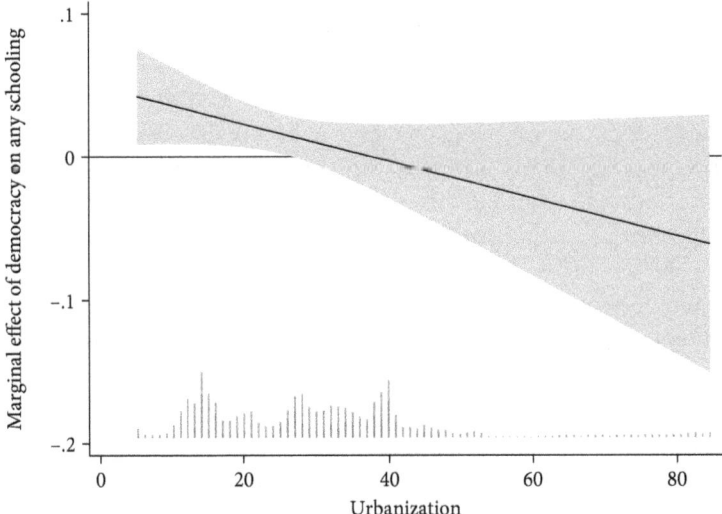

Fig. 4.2 Marginal effects of democracy on access to primary education

Note: Sloped lines show marginal effects of democracy on the probability of a child ever having been to school. Gray areas are 95% confidence intervals. (a) shows effects for urban residents and (b) shows effects for rural residents. Stacked histograms show the distribution of urbanization, with the dark and light portions of the bars showing the distribution of democracy to non-democracy, respectively.

for the urban and rural subsamples. For the education estimates in Table 4.4 there appears to be a significant interaction between multiparty elections and urbanization when estimated for both the urban and rural subsamples. However, separate binning estimates demonstrate that there are not statistically different effects of multiparty elections at typical low and high values of urbanization for either the urban or rural subsamples. What these results suggest then is that, in the absence of an even electoral playing field, multiparty elections may indeed be insufficient to generate incentives for incumbents to fully pursue the types of electoral strategies that lead to pro-rural development.

Democracy in Africa has a positive effect on basic education and health outcomes. Both in terms of infant mortality and access to primary schooling, children are better off under democratic rule. But these positive effects are not universal; the foregoing analysis demonstrates quite clearly that the benefits of democracy for basic education and health outcomes have accrued primarily to those in rural areas. That the extent of these urban–rural differences is conditional on urbanization adds even greater weight to this book's central claim: in Africa's rural democracies, electoral competition creates incentives for governments to court the votes of the rural majority.

4.5 Possible Alternative Explanations

The differential impact of democracy on education and health outcomes across urban and rural areas provides good reason to believe that democracy in Africa is essentially pro-rural. Especially given the conditionality over levels of urbanization, the evidence presented in this chapter strongly supports the idea that democratic elections in Africa have created incentives for rulers to pursue pro-rural policy agendas in order to target the votes of the rural majority. That being said, and despite the robustness of these results, it is important to acknowledge the possibility of alternative explanations for the empirical patterns that have been observed.

In this section I consider two potential accounts that could explain why we see these relationships even if democracy does not create incentives for the pursuance of pro-rural policies. The first possibility is that the estimates are simply picking up pre-trends in education and health outcomes. The second is that the different effects for urban and rural residents could be driven by coethnic favoritism in resource distribution.

4.5.1 Is time a healer?

Although still at levels which lag far behind the rest of the world, basic health and education outcomes across Africa have improved steadily over time, in part due to the intervention of international donors and NGOs. At the same time, since the early 1990s the number of African states holding competitive elections has also risen. Although the estimation strategy employed in the foregoing analysis goes a long way to ensuring that the results are not simply reflecting a temporal correlation between the introduction of democracy and improvements in education and health, causal identification with observational data is never perfect. Therefore it is prudent to consider the possibility, however slight, that the estimates presented in Section 4.4.1 may be simply picking up pre-trends in infant mortality rates and access to primary education, irrespective of regime type. This would be problematic because the effects we are attributing to the introduction of democracy could simply reflect long-term positive trends in access to services across Africa, rather than the impact of strategic incentives induced by electoral competition.

One way to investigate this possibility is to run falsification tests using a placebo treatment variable alongside the democracy variable. The intuition here is that if the *Democracy* variable is simply an arbitrary proxy for time, then any other arbitrary proxy should be just as likely to appear to be a significant determinant of improvements to education and health. For the infant mortality estimates I construct a *Placebo* variable by shifting the *Democracy* variable forwards by two years. As such, the *Placebo* estimates the impact on infant survival of a country becoming democratic two years after a child's birth. Since there is no reason to expect that the positive effects of democracy will be realized *before* the introduction of democratic elections, in this case a large and significant negative coefficient on the *Placebo* variable would suggest that pre-trends in infant mortality rates could be driving the results. By contrast, a small and insignificant coefficient would remove this concern.

For the education estimates I construct the *Placebo* variable by shifting the *Democracy* variable forwards by six years, the average statutory number of primary school age years. This variable therefore estimates the impact on access to primary education of a country becoming democratic after a child passes primary school leaving age. Since it is reasonable to assume that primary education attainment is determined during a child's primary school age years, rather than after, a large and statistically significant positive coefficient on the *Placebo* variable would suggest that pre-trends in access to primary education could be driving the results, whereas a small and insignificant coefficient would provide confidence that the positive education effects being attributed to democracy are not spurious. The results of the falsification tests are presented in Table 4.5.

The results in Table 4.5 quash any concerns that pre-trends in education and health may be driving the estimated effects of democracy. All of the coefficients for *Placebo* are smaller than for *Democracy*, and none positive and are statistically significant. Moreover, these results all hold with a wide variety of alternative placebo specifications, including versions of the placebo variable ranging from one to six years. Even if levels of basic service provision have been increasing across

Table 4.5 Falsification tests of effects of democracy on basic service provision

(a) DV = Infant Death	All (1)	Urban (2)	Rural (3)
Democracy	−0.0032*	−0.0020	−0.0038*
	(0.0018)	(0.0025)	(0.0022)
Placebo	−0.0001	0.0011	−0.0007
	(0.0021)	(0.0028)	(0.0025)
Number of countries	27	27	27
Number of households	231784	75408	156376
Observations	879856	240690	639166
(b) DV = Any Schooling	(4)	(5)	(6)
Democracy	0.0111*	0.0020	0.0200**
	(0.0061)	(0.0068)	(0.0077)
Placebo	−0.0092	−0.0208**	−0.0019
	(0.0077)	(0.0085)	(0.0103)
Number of countries	27	27	27
Number of households	267383	91826	175557
Observations	578695	206204	372491

Note: Estimates from linear probability models of the effect of placebos for democracy on: (a) infant mortality rates; (b) access to primary education. All estimates include gender and birth order dummies, year-of-birth fixed effects, country-specific linear time trends, and either (a) mother fixed effects or (b) household fixed effects. Estimates of infant mortality also include a dummy for multiple births. Estimates of education also include dummies for relationship to household head. Standard errors in parentheses, clustered by country-year-of-birth. *p<.1, **p<.05, ***p<.01.

Africa over time, the healing effects of time itself are not sufficient to explain away the observed impact of democracy.

4.5.2   Is it the ethnicity, stupid?

Ethnicity is undeniably important in African politics, a fact that has been widely recognized and considered at length in scholarly work. One of the many claims about the impact of ethnicity in African politics is that coethnic favoritism has affected the provision of basic education and health services across the continent.[11] Acknowledgment of this suggests another alternative explanation for the evidence that democracy has primarily benefited Africa's rural residents, which is that the differential urban–rural effects actually reflect coethnic favoritism in resource distribution.

Intuitively, this seems unlikely. Two conditions would need to hold for a spurious conclusion of this type to arise. First, it would need to be the case

---

[11] Work by Franck and Rainer (2012) and Kramon and Posner (2016) has provided evidence for this.

that ethnic groups are unevenly distributed across urban and rural areas. And in addition to this, those groups that are predominantly rural would need to be more likely to gain access to power under democracy. While the latter condition could follow from the majoritarian nature of democratic competition, the former is more difficult to envisage. High levels of ethnic heterogeneity across much of Africa mean that in no country are there obviously distinct "rural" and "urban" ethnic groups. Nevertheless, it is worth considering this possibility empirically.

In order to do so, I re-estimate the relationship between democracy and basic health and education outcomes, this time controlling for a measure of coethnicity. Some of the DHS surveys contain information on ethnicity as self-reported by respondents. However, because ethnicity is in many countries a sensitive political issue, this information is often not collected. Therefore it is only possible to carry out the subsequent analysis for nineteen of the twenty-seven countries included in the main sample. For these nineteen countries I construct a *Coethnic Leader* variable that captures the effect of being from the same ethnic group as the president.

An important point to note at this stage is that limiting the sample to these nineteen countries for which information on ethnicity is available alters the significance of the main results, even when coethnicity is not controlled for. In all of the models the direction of the coefficients on the *Democracy* variable remains the same. But reducing the sample of countries results in larger standard errors, meaning that the coefficients no longer all reach the same levels of statistical significance. As such, it is necessary to be somewhat cautious in making conclusions about the impact of including the *Coethnic Leader* variable, given that it is not available for the full sample.

For the infant mortality analysis the *Coethnic Leader* variable is coded 1 if a child was born in a year in which one of her coethnics was in power, and 0 otherwise. Analogous to the *Democracy* variable, for the education analysis *Coethnic Leader* captures the proportion of an individuals' primary school age years spent with a coethnic as president. I use information on the ethnic identities of African leaders up to 2002 from Fearon, Kasara, and Laitin (2007), which I then update to cover all of the years included in the sample. Having constructed this variable, I then include it in the models estimating infant mortality and access to primary education. The results are presented in Tables 4.6 and 4.7.

As the results from the baseline estimates in Table 4.6 show, reducing the sample to nineteen countries undermines the significance of the observed relationship between democracy and infant mortality, irrespective of whether coethnicity is controlled for. But what is also clear is that in all other respects the general pattern of the effects of democracy on both infant mortality and access to primary education holds when the *Coethnic Leader* variable is included. Similarly, the results in Table 4.7 show that for infant mortality the pattern of the conditional effects remains just as they were when estimated using the full sample, though

Table 4.6 Effects of democracy on basic service provision (incl. coethnicity)

	All		Urban		Rural	
	(1)	(2)	(3)	(4)	(5)	(6)
(a) DV = *Infant Death*						
Democracy	-0.0020	-0.0017	-0.0017	-0.0011	-0.0022	-0.0021
	(0.0021)	(0.0021)	(0.0028)	(0.0028)	(0.0024)	(0.0024)
Coethnic Leader		-0.0028*		-0.0028		-0.0025
		(0.0015)		(0.0024)		(0.0020)
Number of countries		19		19		19
Number of households		175588		59689		115899
Observations		676483		195049		481434

	(7)	(8)	(9)	(10)	(11)	(12)
(b) DV = *Any Schooling*						
Democracy	0.0132*	0.0136*	0.0098	0.0087	0.0152	0.0148
	(0.0073)	(0.0072)	(0.0087)	(0.0089)	(0.0092)	(0.0090)
Coethnic Leader		-0.0110***		0.0083*		-0.0250***
		(0.0038)		(0.0048)		(0.0050)
Number of countries		19		19		19
Number of households		198811		72285		126526
Observations		432294		163622		268672

Note: Estimates from linear probability models of the effect of democracy on: (a) infant mortality rates; (b) access to primary education. All estimates include gender and birth order dummies, year-of-birth fixed effects, country-specific linear time trends, and either (a) mother fixed effects or (b) household fixed effects. Estimates of infant mortality also include a dummy for multiple births. Estimates of primary education also include dummies for relationship to household head. Standard errors in parentheses, clustered by country-year-of-birth. *p<.1, **p<.05, ***p<.01.

(a) *Infant Death*	All		Urban		Rural	
	(1)	(2)	(3)	(4)	(5)	(6)
Democracy	-0.0065	-0.0074	-0.0045	-0.0046	-0.0063	-0.0072
	(0.0061)	(0.0061)	(0.0094)	(0.0094)	(0.0067)	(0.0068)
Urbanization	-0.0017**	-0.0017**	-0.0014	-0.0013	-0.0018*	-0.0018*
	(0.0007)	(0.0007)	(0.0009)	(0.0009)	(0.0009)	(0.0009)
Democracy×	0.0002	0.0002	0.0001	0.0001	0.0002	0.0002
Urbanization	(0.0002)	(0.0002)	(0.0003)	(0.0003)	(0.0002)	(0.0002)
Coethnic Leader		-0.0030*		-0.0028		-0.0027
		(0.0016)		(0.0024)		(0.0020)
Countries	19		19		19	
Households	175588		59689		115899	
Observations	676483		195049		481434	

(b) *Any Schooling*	(7)	(8)	(9)	(10)	(11)	(12)
Democracy	0.0657***	0.0641***	0.0778***	0.0768***	0.0625***	0.0573**
	(0.0189)	(0.0188)	(0.0232)	(0.0232)	(0.0237)	(0.0234)
Urbanization	0.0129***	0.0129***	0.0061***	0.0062***	0.0195***	0.0194***
	(0.0024)	(0.0024)	(0.0019)	(0.0019)	(0.0035)	(0.0035)
Democracy×	-0.0019***	-0.0018***	-0.0021***	-0.0021***	-0.0019**	-0.0018**
Urbanization	(0.0006)	(0.0006)	(0.0007)	(0.0007)	(0.0008)	(0.0008)
Coethnic Leader		-0.0100***		0.0084*		-0.0237***
		(0.0038)		(0.0048)		(0.0051)
Countries	19		19		19	
Households	198811		72285		126526	
Observations	432294		163622		268672	

Note: Estimates from linear probability models of the effect of democracy on: (a) infant mortality rates; (b) access to primary education. All estimates include gender and birth order dummies, year-of-birth fixed effects, country-specific linear time trends, and either (a) mother fixed effects or (b) household fixed effects. Estimates of infant mortality also include a dummy for multiple births. Estimates of primary education also include dummies for relationship to household head. Standard errors in parentheses, clustered by country-year-of-birth. * p<.1, **p<.05, ***p<.01.

again the sample restriction means that the coefficients are no longer statistically significant.

For access to primary education the estimates of the conditional effects are significant at standard levels, though here the pattern differs slightly from the main analysis. Specifically, in this case the conditional effects of democracy appear to hold for both the urban and rural subsamples rather than just for rural households. Again though, it is worth noting that this is a function of the reduced sample, and is not due to the inclusion of the *Coethnic Leader* variable. Most importantly for the question to hand, these results provide confidence that the differential urban-rural effects of democracy on infant mortality and access to primary education are not being driven by coethnic favoritism.

4.6 Conclusions

On the basis of this evidence, then, urban unhappiness with incumbents across Africa appears to be justified. If urbanites are upset that democracy seems to be doing more for those in rural areas than it is for themselves, the evidence suggests that they may well have a case. This should not be taken as an indictment of democracy, which by its very nature creates winners and losers. But it does lend solid support to the claim that democracy drives governments in Africa to pursue pro-rural policy agendas.

Evidence from household surveys across twenty-seven countries in Africa shows that children born in democracies are less likely to die before their first birthdays than those born in non-democracies, and individuals who reach primary school age subsequent to the introduction of meaningful democratic elections have a significantly higher probability of attending primary school than those who spend their primary school age years in non-democratic contexts. Moreover, these effects clearly differ for those in rural as opposed to urban areas, with the average effects for both education and health outcomes being driven almost entirely by the positive impact of democracy in the countryside. Finally, and perhaps most crucially for the argument put forward in this book, these urban-rural differences are conditional on, and decreasing in, levels of urbanization.

This evidence therefore supports this book's central theoretical claim, that democratic elections induce governments to implement policies that favor rural interests in order to win votes from the rural majority. For citizens across Africa, both in towns and in the countryside, improving health and education outcomes is vitally important. While for those in the countryside this improvement is being realized as a result of democracy, for urbanites the effect of democracy has not been so positive. Given the incentives created by democratic electoral competition, this is not unexpected. Faced with meaningful elections and large rural majorities, rulers across Africa have pursued pro-rural policy agendas in order to win votes.

Of course, pursuing votes through the provision of public goods and services is not the only way to win elections. And indeed, the prevailing focus on electoral fraud and ethnic mobilization in Africa creates the impression that African voters may not be responsive to electoral strategies involving such programmatic provision of goods. Since the validity of the argument rests on this assumption, that voters in Africa are responsive to the provision of goods and services, in Chapter 5 I provide direct evidence that this is indeed the case. That said, the evidence presented thus far suggests strongly that this impression is wrong; it is unlikely that governments would waste time, effort, and resources on pro-rural strategies of distribution if these strategies did not deliver votes. And based on the evidence in this chapter and Chapter 3, it is clear that governments in Africa's rural democracies do pursue such strategies.

APPENDIX

Table 4.8 Summary statistics

	Obs.	Median	Mean	Std. Dev.	Min.	Max.
Sample: Infant Mortality						
Dependent variable						
Infant death	879,856	0	0.075	0.263	0	1
Independent variables						
Democracy	879,856	0	0.427	0.495	0	1
Multiparty	879,856	1	0.729	0.445	0	1
Female	879,856	0	0.491	0.499	0	1
Multiple	879,856	0	0.033	0.179	0	1
Urbanization	879,856	29.098	29.484	13.784	4.721	86.047
Sample: Education						
Dependent variable						
Any schooling	578,695	1	0.768	0.422	0	1
Independent variables						
Democracy	578,695	0.167	0.436	0.467	0	1
Multiparty	578,695	1	0.728	0.404	0	1
Female	578,695	1	0.524	0.499	0	1
Urbanization	578,695	28.535	28.865	13.475	5.198	84.443

Table 4.9 Effects of democracy on basic service provision—interaction models

	(1)	(2)	(3)	(4)
	(a) infant death		*(b) any schooling*	
Democracy	0.0011		−0.0090	
	(0.0023)		(0.0065)	
Democracy × Rural	−0.0059***		0.0344***	
	(0.0022)		(0.0058)	
Multiparty		−0.0008		−0.0068
		(0.0020)		(0.0058)
Multiparty × Rural		−0.0081***		0.0355***
		(0.0019)		(0.0054)
Number of countries	27		27	
Number of mothers/households	231784		267383	
Observations	879856		578695	

Note: Estimates from linear probability models of the effect of democracy on: (a) infant mortality rates; (b) access to primary education. All estimates include gender and birth order dummies, year-of-birth fixed effects, country-specific linear time trends, and either (a) mother fixed effects or (b) household fixed effects. Estimates of infant mortality also include a dummy for multiple births. Estimates of primary education also include dummies for relationship to household head. Standard errors in parentheses, clustered by country-year-of-birth. *p<.1, **p<.05, ***p<.01.

5

Microfoundations: Voting for Public Goods in Ghana

5.1 Introduction

How do voters in Africa choose? How do voters *anywhere* choose? The question of what determines vote choice is one that has occupied political scientists for decades, and will continue to do so for many more years to come. While I certainly don't venture to provide a definitive answer here, it is nevertheless a crucial question to consider, because an assumption about voter behavior underpins the central argument that I make in this book. Simply put, the argument assumes that voters care about public goods.[1] As a result, the underlying impression of voters is that they engage in a certain type of evaluative voting, basing their electoral choice on the government's performance in providing them with goods and services. This assumption is crucial because without it there would be no reason to think that politicians should implement pro-rural policies in order to win rural votes.

Isn't this assumption obviously valid? Surely voters everywhere base their choices at least in part on the government's performance in office? For democrats the hope must be that they do, and that as a result elections are being used to hold governments accountable. But given the predominant focus of writing on African elections, both in academia and in the media, one must be forgiven for questioning whether this assumption holds, because the widespread impression is that voter choice in African elections is determined predominantly by clientelism and ethnicity. And, since evaluative voting in African elections cannot be taken for granted, the task in this chapter is to show that it happens, and that voters in Africa do care about public goods.

As in Chapter 4, in considering whether voters in Africa use elections to hold governments accountable for the provision of goods and services, the choice of which goods and services to focus on is an important one. In contexts of limited information and weak state capacity, as is the case across much of Africa, it can

---

[1] I use the term "public goods" here loosely, in a manner that may infuriate purists. Strictly speaking, goods are public only if they are non-rivalrous and non-excludable, leaving room for very little at all. General usage of the term tends to accommodate a wide array of goods that don't meet these conditions. For the sake of the argument, the type of good actually matters very little here; what is more important is the nature of distribution, and in particular whether or not receipt of goods and services is conditional on the provision of political support.

Rural Democracy: Elections and Development in Africa. Robin Harding, Oxford University Press (2020).
© Robin Harding.
DOI: 10.1093/oso/9780198851073.001.0001

be hard for citizens to attribute the provision of public goods and services to political action. This matters for two reasons. First, focusing on goods that cannot be attributed in this way does not allow us to identify whether or not the provision of these is a determinant of voter choice. Furthermore, it seems more likely that voters will condition their support on the provision of goods and services which can be attributed in this way than on those which cannot.

As with Chapters 3 and 4, the approach in this chapter is quantitative. But while the analyses in those chapters spanned multiple countries, in this one I narrow the focus to a single country, Ghana. Doing so allows me to account for important contextual variations in how goods are provided, which influence the extent to which responsibility for this provision can be attributed to political action. I use data on two types of goods to evaluate whether Ghanaian voters are evaluative. First I look at education, considering a range of inputs at the district level. Usefully, analysis of this data supports the idea that voters are more likely to condition their support on the provision of goods and services which can be attributed to political action than on those which cannot. Acknowledging limitations on inference resulting from aggregation to the district level, I then turn to roads. Using an original panel dataset containing detailed information on road conditions throughout Ghana, I provide even more robust evidence that electoral support is affected by the provision of public goods.[2]

5.2 Examining the Argument's Microfoundations

The purpose of this chapter is to examine the microfoundations that underpin the book's central argument. In order to do so I analyze the link between electoral support and the provision of public goods and services in Ghana. Before diving into the data it is worth taking a moment to clarify the importance of this exercise, to justify the goods and services on which I focus, and to explain the choice of Ghana as a case.

5.2.1   Why these microfoundations are important

Electoral competition in Africa creates incentives for governments to pursue pro-rural policy agendas, in order to court the votes of the rural majority. The evidence presented in Chapters 3 and 4 supports this claim, but in order to gain greater confidence in the validity of the specified mechanism it is important to evaluate the argument's microfoundations. In particular, the argument rests on

---

[2] Some of the evidence presented in this chapter is contained in Harding (2015). Copyright ©2015 Trustees of Princeton University. Reprinted with permission.

an underlying assumption about the nature of voter choice in Africa: that voters condition their electoral support on evaluations of the government's performance in providing them with public goods and services. Although this assumption may seem innocuous to some, the widespread impression that elections in sub-Saharan Africa are dominated by forms of clientelism and ethnic mobilization means that it is not uncontroversial.

This widespread impression is not unfounded. Whether it has been depicted as patronage, prebendalism, tribute, or straightforward vote-buying, the role of clientelism in electoral competition has been highlighted by numerous studies of African politics.[3] Not only is clientelism present but it is successful; experimental research has suggested that clientelistic campaign messages sway more voters than programmatic alternatives, and that turnout increases with vote-buying.[4] At the same time, the importance of ethnicity has also been widely acknowledged, with multiple analyses suggesting that voting in Africa is often based on ethno-regional identities.[5]

While this research has undoubtedly advanced our understanding of electoral politics in Africa, it has also painted a somewhat pessimistic picture, presenting African elections as little more than contests in corruption and ethnic loyalty. This picture is not false but it is incomplete. A much smaller but growing body of work has also noted other possible determinants of voting behavior in Africa, most notably economic factors.[6] And at the same time, researchers have begun to consider whether votes may also be affected by evaluations of incumbent performance.[7] It is on this work that I seek to build, by providing robust evidence that public goods do have an effect on vote shares.

5.2.2   Focusing on attributable outcomes

As in Chapter 4, the choice of public goods and services to analyze is consequential here. Across Africa voters often have limited access to information. Moreover, weak state capacity means that decisions taken centrally by political actors do not always directly translate into outcomes on the ground. In such contexts, citizens may struggle to correctly attribute the provision of public goods and services to political action. This presents us with a potential inference problem of the following type. If we investigate the link between electoral choice and the provision

[3] See Lemarchand (1988), Lewis (1998), van de Walle (2003), Bratton (2008), and Kramon (2009).
[4] See Wantchekon (2003), Vicente and Wantchekon (2010), and Vicente (2014).
[5] See for example Posner (2005), van de Walle (2007), and Ishiyama (2012). In contrast, Young (2009b) provides evidence that although coethnicity is a very strong determinant of voter choice across Africa, electoral support for coethnics is not always guaranteed.
[6] For example, Nugent (1999), Posner (2005), and Kimenyi and Romero (2008).
[7] For example, Lindberg and Morrison (2005), Young (2009a), Lindberg (2010), and Bratton, Bhavnani, and Chen (2012).

of some unattributable good and find no relationship, we might infer one of two things: either that voters don't care about public goods (or the good in question, at least) and vote instead on some clientelistic or ethnic basis, or that they do care about public goods but that the goods in question provide no relevant information about politicians' effort on which they can condition their electoral support. Since these two possibilities are observably equivalent, this type of evidence would not allow us to say conclusively whether or not voters care about public goods.

What this means is that we need to focus instead on public goods whose outcomes are unambiguously attributable to political action. If we do so, and find that changes to the provision of these attributable goods have no impact on votes, we can then infer with confidence that voters have chosen to ignore this information. This is not to say that voters *never* condition their electoral support on unattributable outcomes. Indeed, recent work by Sances (2017) has shown that voters in Massachusetts punish officials for tax increases over which those officials quite obviously had no control. That being said, I provide evidence below that with regard to education inputs in Ghana, voters only reward incumbents for improvements to attributable inputs, ignoring changes to those that are non-attributable. As a result, it seems doubly prudent to focus on attributable outcomes.

5.2.3   Why Ghana?

The need to focus on attributable outcomes also necessitates the shift from focusing on many countries to analyzing just one. The important issue here is that public goods whose outcomes are attributable to political action in one country may not demonstrate the same characteristic in another. This follows from consideration of the reasons underlying attributability. The extent to which some outcome on the ground can be attributed to action on the part of the executive, for example, may depend on the extent to which decision-making authority for that particular outcome is devolved to lower levels of government. Alternatively, it may be affected by the extent to which funding sources are disaggregated. The discussion of various education inputs in Ghana in Section 5.3 illustrates this nicely. What this means is that the extent of attributability for any particular outcome may hinge on the particular nature of decision-making and funding for the outcome in question.

Acknowledging the potential determinants of attributability highlights an additional implication, which is that the attributability of most outcomes is unlikely to be uniform across countries. Admittedly, some policies are likely to have an attributable impact irrespective of where they are implemented. As Harding and Stasavage (2014) note, for example, the abolition of user fees for primary education has an impact that can be easily and directly traced back to action on the part of the executive. But for most outcomes this is unlikely to be the case, due at least in part to variations in institutional and bureaucratic structures. If we are to investigate the link between voting and changes to the provision of some attributable good, and the attributability of goods is country-specific, it is therefore necessary to limit the analysis to a particular country. I start here with Ghana, but future analyses can and should be done across different countries, identifying attributable outcomes in each.

So why focus on Ghana? As with any question of case selection, there are practical and methodological factors to consider. In order to analyze the impact of changes to the provision of certain public goods on changes to electoral behavior effectively, we need data on votes and public goods over time. This limits the set of useful cases to those in which meaningful elections have been held consecutively, making Ghana a very appealing candidate. Ghana has held regular multiparty elections every four years since 1992. The president and parliament are elected concurrently, the former by direct popular vote in a two-round run-off system, and the latter via single-member constituencies using first-past-the-post. The presidency has changed hands multiple times since 1992, most recently with Nana Akufo-Addo of the New Patriotic Party (NPP) defeating the incumbent President John Mahama of the National Democratic Congress (NDC) in 2016.

Ghana has a stable two-party system, with the presidential candidates of the NPP and NDC having won at least 93% of the votes between them in each of the elections since 1992. While questions were raised about the conduct of the 1992 presidential election, leading to an opposition boycott of the parliamentary elections, elections since then have been widely regarded as free and fair, and competitive.[8] Ghana is also a useful case to analyze because it is possible to obtain good-quality data on the provision of various public goods over time, at a fairly disaggregated level. For the analysis to hand I use data on education inputs and local road conditions, which will be discussed in detail in Sections 5.3 and 5.4.

Practically then, there are good reasons to focus the analysis on Ghana. Methodologically, however, it is important to consider the comparability of the Ghanaian case, and the extent to which findings about how voter behavior therein may generalize across Africa. As was highlighted by the preceding discussion, Ghana is relatively stable and democratic compared to other African countries. One possible concern might be that the extent to which citizens are inclined to use their votes to hold the government accountable is greater in such a context, where elections are more meaningful and competitive. Moreover, it is possible that the stability of the Ghanaian political system increases citizens' ability to hold politicians accountable, perhaps by clarifying the operation of democracy and facilitating the accumulation of information about political effort.

While these are valid concerns, it is important to note that Ghana is not an anomaly in Africa, where many other countries are stable and democratic also.

---

[8] For a discussion of the 1992 elections see Oquaye (2006).

As discussed in Chapter 4, evaluating and measuring democracy is a controversial endeavor, but available indicators provide us with some useful metrics here. In 2011, almost twenty years after the return to multiparty politics, Ghana was just one of eighteen countries (38% of the total) in sub-Saharan Africa coded as democratic by the Polity IV index, and one of fourteen (30%) coded as electoral democracies by Freedom House. Of these eighteen countries coded as democratic by the Polity IV index, six achieved the same score as Ghana or higher on the Polity Index.[9] In 2006 Ghana was one of thirty-six countries (80%) coded as having an executive elected via competitive multiparty elections by the World Bank's Database of Political Institutions (Beck et al. 2001), and in 2008 Ghana was one of seventeen (36%) coded as democratic by Cheibub, Gandhi, and Vreeland (2010). Whilst it is always important to be cautious in generalizing any findings from a single case, Ghana is therefore clearly not a democratic outlier.

5.3 Education Inputs

In assessing whether or not voters care about public goods, the first area that I consider is education. As discussed in Chapter 4, access to basic education services is limited across much of Africa, and demand is high. This story holds true when we narrow the focus to Ghana; in the third round of the Afrobarometer Series, undertaken in 2005, 42% of Ghanaian respondents had not completed primary school, and education was cited as the second most important problem facing the Ghanaian government, behind only unemployment. Education inputs therefore seem like very much the type of issue that voters would take into account, if they do condition their electoral support on the provision of public goods. This makes the provision of education inputs a useful policy area to consider when evaluating whether voters care about public goods. Furthermore, in Ghana there is variation in the extent to which different types of education inputs are attributable to executive action. This is also helpful, because it allows investigation of whether the extent to which voters care about education inputs varies according to whether inputs are attributable or not.

5.3.1   Which education inputs are attributable?

Some education inputs in Ghana, such as classrooms and textbooks, are harder than others to attribute to executive action, because their provision is determined by decentralized decision-making processes and fragmented funding flows.

---

[9] Data from http://www.systemicpeace.org/polity/polity4.htm and http://www.freedomhouse.org.

Central government transfers may well determine the amount of resources available locally, but where local authorities have power over the allocation of these resources there may be opportunities for corruption and "leakages." As a result, outcomes on the ground may not truly reflect inputs from the center. Reinikka and Svensson (2004) provide evidence of this in Uganda, where between 1991 and 1995 capture by local government officials and politicians meant that schools received only 13% of allocated central government spending.

Since 1951 responsibility for education in Ghana has been split between the central government and local authorities (Darvas and Krauss 2011). More specifically, decentralization means that responsibility for the construction of classrooms and the management of services such as water and sanitation rests at the district level. Funds for these inputs flow through the District Assemblies and District Education Offices from various central government offices, and from donors. Textbooks and other learning resources are provided both centrally by the Ministry of Education, and at the district level using donor funds. Taken together, this decentralization of responsibility, and the fragmentation of funding sources, means that responsibility for education inputs including numbers of classrooms, textbooks and seats, and school services and facilities, cannot be attributed directly to the executive.

What the executive can be held directly accountable for is supplying teachers and building new schools. The central government in Ghana directly distributes and controls any investments to fund new school construction. Furthermore, teachers are hired, trained, deployed, and paid centrally, with no involvement at the district level (Steffensen 2006). What this means is that both pupil–teacher ratios and the number of schools are inputs that can be directly attributed to executive action. Interestingly, newspaper reports from the 2004 presidential campaign suggest that the incumbent specifically tried to cultivate this, by reminding voters of new schools that the government had built.[10]

5.3.2   Analyzing the impact of education inputs on votes

The Ghanaian Ministry of Education carries out an annual schools census, which collects data and information on the number of institutions, enrollment, teachers, classrooms, textbooks and examination results, at the basic, secondary, and higher education levels. The census is a central part of the Education Management Information System (EMIS) Project, which was launched in January 1997 with technical support from Harvard University and funds from the World Bank and the Government of Ghana. Since then multiple censuses have been carried out, providing detailed education statistics at the district level that are comparable over

---

[10] "Students Subject Parties to Hot Debate Ahead of December Polls," Ghanaian Chronicle, October 6, 2004; "Akuffo-Addo Storms Keta-Somey," Ghanaian Chronicle, November 23, 2004.

time. Although the data from some years was inaccessible at the time of writing, there is sufficient coverage to permit rigorous analysis. Linking this data to vote shares at the district level, it is possible to investigate the relationship between electoral support and a range of different education inputs.

In order to evaluate the impact of education inputs on votes I aggregate electoral data to the district level. Elections in Ghana are administered via a nested structure. Ballots are cast and counted at polling stations, which are nested within Electoral Areas for administrative purposes. The counted results are taken to Constituency Collation Centers, and once collated the constituency results are sent to the relevant District Electoral Officers for onward transmission to the Regional Offices of the Electoral Commission. The Regional Offices then communicate the results to the Commission's headquarters in Accra. This means that although districts are not natural electoral units (they are not electoral districts that demarcate the boundaries for electing members of parliament), they do nest one or more constituencies. Although it would be preferable to disaggregate the electoral data further, the aggregation of education data to the district level means that this is not possible.

Combining data on education inputs and election results over time, it is possible to rigorously estimate the relationship between them using first difference models. Taking the difference in the variables of interest over two time periods for each district, this approach allows us to estimate the impact of changes to a variety of education inputs over time on changes to electoral support for the incumbent party. Moreover, by differencing over time within districts we are holding constant any time-invariant district-level factors that might affect vote shares.

Using these data I estimate a series of linear models where the outcome of interest is change to the vote share of the incumbent party (the NPP) between the 2004 and 2008 elections. The choice of this time period is informed by the availability of education data, as well as the fact that the identity of the incumbent was constant during this period. I begin by looking at the impact on vote shares of education inputs that represent major infrastructure investments, namely the numbers of *Primary schools* and *Classrooms per school*. The second model investigates the impact of changes to school facilities and services, looking specifically at the proportions of *Schools with toilets* and of *Schools with drinking water*. The third model estimates the impact of three different learning inputs, these being the numbers of *Books per pupil* and *Seats per pupil*, and the *Pupil–teacher ratio*. In the fourth model I include all seven different education inputs together.

5.3.3   Do education inputs affect votes?

Results from estimates of the impact of education inputs on vote shares are presented in Table 5.1. From the first column we can see that there is a significantly

Table 5.1 Education inputs and incumbent vote shares—district-level data

	(1)	(2)	(3)	(4)
		Incumbent vote share		
Investments/Infrastructure:				
Primary schools	0.0963**			0.0844**
	(0.0354)			(0.0367)
Classrooms per school	1.0853			1.9678*
	(0.8067)			(1.0732)
Facilities/Services:				
Schools with toilets		−0.2960		0.3313
		(1.9304)		(1.7909)
Schools with drinking water		6.0605*		2.9128
		(3.2912)		(3.0928)
Learning Inputs:				
Pupil–teacher ratio			−0.2664***	−0.2913***
			(0.0889)	(0.0851)
Books per pupil			0.4427	−0.4244
			(1.6262)	(1.6455)
Seats per pupil			2.9793	2.2142
			(2.7841)	(2.7309)
Districts	109	109	109	109

Note: Dependent variable is incumbent vote share change between 2004 and 2008 by district. Robust standard errors in parentheses. *$p<.1$, **$p<.05$, ***$p<.01$

positive relationship between new school construction and electoral support for the incumbent party. It is worth noting that substantively the implied effect of new primary schools is quite small, with the implication from model (1) being that each additional school built in a district correlates with a 0.1 percentage point increase in the incumbent party's share of the vote therein. This is not a huge effect, but given the stability of vote shares in Ghana (the average district-level change in the incumbent's vote share was only 2.7 percentage points), and the high likelihood that voters condition their support on a multitude of different factors, the fact that we find any significant effect at all is worth acknowledging.

The results in the second column of Table 5.1 suggest that presidential vote shares are largely unaffected by changes to school services and facilities. The coefficient for the variable capturing change in the number of schools with drinking water is positive and significant at the 10% level, but when all the education inputs are included together (in the fourth column) this coefficient loses significance. Looking at learning inputs, we can see that changes to numbers of books and seats per pupil are similarly unrelated to vote shares. What voters do seem to care about are teacher numbers; the coefficient on the variable measuring pupil–teacher ratios is negative, suggesting that voters reward the incumbent for reductions to the number of pupils per teacher. This coefficient is significant at the 1% level, and its magnitude implies that for every fewer pupil per teacher the incumbent party's vote share increases by roughly one quarter of a percentage point. From the final column of Table 5.1 we can see that these results hold when all seven education inputs are included together.

As far as education is concerned, voters in Ghana do seem to care about public goods. Improvements to both the number of schools and the number of teachers per pupil are both significantly related to an increase in the incumbent party's share of the vote, suggesting that voters reward the incumbent for efforts to increase the provision of these particular education inputs. Interestingly, these results also suggest that only outcomes that can be attributed to executive actions are significantly related to changes in vote shares. As discussed in Section 5.3.1, in Ghana the division of responsibility between the central government and local authorities means that the executive can only be held directly accountable for supplying teachers and building new schools. That these are the only two inputs significantly related to presidential vote shares therefore suggests that voters are indeed more likely to condition their electoral support on outcomes that can be attributed to the relevant political actors.

By demonstrating a significant link between electoral support and the provision of public goods, this evidence provides useful support for the microfoundations underpinning the central argument of this book. But it is not perfect; a major problem with this analysis is the aggregation of the data to the district level, which raises potential concerns about ecological inference.[11] Analyzing voting behavior at this level of aggregation also makes it difficult to rule out the possibility that the observed relationships between education inputs and vote shares are not being driven by some other unobserved time-varying factor at the district level, which could lead us to make spurious conclusions about the impact of these inputs on electoral behavior. Therefore in order to bolster this support for the theoretical microfoundations, I turn now to another outcome for which more highly disaggregated data is available: roads.

5.4 Roads

Like education, roads are a salient issue for citizens across Africa. Not only can bad roads be dangerous and inconvenient but they can also have a severely detrimental impact on poverty alleviation and development. In largely agrarian societies poor transport infrastructure can increase agricultural costs, threatening both livelihoods and food security (Blimpo, Harding, and Wantchekon 2013). Furthermore, poor quality roads can bring a wide array of negative externalities, with just one example being that high transport costs can undermine improvements

---

[11] On ecological inference and aggregation bias see Achen (1995) and King, Rosen, and Tanner (2004).

to education and healthcare. This salience makes roads a useful outcome to consider when evaluating whether voters care about the provision of public goods. Moreover, in the Ghanaian context focusing on roads brings two added benefits. First, the particular type of roads that I analyze are directly attributable to the executive. In addition to this, high-quality data on the condition of these roads is available at a very disaggregated level, making it possible to robustly identify the impact of roads on votes in Ghana.

5.4.1   Roads in Ghana

In the third round of the Afrobarometer Series, more than 15% of respondents cited infrastructure and roads as one of the three most important problems facing their country. In Ghana specifically, this proportion was almost 24%, with infrastructure and roads cited behind only unemployment, education, and the economy as the single most important problem the government needed to address. Clearly then, Ghanaians care about the state of their roads. In the analysis that follows I focus on Ghana's trunk road network, which in 2004 consisted of 13,367 kilometers of major roads that connect towns and cities throughout the country.[12] The quality of these roads varies widely, with surfaces ranging from asphaltic concrete to gravel, all of which are prone to subside, crack, and develop pot-holes. This variation significantly affects citizens in the course of their daily lives, influencing the ease, speed, and safety of travel, and affecting the ability of producers and traders to get goods to and from markets.

As well as being highly visible to citizens, variation in the condition of Ghana's trunk roads is also directly attributable to the office of the executive. Responsibility for the development and maintenance of the trunk road network is highly centralized, and ultimately rests with the Ghana Highways Authority (GHA). The GHA has regional and district offices, and these are responsible for minor ongoing road maintenance. But all major periodic maintenance and construction projects of the type that lead to significant improvements in road quality are determined at the center. The allocation of funds for these projects is done on the basis of need, according to publicly available criteria.[13] Analysis of road maintenance outcomes suggests that these formal criteria do determine the distribution of road maintenance—need, measured as the quality of roads in a given constituency in

---

[12] Ghana also has urban roads (4,000km) and rural feeder roads (32,000km). Data on road network distances, correct as of 2004, was provided by the Ghana Highways Authority.

[13] Specifically, each year the GHA's regional directors send a list of roads that need attention to the Ministry of Roads and Highways. The Ministry sets a ceiling budget for the Maintenance Department at the GHA, which then allocates this budget based on need. The Ministry also provides emergency budgets to repair unexpected damage. Information on the process of road maintenance budgetary allocations was collected during an interview with the Director of Road Maintenance at the GHA in Accra, in December 2010.

2004, is the only significant correlate of subsequent changes to road conditions in that constituency (results of this analysis are presented in the Appendix).

Actual maintenance work is routinely undertaken by contractors, but this work is governed by a uniform performance-based contracting process, and subject to careful monitoring and control procedures with penalties for non-compliance. As a result, there is very little scope for variation in the quality of maintenance works carried out by different contractors.[14] Similarly, although Regional Tender Boards are responsible for maintenance contracts, these are allocated according to well-established bidding and monitoring procedures, which again minimizes variation across regions. Taken together, this highly centralized process means that the key factor determining road conditions is the allocation of funds at the ministerial level. And as a result, changes to road conditions in Ghana can be attributed directly to the actions of the executive. Moreover, there is evidence that Ghanaians do in fact draw direct lines of accountability from road conditions to executive action.

During the 2004 Presidential election campaign, for example, citizens directly credited President Kufuor with improving road conditions, citing his efforts in this area as a reason to re-elect him.[15] Somewhat more dramatically, the run-up to the 2008 election saw numerous protests throughout the country about the state of roads, with citizens displaying placards bearing the slogan, "No Road, No Vote." Reports recorded the use of this slogan by protestors in 2007 in Anlo Beach, Western Region, in 2008 in Bunkpurungu and Yendi, Northern Region, and in Kintampo North, Brong Ahafo Region. Protests continued after the election, with reports of the same slogan being seen in 2010 in Bimbilla, Northern Region, and in 2011 in Aflao, Volta Region. While the "votes" being referred to need not necessarily be for the president, other slogans seen at the same demonstrations included, "Mr. President our road our better Ghana," "Be a father to us also," and "Mr. President stop this terrifying deaths [sic]." Clearly then, as noted by an official at the Ministry of Roads, "people blame the president."[16]

In actively demanding better roads from the president, and threatening to withhold their votes if these demands are not met, Ghanaians are directly attributing the condition of their roads to the actions of the executive. This attribution is re-enforced by presidential candidates themselves, who often focus on roads while campaigning. In 2004 President Kufuor and his running-mate Vice President

---

[14] Information on contracting and monitoring of maintenance procedures comes from the Road Maintenance Work Procurement Operations Manual, Ghana Highways Authority, February 2001.

[15] "Ghana: Kufuor Faces Old Opponent in His Bid for a Second Term," All Africa, September 15, 2004. "Strong Turnout in Ghana's Presidential Vote Marks Steadying of Africa's Older Democracies," Associated Press, December 8, 2004.

[16] Interview with Principal Engineer, Department of Urban Roads, Accra, December 2010.

Mahama both sought to claim credit for improvements to the road network.[17] And again in 2008, President Kufuor highlighted his government's achievements with regard to roads when urging citizens to vote for his successor as the NPP's presidential candidate, Nana Akufo-Addo.[18]

Given the evidence presented in Section 5.3.3, that voters are more likely to condition their support on those outcomes that are attributable to political action, it is helpful that roads demonstrate this characteristic. More importantly, if we are to make any valid inference about whether changes to the provision of some good actually influence voter choice, it is essential that these changes can be attributed to the political office for which votes are being cast. There is good reason to think that this is true of the condition of trunk roads in Ghana, changes to which can be attributed to the presidency. The task ahead is therefore to evaluate whether changes to road conditions actually affect the way that citizens vote in Ghana.

5.4.2   Analyzing the impact of roads on votes

While the analysis of education inputs provided useful evidence to support the idea that voters care about public goods, the ability to identify a causal impact of changes to education inputs on electoral support was hampered by the level at which the data was aggregated. One reason to analyze the impact of roads is therefore to achieve a greater level of disaggregation. This is made possible by the use of finely-grained data on both roads and votes.

Election Results

Election results in Ghana are reported at the constituency level, and until recently results from individual polling stations were not transmitted to the head office of the Electoral Commission, instead being kept locally in district or regional offices. Therefore in order to shift the analysis to the lowest possible level of aggregation I collected original electoral returns from more than 3,000 polling stations for the 2004 and 2008 presidential elections, from a sample of 700 Electoral Areas (EAs) throughout the country. This minor aggregation (from polling stations to Electoral Areas) was necessary to link the results geographically to data on road conditions, but EAs are very localized units, containing on average five polling stations in each. Unfortunately, though perhaps not unexpectedly, not all of the data was available.

Serious resource constraints make it difficult for local Electoral Commission offices to effectively maintain archives of election results, and in many districts

---

[17] "NPP Survives First Term," Ghanaian Chronicle, September 20, 2004, "Students Subject Parties to Hot Debate Ahead of December Polls," Ghanaian Chronicle, October 6, 2004, "Vote with an Open Mind," Ghanaian Chronicle, November 12, 2004.

[18] "President Kufuor Urges Citizens to Vote for Akufo-Addo," All Africa, December 18, 2008.

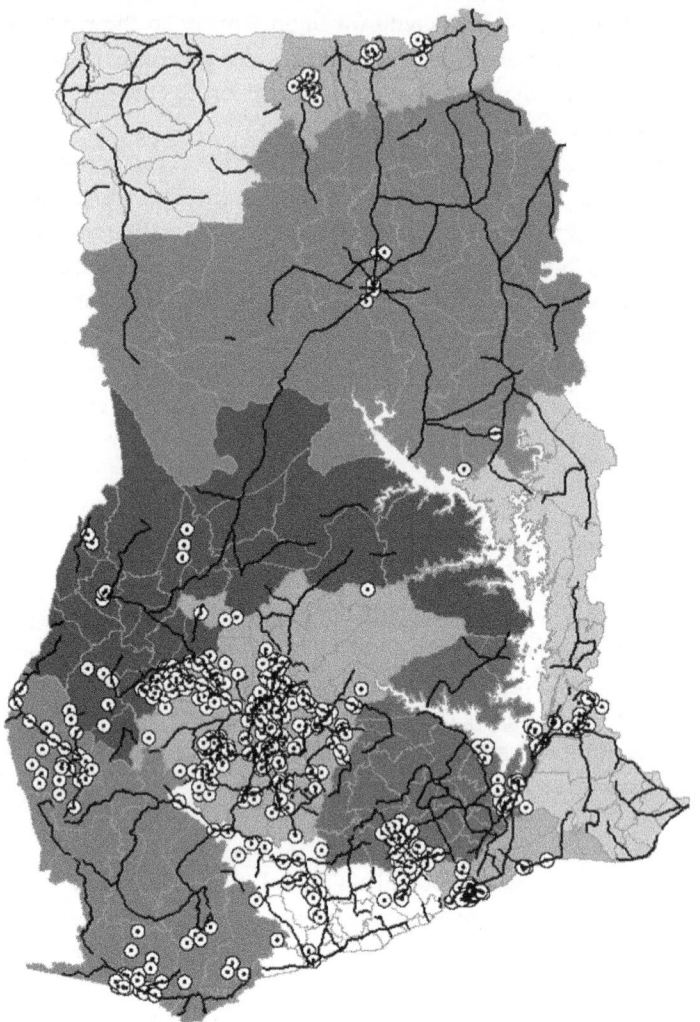

Fig. 5.1 Map of sample distribution by region

Note: Dots represent sampled electoral areas, white circles are 5km buffers. Black lines are trunk roads. Shading reflects regions, and gray lines mark constituency boundaries

the 2004 results have been lost or are incomplete.[19] However, as the maps in Figs. 5.1 and 5.2 show, the coverage of the data is still broad. From the original sample of 700 I was able to collect electoral data from 438 EAs, spread across fifty-three different districts, in nine of Ghana's ten regions.[20] For each EA I construct a

[19] Analysis of the areas where data was unavailable shows no significant differences in the variables of interest between these areas and those from which data was collected.

[20] In early 2019 the number of regions in Ghana was increased from ten to sixteen.

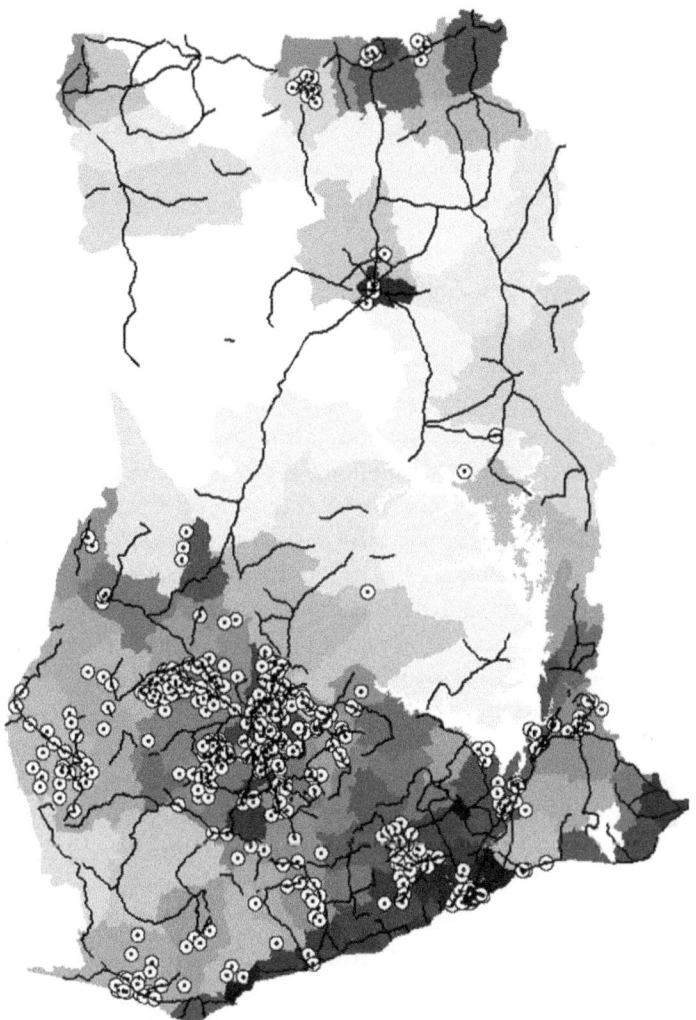

Fig. 5.2 Map of sample distribution by population density

Note: Dots represent sampled electoral areas, white circles are 5km buffers. Black lines are trunk roads. Shading reflects population density by constituency (darker is denser).

measure of *Incumbent vote share change*, defined as the difference in the share of the votes won by the NPP in the first rounds of the 2004 and 2008 presidential elections.

From the maps in Figs. 5.1 and 5.2 we can see that the sample is well distributed throughout the country, and provides good coverage of the population. In Fig. 5.1 the shading demarks the ten administrative regions; unfortunately no polling station returns were available from Upper West Region, but the other nine regions are all included. In Fig. 5.2 constituencies are shaded according to population density, demonstrating that the sparse coverage in the largest geographical region (Northern) reflects the very low population density therein. Certainly the distribution of the sample is not perfect—Fig. 5.2 highlights the lack of data in the densely populated border area around Aflao, in the south-east corner of the country, as well as the apparent over-representation of the Ashanti Region (in the center of the country). Overall though, these maps demonstrate a high degree of data coverage.

Road Conditions

In order to assess the impact of roads on votes we require high-quality localized information on road conditions, which varies over time. I take this information from the annual road condition report produced by the GHA, which provides detailed, systematic, and objective information on the condition of the entire trunk road network at the same period of time each year. In order to compile this report the GHA surveys the condition of each of the more than 2,400 road segments in the network between March and April each year, taking measures of road surface distresses and roughness.[21] These two measures are combined to produce an annual condition score (0 to 100) for each road segment.

As with the education analysis in Section 5.3, in order to robustly estimate the impact of road conditions on how people vote I need a measure of how the condition of roads changes between elections. Having annual, localized road condition scores allows me to construct two different measures. The first is a measure of the change in the average condition of roads in the precise vicinity of each EA, created by averaging the condition scores of all road segments that intersect a five kilometer buffer around the centroid of the EA, and then taking the difference between the mean 2004 condition score and the mean 2007 score.[22]

One concern with this measure of *Average road condition change* is that since some EAs have no road segments within a five-kilometer radius, these EAs get omitted from the analysis. As an alternative I construct a second measure which captures changes to the condition of the road segment that is closest to the centroid of each electoral area. Although this measure of *Closest road condition change* only

---

[21] Distress is measured via a "Windshield" visual road condition survey. In this survey, raters traveling in a slow-moving vehicle (at about 30km/h) observe the road surface for distresses, and determine their severity and extent based on clear guidelines set by the GHA. The raters also disembark from the vehicle and inspect distressed sections on foot in order to get more detailed measurements of slight distresses (e.g. cracks), which are not visible from the moving vehicle. Roughness is measured using a vehicle-mounted electronic measurement device, which measures the severity of bumpiness in a given road segment.

[22] The 2008 data is not directly comparable with other years because in 2008 the condition survey was carried out between May and June. This is problematic because the rainy season starts in May, and variations in climate throughout the country mean that electoral areas are not affected equally. Therefore I look instead at the change in condition scores between 2004 and 2007. When the models are estimated using the 2008 data the coefficient for the road conditions variable is positive but not always significant at standard levels. Since the rains have such variable impact on roads across Ghana, it is unclear how these results should be interpreted.

contains information about one road segment for each electoral area, it does not necessitate dropping any electoral areas from the analysis. For robustness I also look at additional measures of *Average road condition change*, with buffer sizes varying from 3km to 7km.

Summary statistics for changes to vote shares and road conditions are presented in Fig. 5.3 (full summary statistics are included in the Appendix). These show that on average, between 2004 and 2007 the condition of Ghana's trunk roads improved. At the same time, between the 2004 and 2008 elections support for the incumbent NPP party deteriorated. It is worth noting that for the most part changes to vote shares during this period were very small. This reflects the high degree of stability in Ghanaian electoral politics that was noted in Section 5.2.3. We see much greater variation in the condition of roads; although improvement or deterioration in the condition of most road segments was fairly modest, road conditions in some areas changed dramatically, both for better and for worse.

Estimation Strategy

As with the analysis of education inputs, having data on road conditions and votes over time allows me to estimate linear first difference models, a strategy which

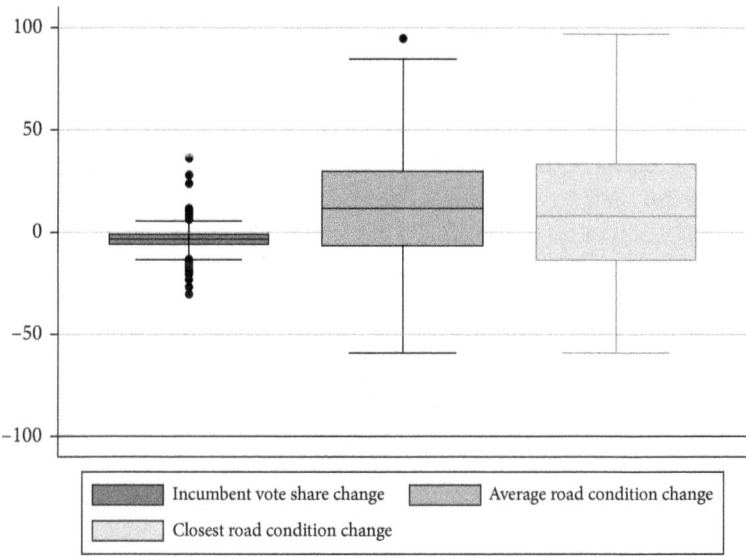

Fig. 5.3 Summary statistics

Note: Changes in presidential vote shares won by the incumbent party, the NPP, between the 2004 and 2008 elections, for the sample of 438 electoral areas. Also average changes in road condition scores between 2004 and 2007 across all road segments within a 5km buffer for the 280 electoral areas that have road segments within 5km, and changes to condition scores between 2004 and 2007 for the closest road segment to each of the 438 electoral areas in the sample.

controls for any unobserved time-invariant characteristics of EAs. If we assume that any unobserved but potentially confounding factors at the EA level are fixed over time, the estimates from these models identify the causal effect of changes to road conditions on electoral support.[23] Although such an assumption is not uncontroversial, it is more reasonable to make at a level as disaggregated as EAs, especially when compared to the district-level analysis of education inputs.

With any analysis of this type, a major obstacle when attempting to estimate how the distribution of some good affects votes is the potential for endogeneity. In this case what we might worry about is the possibility that instead of voters responding to improved roads, any positive relationship between roads and votes might be driven by incumbents rewarding their supporters by improving roads in areas where they win more votes. This is overcome to a great extent by the first difference model, which alters the empirical focus to *trends* in road improvements and vote shares within EAs, rather than *levels* across them. As a result, our concern is reduced to the possibility that the incumbent is targeting road improvements to EAs where its support is known to be increasing between the elections. Since good information about changes to incumbent support at a level as localized as EAs is unlikely to be available, this is far less worrying.[24]

Since the first difference models control for any time-invariant factors at the EA level, there is no need to include measures of any other fixed characteristics of EAs. However, in order to control for the possibility of unobserved time-varying confounding factors I include a set of district-specific time-trends. The primary model that I examine therefore estimates the change in vote shares as a function of the change in *average* road condition scores for each EA. In addition to this, I also examine the impact of changes to the condition of the single *closest* road segment. This is a useful alternative because it does not necessitate dropping any EAs from the analysis, but it raises the possibility of heterogeneity in the effects, because for some EAs the closest road segment is not very close—for the most remote electoral areas in the sample, the closest road is twenty-four kilometers away. It is possible that the effect of road conditions varies by distance, perhaps because citizens only have limited information about the condition of distant roads, or because they are less concerned about roads that are far away. I account for the possibility of such heterogeneity by interacting the condition of the closest road segment with a measure of its proximity to the EA. Because EAs are nested within districts, I cluster standard errors at the district level to counteract potential within-district correlation in the errors.

---

[23] See Angrist and Pischke (2009) for a useful discussion of the benefits of fixed-effects models for causal inference.

[24] In Ghana there are no local opinion polls for the incumbent to base this kind of targeting on, and political parties have very limited local infrastructure outside of election campaigns. Moreover, although there are local district elections, these are non-partisan, so they provide no direct information about changes in partisan support at the local level.

5.4.3   Do road conditions affect votes?

Estimates of a series of models demonstrate that changes to road conditions have a significant effect on the incumbent's electoral support. Fig. 5.4 presents the estimated marginal effects of a one standard deviation increase in road conditions on the incumbent party's share of the vote. These estimates are from models looking at the impact of average changes to the condition of all road segments within a certain distance of the EA (with buffer sizes ranging from 3km to 7km), as well as the impact of changes to the condition of the single closest road segment.

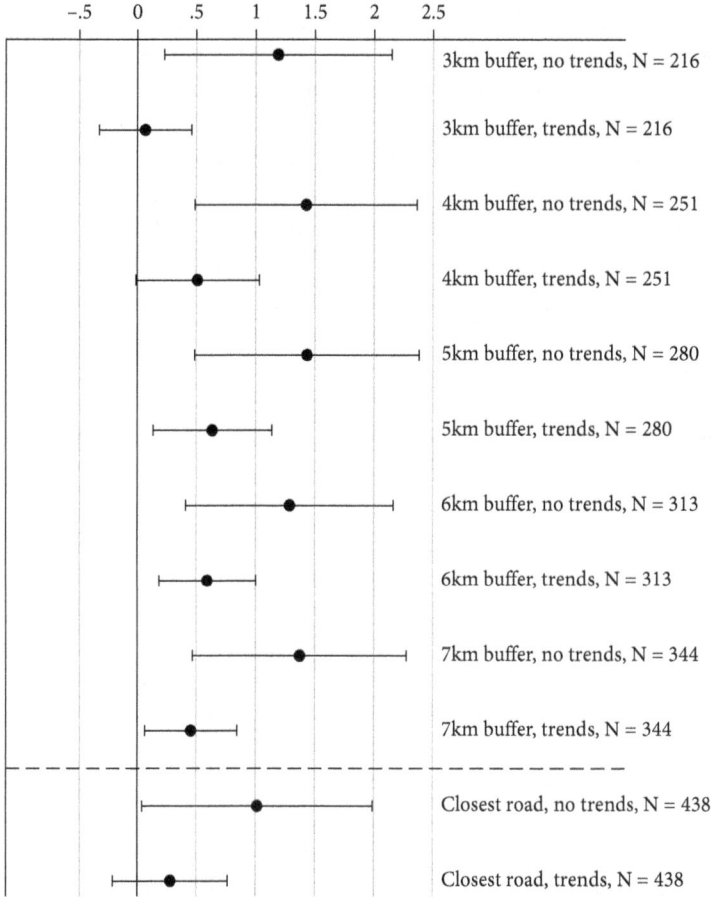

Fig. 5.4 Effects of change in road conditions on incumbent vote shares

Note: Dots show incumbent vote share change given a one-standard deviation increase in road conditions. Bars shows 95% confidence intervals. Estimates above the dashed line are for models of changes to average road conditions within varying-sized buffers around EAs, with and without district-specific time trends. Estimates below the dashed line are for models of changes to the condition of the closest road segment, with and without district-specific time trends.

From the estimates presented in Fig. 5.4 it is clear that changes to average road conditions are positively and significantly related to changes in the share of the presidential vote won by the incumbent party (coefficients are presented in Table 5.4 in the Appendix). In Fig. 5.4, the dots plot the increase in the incumbent party's share of the vote that is estimated to result from a one-standard deviation improvement in road conditions. The lines and bars surrounding the dots represent 95% confidence intervals around these estimates. What we can see quite clearly is that the positive effect of changes to road conditions holds across the range of buffer sizes (the estimates above the dashed line in Fig. 5.4), and for all but the smallest buffer sizes the estimates are statistically significant both with and without district-specific time trends.[25] For all of the models the magnitude of the estimated effect of changes to road conditions is reduced with the inclusion of district-specific time trends, which take account of unobserved time-varying factors at the district level that may confound the impact of road conditions on voter behavior.

Taken together, the consistency of these results and the nature of the estimation strategy make for convincing evidence that changes to road conditions significantly affect vote shares in Ghana. Moreover, as well as being statistically significant these effects are also substantively meaningful. Looking at the estimates using five-kilometer buffers, the mid-point in the range, without time trends the implied effect of a one-standard deviation increase in average road conditions is to increase the incumbent party's vote share by 1.4 percentage points. When time trends are included the effect is slightly more than 0.6 percentage points. While this may not sound huge in absolute terms, the stability of vote shares over time demonstrated in Fig. 5.3 means there is only limited variation to be explained here. As such, the fact that changes to road conditions account for any of this variation is an important finding.

It is also worth noting that the NPP's presidential candidate Nana Akufo-Addo won 49.13% of the first round votes in the 2008 presidential election. Given Ghana's two-round runoff electoral system, the results therefore suggest that had the NPP invested in only a little more than one additional standard deviation improvement in road conditions across the country, they could have won the 2008 election in the first round, rather than losing it in the second. Viewed in this light, it is hard to deny that the effect of roads on votes is substantively as well as statistically meaningful.

While the estimates presented in Fig. 5.4 represent average effects across the sample, further analysis shows that this masks a degree of heterogeneity in the effects of changes to road conditions across EAs. As was shown in Fig. 5.3, changes to road conditions vary substantially across the EAs in the sample, raising the possibility that the effects of these changes vary with their extent. This possibility

---

[25] The sample size reduces with smaller buffers because fewer EAs have sufficiently close road segments. This means that statistical power reduces as the size of the buffers decreases.

is borne out by restricting the analysis to EAs in which road conditions improved by at least one standard deviation (twenty-nine points on the 0–100 scale of road condition scores). This restricted subsample contains 28% of the EAs in the total sample, but accounts for 71% of *all* observed improvements to road conditions. When this subsample is analyzed separately, the implied effect of a one-standard deviation improvement to road conditions is to increase the incumbent's vote share by 1.77 percentage points (or 3.19 percentage points if district time trends are omitted from the model), which equates to almost 50% of the average change in vote shares across the sample. This is interesting because it suggests that, up to a point at least, there may be increasing marginal electoral returns to investments in road maintenance.

The estimates below the dashed line in Fig. 5.4 show the effect of changes to the condition of the single closest road segment to the EA, irrespective of distance. Broadly speaking these reflect the estimates of changes to average road conditions. Although the estimate which includes time trends is not statistically significant, the implied effect of improvements to the condition of the single closest road segment is similar in size to that of improvements to local average road conditions. The benefit of using this alternative measure is that it avoids dropping EAs, thereby increasing the size of the sample. But doing so comes at a cost, because as noted in Section 5.4.2 for some EAs the closest road segment is not very close. This cost can be seen as an opportunity, however, in that it allows us to investigate an additional source of potential heterogeneity in the effect of road conditions. Therefore to evaluate whether the impact of road conditions varies by distance to the road, I interact the condition of the closest road segment with a measure of its proximity to the EA.

Fig. 5.5 presents the effects of changes to road conditions by distance to the closest road (coefficients are presented in Table 5.5 in the Appendix). These plots show the marginal effect of a one-standard deviation improvement to the condition of the closest road segment on the incumbent's vote share, up to a distance of five kilometers. Panel (a) shows the effect without district-specific time trends, and panel (b) shows the effect when they are included. What is clear from these graphs is that the magnitude of the effect of road conditions diminishes with greater distance to the road, suggesting that voters care more about improvements to roads that are closer to them.

As the magnitude of the effect of improved roads diminishes with distance, so too does its significance. Without time trends the effect remains significant at the 95% level up to a distance of about four kilometers. When time trends are included, the effect is significant for roads within one kilometer. Beyond a certain distance, then, voters no longer appear to condition their electoral support on changes to road conditions. This heterogeneity could be explained by motivations, or by information. It is possible that voters only care about proximal road segments because these are the roads that they are most likely to use. Alternatively, it may

(a)

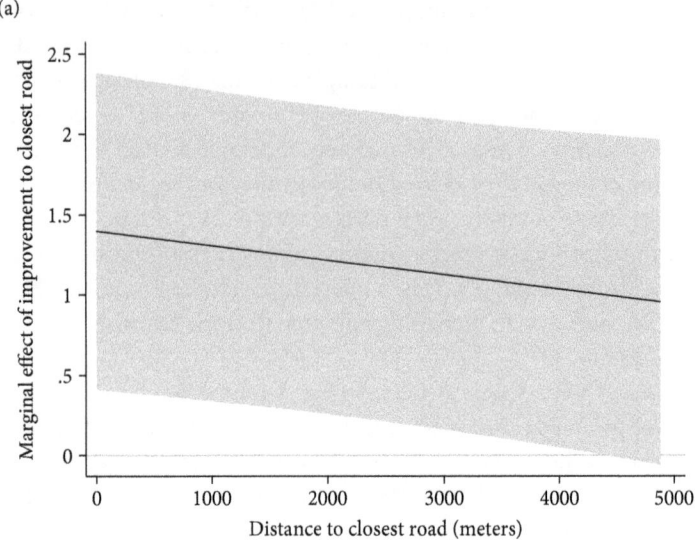

(b)

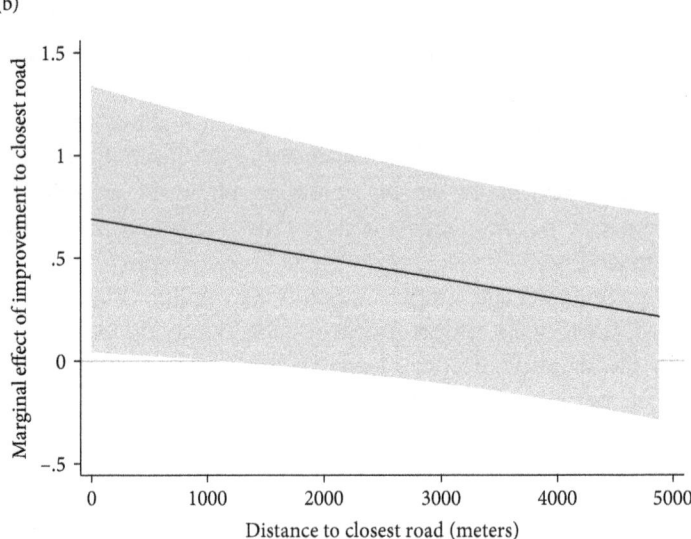

Fig. 5.5 Marginal effect of increase in road conditions by distance to closest road

Note: Dependent variable is incumbent vote share change. Graphs show the marginal effect of a one-standard deviation increase in the condition of the closest road segment to each electoral area, by the distance in meters from the centroid of the electoral area to the closest road segment. Panel (b) shows the effect when district-specific time trends were included, and panel (a) shows the effect without these time trends.

be that while citizens remain concerned by the state of more distant roads, the fact that they use these roads less frequently means that they have less information about their condition, thereby reducing voters' ability to effectively condition their electoral support on this outcome.

Whatever the reason, this heterogeneity provides further vindication of the argument that locally disaggregated data is necessary if we are to effectively evaluate the extent to which citizens condition their electoral support on the provision of public goods and services. In the case of roads in Ghana, it is clear that voters do behave in this way. The results presented in Figs. 5.4 and 5.5 provide consistent evidence of a significant and positive impact of changes to road conditions on incumbent vote shares. These results are generated via a very robust and conservative estimation strategy that controls for unobserved time-invariant characteristics of EAs, as well as any time-varying factors at the district level.

Nevertheless, one potential weakness of these results could stem from the possibility that vote shares are affected by unobserved changes to wealth. Increased wealth may make citizens more prone to reward the incumbent with greater electoral support, while at the same time increasing their ability to lobby for improved roads, leading us to spuriously attribute increased vote shares to the effect of road conditions. Estimates including a time-varying measure of wealth constructed from data on household wealth from the DHS surveys show that the impact of roads on votes is robust to this possibility (results are presented in Table 5.6, in the Appendix). It is also robust to alternative estimates that down-weight the potential impact of outliers.

This evidence of the impact of roads on votes therefore provides further, and even more robust, support for the microfoundations underpinning the book's central argument. Disaggregating the analysis to a much more localized level helps reduce concerns of ecological fallacies, that we might be making false conclusions about individual behavior on the basis of aggregate data. Moreover, it makes it easier for us to rule out the possibility that the observed relationship between roads and votes is being driven by some other unobserved factor. As such, we can be confident that the effect we are identifying is not spurious; among other things, Ghanaian voters condition their electoral support on changes to road conditions, because they care about the government's performance in providing them with goods and services.

5.5 Conclusions

Voters in Africa care about public goods. Of course, voters everywhere care about a multitude of things, and even within a single family the determinants of electoral choice are likely to vary from one individual to the next. But on the basis of the evidence presented in this chapter, electoral choice is affected by the government's performance in providing public goods. Given the overwhelming focus on issues of ethnicity and clientelism in studies of African electoral politics, this is an important conclusion in and of itself. And in the context of this book, it is crucial. If citizens in Africa do not engage in evaluative voting of this type, it would not make sense to think that politicians implement pro-rural policies in order to win the votes of the rural majority, because such policies would be ineffective in achieving that end. That citizens in Africa do behave in this way suggests that, at the micro-level, the argument in this book rests on solid foundations.

The evidence in this chapter comes from Ghana, but while the determinants of electoral choice will vary by country, there is little reason to think that Ghana is unique in this regard. Where it may be unique is in the extent to which the provision of particular goods and services can be attributed to political action. What this means is that while voters in other African countries are also likely to condition their electoral support in part on goods and services, the specific outcomes that they care about may differ from those that matter in Ghana, and any replication of this analysis in other countries should bear this in mind. Looking across different education inputs, citizens in Ghana are more likely to condition their presidential votes on those things that can be directly attributed to executive action, in this case the construction of new schools and the number of teachers. This may not be true elsewhere, if for example local authorities have greater control over the recruitment and allocation of teachers, or the location of new schools. Similarly, changes to road conditions elsewhere may not have quite the same impact on executive support, if responsibility for road maintenance is not so centrally controlled.

What matters most here, though, is that voters care about *any* public goods. This chapter provides robust, consistent evidence that they do. Whether it be road conditions, education inputs, or something else, there is good reason to think that voters in Africa condition their electoral support on their government's performance vis-à-vis the provision of goods and services. The extent to which this is true may vary for any particular individual—some may be driven by strong partisan attachments, others by ethnic loyalties, and yet others by some one-time, conditional material incentive. But the evidence presented in this chapter demonstrates that alongside these dynamics exists a degree of evaluative voting, on which this book's central argument is predicated.

Building on the evidence presented in the preceding chapters, these findings add further empirical weight to the book's central argument. Across Africa the introduction of meaningful electoral competition has created incentives for governments to court rural votes by implementing policies that primarily benefit rural interests. In Chapter 6 I turn to historical evidence from the case of Botswana in the decade immediately following independence, in order to more effectively illuminate the mechanism underlying this argument about Africa's rural democracies.

APPENDIX

Table 5.2 Summary statistics

	Obs.	Mean	Std. Dev.	Min.	Max.
Electoral Area-Level Data					
Dependent Variable:					
Incumbent vote share change	438	−4.006	6.298	−30.692	35.825
Independent Variables:					
Average road condition change (3km)	216	12.443	30.388	−59	95
Average road condition change (4km)	251	12.941	29.923	−59	95
Average road condition change (5km)	280	12.433	29.008	−59	95
Average road condition change (6km)	313	12.471	28.183	−59	95
Average road condition change (7km)	344	12.702	28.971	−59	95
Closest road condition change	438	12.011	33.3	−96	97
Constituency-Level Data					
Independent Variables:					
Wealth change	256	−0.207	0.631	−1.834	1.002
Water change	256	158.63	246.81	−18.03	988.11
Electricity change	256	0.040	0.284	−0.654	0.937
District-Level Data					
Dependent Variable:					
Incumbent vote share change by district	109	−2.705	6.575	−22.966	14.543
Independent Variables:					
Primary schools	109	12.376	17.747	−44	88
Classrooms per school	109	0.628	0.697	−0.811	5.029
Schools with toilets	109	−0.094	0.279	−0.651	0.777
School with drinking water	109	0.252	0.215	−0.216	0.779
Pupil–teacher ratio	109	−1.958	8.709	−48.813	7.887
Books per pupil	109	0.397	0.321	−0.699	1.818
Seats per pupil	109	−0.0004	0.219	−0.7	1.005
Average road condition change by district	109	9.670	21.769	−96	77.75

Table 5.3 Estimates of changes to road condition scores

	(1)	(2)	(3)	(4)	(5)	(6)
Average road condition, 2004	−0.427**	−0.436***	−0.441**	−0.438***	−0.758***	−0.692***
	(0.161)	(0.130)	(0.147)	(0.124)	(0.132)	(0.145)
Incumbent vote share, 2004	−0.012	−0.095				
	(0.108)	(0.153)				
Margin of victory, 2004			0.090	0.005		
			(0.087)	(0.109)		
Akan % of population					6.188	12.675
					(5.195)	(7.214)
Region fixed effects	No	Yes	No	Yes	No	Yes
Constituencies	230	230	230	230		
Districts					110	110

Note: Dependent variable is change in average road conditions between 2004 and 2007. Standard errors in parentheses, clustered by region. *p < 0.1; **p < 0.05; ***p < 0.01.

Table 5.4 Changes to average road conditions and incumbent vote shares

Buffer Size	Average Road Change	Standard Error	District Trends	EAs	Districts
3km	0.040**	(0.017)	No	216	45
	0.002	(0.007)	Yes	216	45
4km	0.048***	(0.016)	No	251	47
	0.017*	(0.009)	Yes	251	47
5km	0.049***	(0.017)	No	280	51
	0.022**	(0.009)	Yes	280	51
6km	0.046***	(0.016)	No	313	52
	0.021***	(0.007)	Yes	313	52
7km	0.048***	(0.016)	No	344	52
	0.016**	(0.007)	Yes	344	52

Note: Dependent variable is incumbent vote share change. District-clustered standard errors in parentheses. * p<.1, ** p<.05, *** p<.01

Table 5.5 Changes to closest road conditions and incumbent vote shares

	(1)	(2)	(3)	(4)
Closest road condition change	0.030**	0.008	0.042***	0.021**
	(0.015)	(0.007)	(0.015)	(0.009)
Closest road condition change X distance to closest road			−0.003	−0.003*
			(0.002)	(0.002)
District-specific time trends	No	Yes	No	Yes
Electoral areas	438	438	438	438
Districts	53	53	53	53

Note: Dependent variable is incumbent vote share change. District-clustered standard errors in parentheses. *p<.1, **p<.05, ***p<.01

Table 5.6 Changes to average road conditions and incumbent vote shares—controlling for wealth

	1	2	3	4	5	6
Average road condition change (5km)	0.046**	0.024**	0.038***	0.024**	0.039**	0.024**
	(0.017)	(0.009)	(0.014)	(0.009)	(0.016)	(0.009)
Wealth change			−2.129*	−0.038	−1.605	−0.425
			(1.161)	(0.184)	(1.179)	(0.254)
Water change					0.002	0.003***
					(0.002)	(0.0004)
Electricity change					−2.212	1.869
					(2.145)	(1.696)
District-specific time trends	No	Yes	No	Yes	No	Yes
Electoral areas	256	256	256	256	256	256
Districts	44	44	44	44	44	44

Note: Dependent variable is incumbent vote share change. District-clustered standard errors in parentheses. *p<.1, **p<.05, ***p<.01

6

Mechanisms: Historical Evidence from Botswana

6.1 Introduction

At independence Botswana was a poor country. Like other countries in Africa, years of colonial neglect had left it ill-prepared for self-government. Also like other African countries, Botswana at independence had a government that sought to transform its agricultural economy. Across Africa's new states, and indeed across developing areas of the world more generally, the broad objective was to shift economic resources from agriculture to industry in order to build a "modern" economy (Bates 1981, 4). What set Botswana apart from other countries in Africa, however, was the persistence and stability of electoral competition. While rulers across the continent were jettisoning democracy in favor of one-party states, the government of Botswana remained accountable to its electorate throughout the post-colonial period. Even in the early years of independence, this had important consequences for rural development.

The purpose of this chapter is to illuminate the mechanisms by which electoral incentives lead to pro-rural development. Of course, all cases are unique, and nowhere else will the dynamics highlighted in Botswana be replicated like for like. Nevertheless, highlighting them in this particular case provides insights into their plausible operation elsewhere, in one flavor at least. Doing so also conveys the additional benefit of controlling for the potentially confounding influence of donor pressure. Unlike donors in the 1990s and 2000s, but much like the governments they were lending to at the time, donors in the early years of African independence placed far greater emphasis on economic modernization than on rural development. The first decade of independence in Botswana therefore presents a useful case in which to examine the impact of electoral incentives on rural development.

The initial emphasis on transformation and modernization is clear from the policies pursued by Botswana's government at independence in 1966. After considering the economic and political context in which policy making was being undertaken, the chapter will trace through the country's development over much of the subsequent decade, differentiating between two very distinct periods. In the years immediately following independence through to the elections of

Rural Democracy: Elections and Development in Africa. Robin Harding, Oxford University Press (2020).
© Robin Harding.
DOI: 10.1093/oso/9780198851073.001.0001

1969 Botswana's government was content to largely ignore rural development concerns, emphasizing instead the achievement of financial independence through economic development and modernization. Jolted by a significant reduction to the ruling Botswana Democratic Party's (BDP) vote share in the 1969 elections, however, the period 1969–74 saw a stark shift in policy and rhetoric, culminating in the implementation of the Accelerated Rural Development Program (ARDP) in 1973.

Evidence from archival materials, including government documents, contemporary newspaper reports, and BDP manifestos, all points to the central role of electoral incentives in driving this clear shift in emphasis. Bolstered by secondary material, and by consideration of the distribution of electoral support and development resources, this evidence from Botswana's first decade of independence usefully illuminates the mechanisms linking electoral accountability to rural development. To be clear, the argument here is not that the pursuance of rural development policies in post-independence Botswana was entirely cynical or opportunistic. Government rhetoric from independence onward suggests a long-standing and persistent acknowledgment of the need for such development, and the easing of financial pressures in the early 1970s certainly facilitated its realization. But what distinguished Botswana's program of rural development at that time from a mere set of rural projects was "the political impetus behind it" (Colclough and McCarthy 1980, 233). Development policy in Botswana during the early 1970s represented an explicit and wholesale change in emphasis, and this change occurred because the government was worried about elections. As such, this case very nicely illustrates the mechanisms underlying this book's central argument about Africa's rural democracies.

6.2 Case and Context

Before considering the nature of development policy in Botswana in the period immediately following independence, it will be helpful to clarify the value of the case for the purpose at hand, and to provide some important background information.

6.2.1 Case

Today Botswana is a rich African country. With the fifth highest per capita GDP in sub-Saharan Africa, upper middle-income status, and a stable democratic system, it is rightly viewed as being something of an outlier on the continent. But the situation in Botswana was not always quite so rosy. At independence in 1966 Botswana was one of the world's poorest states, boasting only twelve kilometers of paved road in a territory of over six hundred thousand square kilometers. Among its population of 550,000, only one hundred Batswana had completed secondary school, and a mere twenty-two had graduated from university. This level of under-development was representative of the contemporary African experience, but what set Botswana apart from other African states in the 1960s was its commitment to multiparty electoral competition. The reasons for this commitment are for others to scrutinize. What matters for the purpose at hand is that Botswana's first decade of independence provides a unique historical case in which to explore the impact of electoral competition on rural development.

That it is a historical case is important because it provides an opportunity to rule out the possibility that the link between elections and rural development results not from electoral incentives but from contemporaneous donor pressure. Much like the governments they were lending to, donors in the early years of independence were concerned much more with economic modernization than with rural development. This had begun to change by the mid-1970s as donors started to pay greater attention to rural poverty alleviation, in particular through agricultural development (Eicher 2003), but in the period under examination here there is little reason to think that Botswana was under great external pressure to emphasize rural development. Donors during this period tended to give on a project rather than a program basis, with a large proportion of aid funding imported capital goods to support projects located in or primarily beneficial to urban areas (Colclough and McCarthy 1980, 105). This makes the case a very useful counterpoint to African countries in the 1990s and 2000s, during which time the re-introduction of multiparty elections occurred contemporaneously with a shift in emphasis of the aid agenda to focus on poverty alleviation and rural development.

6.2.2   Context

Botswana is a landlocked and mostly arid country. Less than 1% of its land is designated arable, with roughly 80% of the territory being desert area that is only usable as seasonal grazing lands. As a result, much of the population is concentrated in a narrow strip to the east of the country. Fig. 6.1 shows the distribution of the population throughout the country, based on data from the 1964 population census. Four-fifths of the population belong to the eight Tswana tribes (the largest of which is the Bangwato), whose chiefs traditionally exercised authority through hierarchical structures while governing with the consent of the *Kgotla*, a form of tribal assembly that provided a counterpoint to the power of the chief. Fig. 6.2 shows the location of tribal territories in Botswana, along with an approximation of their geographic sizes. Although the importance of *Kgotlas* to their traditional system of government set the Tswana apart from other precolonial

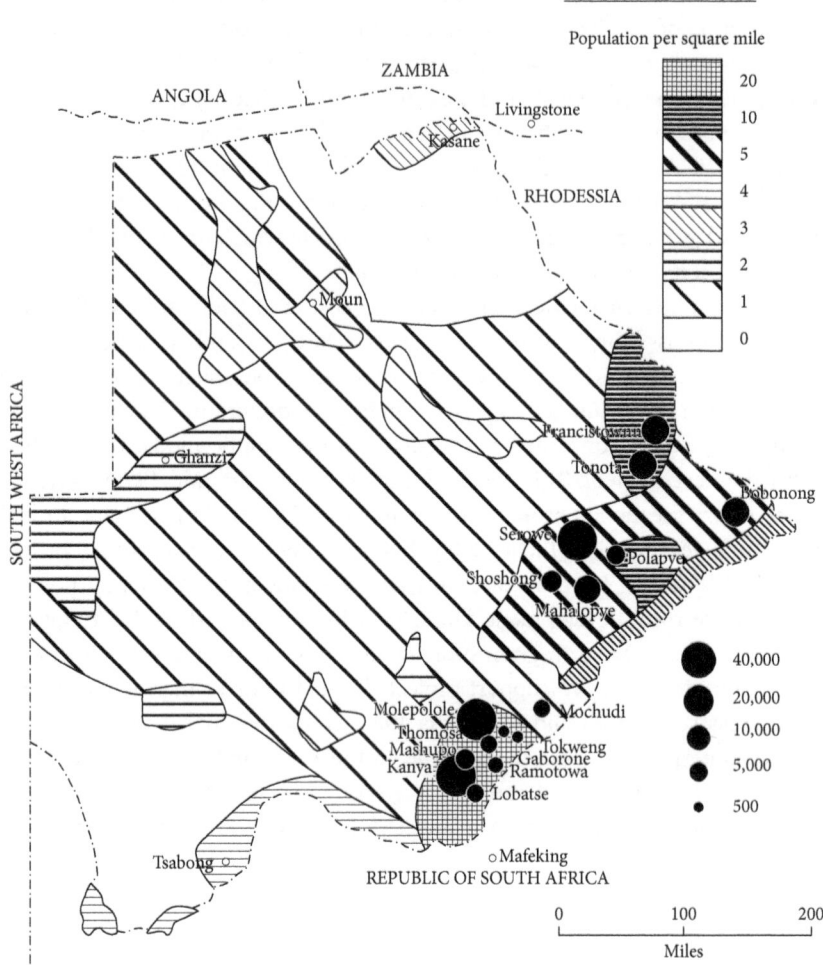

Fig. 6.1 Map of population density in Botswana at independence

Note: Population data from 1964 population census. Map copied from the National Development Plan 1970–75 (RB 1970).

African societies (Robinson, Acemoglu, and Johnson 2003), it has been argued that the extent of the *Kgotlas'* countervailing influence was undermined by British support for the chiefs during the colonial period (Colclough and McCarthy 1980, 36). While this may have been true to a degree, it seems reasonable to assert, as Hjort (2010) does, that important aspects of traditional Tswana culture and institutions nevertheless survived the colonial period.

From 1885 through to independence in 1966, Botswana had been under British protection as the Bechuanaland Protectorate. The protectorate had been

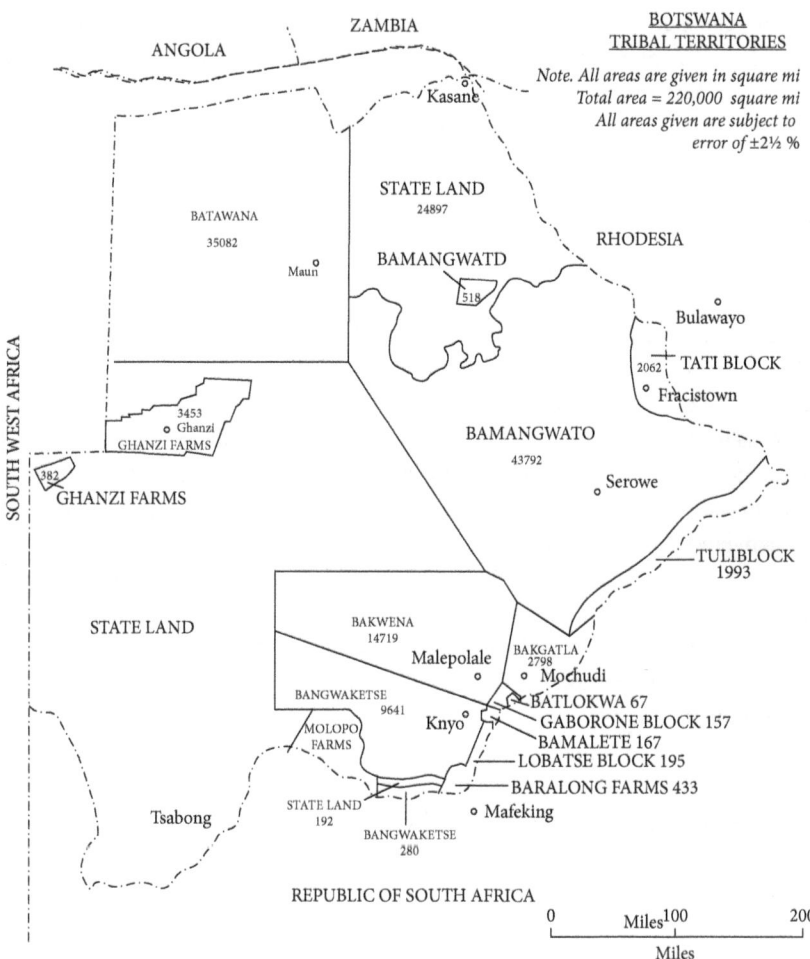

Fig. 6.2 Map of tribal territories in Botswana at independence

Note: Map copied from the National Development Plan 1970–75 (RB 1970).

established somewhat reluctantly, not to exploit the territory economically or to establish settlement but to secure the trade route for British commercial interests in the north. Moreover, it was welcomed by the principal Tswana chiefs in the face of persistent expansionary efforts by the Boers, especially given the expressed British intention to restrict involvement in the territory to the bare minimum, doing in the words of the High Commissioner "as little in the way of administration or settlement as possible" (Picard 1987, 36). A firm commitment to this policy of non-intervention had the dual consequences of leaving traditional Tswana authority largely intact, while contributing to the extreme underdevelopment already discussed.

While the political changes necessitated by independence would require a reduction in the power of chiefs, the continued relevance of traditional authority explains in part the political success of Seretse Khama, who as leader of the Botswana Democratic Party (BDP) became the country's first president in 1966. Although hereditary heir to the Tswana chieftancy, Seretse Khama had studied in the United Kingdom and married a European woman in 1948, leading to a chieftancy dispute that saw him exiled from the protectorate until 1956. At this point both Seretse and his uncle Tshekedi Khama, who had been acting as regent, renounced their claims to the chieftancy in order to create a tribal council, which, as Leith (2005) argues, effectively formalized democratic constraints on the chief.

The combination of his hereditary claim to traditional authority and his modern and modernizing political approach proved effective for Khama's appeal, and under his leadership the BDP was able to draw support in the 1965 elections from both emerging educated elites and traditional rural structures of loyalty to chiefs. Such a broad base of support set the BDP in contrast to its primary opponent, the Bechuanaland People's Party (BPP), which despite having a degree of international recognition as Bechuanaland's liberation party had a much narrower domestic appeal, with its support being concentrated among urban groups and workers (Robinson, Acemoglu, and Johnson 2003, 97). As a result, the BDP won the 1965 elections convincingly, taking over 80% of the votes and twenty-eight of the thirty-one parliamentary seats.

Yet while its government approached independence from a position of great political strength, Botswana's economic prospects at this time were bleak. The early 1960s saw the onset of the worst drought that the country had faced for over half a century, leading to repeated crop failures and the death of about one-third of the national cattle herd. The impact on agricultural productivity was disastrous, and generated such widespread rural poverty that at independence fully one-fifth of the population were dependent on famine-relief programs for their food supplies (Colclough and McCarthy 1980, 54). Needless to say, the economic outlook at this time was broadly pessimistic.

6.3 Botswana 1966–69

At independence, the Government's approach to development was to prioritize rapid industrialization at the expense of improving living standards. This was set out clearly by the President, Seretse Khama, in the foreword to the National Development Plan 1968–73:

> The primary aim of my Government, as I stated in the Transitional Plan, is to create a strongly united nation, to overcome all parochial, tribal and racial rivalries . . . increased efforts will be made to establish an industrial sector . . . At

the village level the spirit of self-help will be fostered ... The time has come for everyone to realize that immediate improvements in living standards can be achieved through individual effort and initiative, rather than through the charity of others.   (RB 1968)

Throughout Botswana, and especially so in rural areas, living standards at independence were incredibly poor. Yet during the period 1966–69 the government was happy to leave it to the people to realize any improvements in their living standards, encouraging a "spirit of self-help" while government efforts and resources were directed towards promoting industrialization.

6.3.1   Development in the early years

In the shadow of drought, famine, and widespread poverty, the early years of independence were in many ways remarkable. After five years of drought-induced decline Botswana's economy appeared to embrace political liberation with vigor, recording rapid and accelerating growth. In the first year of independence the country experienced an annual growth rate of nearly 7%, which increased to over 10% in 1967/8 and topped 15% the following year, such that the value of domestic production had doubled in real terms between 1965 and 1970 (Colclough and McCarthy 1980, 57–8). Some part of this growth was due to the expansion in public sector employment necessitated by the establishment of new government departments. Central government employment grew by a massive 70% between 1964 and 1969, an increase that was funded largely by greater aid revenues. But the bulk of Botswana's economic development in the early years of independence came from the countryside, as a result of significant increases to agricultural output.

Following the years of drought that blighted the early 1960s the second half of the decade was a period of recovery for Botswana's rural areas, as farmers sought to build up their cattle herds while rainfall was plentiful. Despite a partial drought in 1967/8 the agricultural sector grew by an average of 28% per year between 1965 and 1968/9, a period over which international beef prices increased by 27%.[1] However, although growth during this period was driven by gains in agricultural productivity, this did not translate into improvements to the livelihoods of all those living in rural areas. Inequalities in cattle ownership had always existed, and had increased during the drought years such that by the end of the 1960s almost half of all rural households owned no cattle at all, while ownership of around three-quarters of the national herd was concentrated in the hands of less than 20% of rural households (a group that included Seretse Khama, as well as

---

[1] Data on international beef prices from the World Bank, accessed at https://www.worldbank.org/en/research/commodity-markets on May 23, 2018.

his Vice President Quett Masire). The years of abundant rainfall were still of some benefit to most rural dwellers, as the system of loaning cattle for plowing meant that arable farming was also more productive during this period. But while famine-relief programs were no longer required, living standards for most rural Batswana remained low, and poverty was widespread.

Throughout the country access to basic services was incredibly limited. This was true at independence, and remained so through the rest of the decade. In 1966 Botswana had 247 primary schools with a total enrollment of a little over 70,000 pupils, which accounted for somewhere between 50%–70% of the school-age population.[2] This level of enrollment resulted from large increases over recent years, such that resources were stretched, and the average pupil/teacher ratio was over 45:1. The situation with regard to healthcare told a similar story. At independence there were about twenty registered doctors in Botswana, or roughly one per 26,000 people, covering seven hospitals and thirteen health centers (RB 1966, 38). Given the concentration of health services in urban centres, and the uneven distribution of the population, the ratio of doctors to people was estimated to be as high as 1:67,000 in some areas (RB 1968, 60).

Despite acknowledging the need and demand for improved services, however, the Government's National Development Plan of 1968 prioritized rapid economic development in order to achieve self-sustainability, with policies designed primarily to further this end. In education, for example, this meant a focus on expanding the secondary sector in order to create the human capital necessary to speed up localization of the bureaucracy. In contrast, very little emphasis was given to primary education, and what there was tended to focus on improving quality rather than access. While these policies may have been well designed to meet the stated goal of rapid economic development, their short-term benefits would clearly be concentrated in urban areas, given the greater demand for secondary education among urbanites.[3]

This pattern was reflected in other sectors also. In the early years of independence the government acknowledged that water shortages and associated problems affected the lives of the population more than any other factor (RB 1968, 14). Nevertheless, of the 558,000 rand committed to capital expenditure for the Water Branch in 1969/70, 499,500 rand (90%) was allocated to urban water projects that would only directly benefit the 8% of the population living in urban areas at that time. Likewise concerning healthcare services, in the latter half of the 1960s the vast majority (more than 70% in 1968/9) of the Medical Department's capital

---

[2] While the Government's Transitional Plan of 1966 cited an enrollment rate of roughly half the school-age population in 1966 (RB 1966, 33), the National Development Plan of 1968 claimed that the same number of pupils represented in 1967 an enrollment rate of approximately 70% (RB 1968, 53).

[3] On differential preferences for education across urban and rural areas see Stasavage (2005a).

expenditure was allocated to the urban hospitals (RB 1968, 150–1). Certainly the BDP was conscious of the clamor for improvements to service provision, noting in the National Development Plan of 1968 that the "Government is aware of the widespread desire for better medical services" (RB 1968, 9). With equal certainty it can be said that the government was working to extremely tight budgetary constraints during this period. Yet while the expressed desire to do more may well have been sincere, the focus of development during this period was quite distinctly pro-urban.

Notwithstanding the Government's awareness of rural poverty and the pressing need for investment in rural development, the 1968 National Development Plan devoted much of the development budget to the Shashi Complex, a huge industrial development project. This followed the commitment in the Government's Transitional Plan, published at independence in 1966, to invest a large proportion of development expenditure in the infrastructure necessary to develop copper mining at Matsitama in Central District, and copper–nickel mining at the adjacent deposits identified at Selebi and Phikwe, also in Central District. By the end of the decade better understanding of the various mineral prospects led to the Shashe Project being readjusted to focus solely on developing a mine at Selebi-Phikwe. But this still remained an enormous undertaking, requiring the construction of a new town, with its own electricity, water, and transport infrastructure. Delays meant that construction did not begin until 1970, after which time the project would for a number of years represent a significant proportion of capital expenditure, as is reflected by the data on expenditure patterns presented in Table 6.1.

While the decision to prioritize industrial development was understandable given the government's stated goal of achieving rapid economic growth and self-reliance, it necessarily implied that attention and resources would be directed away from the needs of the countryside. This commitment of resources to industrial development stood in fairly stark contrast to the government's emphasis on "self-help" for rural development in the 1968 National Development Plan, and its explicit statement that reducing inequalities in incomes was only "a long range objective of government policy." The government sought to justify this by highlighting the lack of available resources, pointing out in the National Development Plan that "there are therefore very few local funds to be spent on development" (RB 1968, 8). Although Khama's government during this period may have expressed rhetorical plans to develop the whole country, meaning the rural as well as the small but rapidly expanding urban centers, the realization of these plans was being punted to some distant affordable future.

The rhetoric and proposals set out in the National Development Plan matched patterns of actual government expenditure during this period. As Table 6.1 shows, between 1966/7 and 1969/70 the proportion of annual capital expenditures directed to or primarily benefiting urban areas was almost double that for rural

Table 6.1 Capital expenditure by location and/or main beneficiary group, 1966/7–1975/6

	1966/7	1967/8	1968/9	1969/70	1970/1	1971/2	1972/3	1973/4	1974/5	1975/6
Rural	1.44	1.48	0.85	1.00	1.39	1.00	1.63	3.32	12.31	13.40
	(26)	(39)	(25)	(20)	(16)	(8)	(5)	(10)	(33)	(32)
Urban	2.79	1.69	2.12	2.19	5.34	9.03	25.39	23.86	13.67	17.69
	(49)	(45)	(64)	(45)	(63)	(74)	(85)	(70)	(37)	(42)
Communications	1.43	0.62	0.37	1.71	1.80	2.22	2.86	6.93	11.00	11.00
	(25)	(16)	(11)	(35)	(21)	(18)	(10)	(20)	(30)	(26)
Total	5.66	3.79	3.34	4.90	8.53	12.25	29.88	34.11	37.00	42.09

Note: Pula millions (percentages). Data from the Republic of Botswana's Annual Statements of Accounts, 1967–76, recorded in Colclough and McCarthy (1980).

areas, despite less than 8% of the population living in urban areas.[4] As already discussed, a large part of this urban expenditure was driven by the rapid expansion of the public sector, with spending on government administration accounting for an average of 17.5% of annual current budget expenditure. Indeed, urban housing alone soaked up around 3.5% of annual expenditure during this period. This urban skew in capital expenditures was exacerbated by the scaling down of famine relief and institutional feeding programs by 1967, a saving that was not followed by any substitute expenditure that would benefit the rural areas.

In a classical sense it is true that Botswana avoided "the African disease" of urban bias during this period (Hjort 2010); the government was not using distortionary agricultural policies to divert resources from rural areas to the urban centers. Yet it is clear that despite being home to only a fraction of the population, urban areas were benefiting far more from the country's fairly limited revenues than the countryside was. This was part and parcel of the government's explicit strategy for development, and it is likely that this was at least implicitly encouraged by donors who were happy to fund "projects rather than programs." Much like elsewhere in Africa at the time, the emphasis was on modernization rather than rural development, and this emphasis came through loud and clear in the BDP's campaign for the 1969 election.

6.3.2 The 1969 election

In October 1969 Serestse Khama's BDP Government faced the electorate for the first time since the party's overwhelming victory in 1965. After three years of independence the people of Botswana would have the opportunity to express their verdict on the government's performance. As in 1965, the BDP was opposed in 1969 by the BPP, which had won three parliamentary seats in the previous elections, and the Botswana Independence Party (BIP). The BIP was led by Motsamai Mpho, who hailed from one of the non-Tswana tribes located in the north-west of the country. Although it had not won any seats in 1965, the BIP had polled well among the non-Tswana in the north-west.

These three parties were joined in 1969 by a new party, the Botswana National Front (BNF), which had formed in an effort to unite opposition to the BDP but whose presence may have had the unfortunate impact of further fragmenting opposition support. The inherent difficulty of uniting diverse opposition interests was reflected by the fact that the BNF represented an uneasy balance of radical and traditionalist views, calling for both nationalization of industry as well as greater political representation of tribal interests. Perhaps by virtue of the latter, the party

---

[4] Colclough and McCarthy (1980, 88) also provide a useful breakdown of expenditures across sectors during this period.

was joined by Chief Bathoen II of the Ngwaketse, one of the principal Tswana tribes, who resigned his chieftancy and ran as a parliamentary candidate in the South Kanye constituency, in Ngwaketse District.

Campaign

The BDP approached the campaign with very little pretense about its development strategy. Reflecting its rhetoric of the early independence years, the BDP's 1969 election manifesto was notable for the lack of attention paid to the provision and expansion of rural services. The manifesto opened with a legacy pitch, highlighting the party's role in leading Botswana to political independence, before emphasizing its efforts to achieve financial independence for the nation through the development of the mining industry. Echoing the National Development Plan this was framed as the means to fund other forms of development in the long-term, but the realization of any such development was explicitly punted into the long grass, being said to be achievable "by the end of the 1970's" (BDP 1969, 5).

The expectation that the rural majority would wait patiently for development was reproduced physically in the manifesto, which did not begin to consider rural development directly until page twenty-eight (of fifty-three). Even then discussion of rural development remained somewhat vague, and lacked explicit promises of rural investment. Instead it served to re-emphasize that although investments in areas such as education and communications were being directed towards the goal of financial independence, the BDP's chief objective was still to modernize and increase the productivity of agricultural industries. Broad discussion of policies to establish new stock routes and provide protective services to ward against livestock diseases formed part of a set of proposals to help further this objective, but no focus was given to the development of more widespread access to basic services such as education and healthcare.

Reflecting the policies of previous years, proposals for primary education emphasized improving quality for the few rather than widening access for the many, with far greater priority given to the expansion and improvement of secondary education. More tellingly still, no promises whatsoever were made to expand medical services beyond the existing urban-centered provision, on the basis that "Botswana is a poor country" (BDP 1969, 39). Likewise for rural roads the BDP declined to promise any investment, stating simply that the party "scorns to win easy popularity by encouraging unproductive expenditure which is not justified by concrete gains, economic or social" (BDP 1969, 26). As we shall see, this tune would change in the not-too-distant future.

Just as with the rhetoric of its early development plans, the BDP did not demonstrate ignorance of rural needs and demands in its manifesto of 1969. Instead, while rural interests and issues of rural development were noted, they were de-prioritized beneath a focus on rapid economic development, and a message of self-help and national unity. The final element of this may well have reflected a concern that the BNF was drawing support away from the BDP along tribal lines, given Bathoen's strong support among the Ngwaketse. This concern came through clearly in the BDP's statements during the lead-up to the election, and on the campaign trail around the country.

In what seems a thinly-veiled threat to the BNF, two months prior to the election the Minister of State told the National Assembly that "action would be considered and taken against any individuals found working against the Government's policy of National Unity and promoting tribal antipathies."[5] At BDP meetings the following week in Kanye, the traditional capital of the Ngwaketse tribe, speakers strenuously denied BNF allegations that the government had no relations with the local chiefs.[6] And a month later the President called for national unity at a speech in Mmadinare, in Central District, saying that "anyone who tries to divide the people according to tribes is leading the country to a wrong destiny."[7]

Launching the BDP manifesto at the end of September 1969, President Khama and Vice President Masire emphasized the importance of national unity and self-reliance,[8] and in a speech at the start of October the President stressed that in contesting the elections political parties "must not employ the self-destructive weapon of racialism and tribalism."[9] These themes were recurrent throughout the campaign period, with BDP representatives repeating their calls for unity and self-reliance to crowds throughout the country. While these calls likely reflected a sincere concern about the BNF's ability to draw support away from the BDP along tribal lines, they may also have been in part an attempt to present the BNF as a narrowly tribal party in order to deflect attention from its potentially threatening policy positions.

At an event at Totome attended by Khama in early October one of the founders of the BNF, Daniel Kwele, championed the issue of free education.[10] Addressing crowds at multiple locations in the following days the President attacked opposition parties for irresponsibly proposing policies such as free education without explaining how such policies could be paid for.[11] He would return to this issue repeatedly in the run-up to the vote, warning voters just two days before the election to "be aware of politicians who attempted to bribe them with policies they cannot fulfill."[12] Given the tight financial constraints facing the country at this time, Khama's conservative rhetoric may well have been a responsible position, but the need to reiterate its defense reflects an acknowledgment of the likely traction that the BNF's policies would have with the electorate. Through repeated decrials of tribalism and reckless promises, the BDP sought to undermine popular opposition policies while painting the BNF as a narrow, tribalist party of the Ngwaketse.

---

[5] Botswana Daily News, August 18, 1969.   [6] Botswana Daily News, August 25, 1969.
[7] Botswana Daily News, September 17, 1969.   [8] Botswana Daily News, September 29, 1969.
[9] Botswana Daily News, October 1, 1969.   [10] Botswana Daily News, October 3, 1969.
[11] Botswana Daily News, October 6, 1969.   [12] Botswana Daily News, October 16, 1969.

On the final day before the election, the President reiterated his rejection of tribalism one last time, reminding people that "they should not vote for someone because they were a friend, a relation or a chief," and calling again for unity.[13] Like the party's election manifesto, newspaper reports of the BDP's campaign are distinctly devoid of promises by the government to bring tangible development outcomes to the masses in the short term. Save for some very general early pronouncements about the importance of rural development by the President and the Minister of Local Government,[14] and a reminder of an increase in secondary school places by the Vice President,[15] the BDP's campaign accurately reflected its lack of attention to rural development. This focus on unity and self-reliance over short-term development may have been a mistake; a subsequent and quite dramatic shift in the emphasis of both its rhetoric and policies would later suggest that the BDP thought as much.

Results

In retrospect the BDP had little reason to be overly concerned, easily winning the 1969 election. It took 68% of the votes, and won 24 (or 77%) of the 31 parliamentary seats. The BPP took 12% of the votes, retaining the 3 seats it had won in 1965, while the BIP's 6% share of the votes this time round gave it a single parliamentary seat, in the north-west of the country. The big change compared to 1965 was the arrival of the BNF. Despite the Government's efforts to paint the BNF as reckless and tribalist the new party garnered 13.5% of the votes, enough to give it victory in three constituencies, all in Ngwaketse District. Most strikingly, this included the Kanye South seat held by the Vice President, Quett Masire, who was defeated by Bathoen himself.

While its overall victory was comfortable, and its tenure in government never really under threat, the BDP's electoral losses were significant. Along with the loss of four parliamentary seats, including that of none other than the Vice President, its share of the vote had fallen by 12%. And although the BNF's parliamentary seats were concentrated in a single district, support for the government had fallen throughout the country. In the concurrent local elections the BDP lost seats in eight of the twelve councils. While the BDP's parliamentary vote share increased in almost as many constituencies as it fell, the magnitude of losses far outweighed any gains.

Across the seventeen constituencies where the BDP lost support the average decline in vote share was more than 23% (with the median loss being 18%).

---

[13] Botswana Daily News, October 17, 1969.
[14] Botswana Daily News, August 20, 1969 and September 2, 1969.
[15] Botswana Daily News, September 9, 1969.

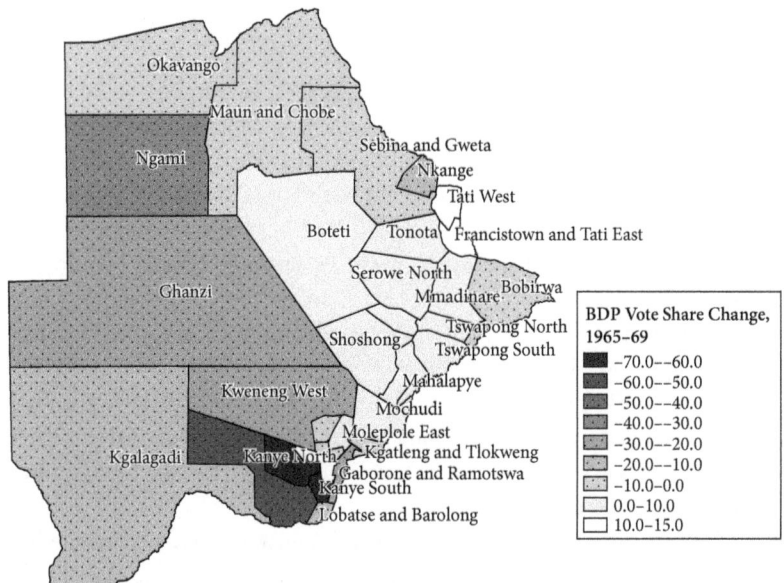

Fig. 6.3 Changes to BDP vote shares, 1965–69, by constituency

Note: Map drawn using boundaries set by 1972 Delimitation Commission. This exercise resulted in minor changes to some of the constituencies. Specifically, Gaborone and Ramotswa was split into two constituencies, but here are merged back together. In addition, a small number of polling areas were reallocated between Tati West and the Francistown and Tati East constituencies, and between Molepolole North and Molepolole East.

By contrast, the average increase in its vote share in the fourteen constituencies where the BDP made gains was less than 4% (with a median increase of only 2%). The spatial distribution of this decline in support can be seen in Fig. 6.3, which highlights both the geographic spread of the decline as well as its extent in many areas of the country. Notably, and despite the portrayal of the BNF as a tribalist party, comparing this to Fig. 6.2 shows that the constituencies in which the BDP's support rose between 1965 and 1969 were largely concentrated within Khama's own Bamangwato tribal territories.

Belying Khama's apparent efforts to paint it as a narrow tribalist party, support for the BNF was widespread. The party won votes in twenty-one of the thirty-one constituencies, including four of the five in Ngwaketse District (in the remaining constituency the BDP candidate ran unopposed), averaging more than 20% of the votes across these (with a median share of 9.3%). As well as the three Ngwaketse parliamentary seats, the level and breadth of its support was sufficient to win the party seats on half of the District and Town councils. The President may have been correct to portray the election in Kanye as "a tribal issue rather than a political one,"[16] but throughout the country support for the BNF was clearly more broadly-based than this, transcending tribal or regional concerns.

Breaking the results down in this way suggests a substantial, albeit not fatal, decline in BDP support between 1965 and 1969. The extent of this decline may be seen as greater still if we consider the fall in voter participation over this period. From a high of 75% in 1965, turnout fell to less than 55% in 1969 (Parson 1977). While this may have been in part due to a lack of understanding of the voter registration process, survey evidence from the 1970s suggests that it was not due to a widespread belief that politicians, like chiefs, do not need to have their mandates renewed to remain in office, as BDP supporters had suggested at the time (Parson 1977; Colclough and McCarthy 1980). More worryingly for the government, the precipitous decline in turnout may have reflected the growth of "apathy in the face of intractable poverty or actual dissatisfaction but without any perception that this may be expressed through the behavior of voting" (Parson 1976, quoted in Colclough and McCarthy 1980).

What is quite clear is that the BDP Government was concerned by the loss of support. Sufficiently so that in the days immediately following the election, while continuing to depict the BNF's rapid rise as the result of tribalism, the government's rhetoric with regard to rural development shifted dramatically. Just two days after the election, the Vice President announced that the government's priority over the next five years would be to further educational expansion.[17] This marked a notable shift from the previous policy of quality over quantity, and a clear appropriation of the position expounded by the BNF during the election campaign. Later that week the President reiterated this priority in a broadcast to the nation, noting in addition that "the provision of improved medical facilities is also a matter of urgency."[18]

All the while, the BDP persisted in painting BNF support as tribalist rather than programmatic, with Khama expressing regret that voters in Ngwaketse District supported "a man rather than a policy."[19] Arguing that "those Bangwaketse who voted BNF did not vote for the Front, because they approved of its policies or those of its presidential candidate, but because Bathoen Gaseitsiwe had been their chief for forty-one years," the President denied the BNF's claim to be a truly national party, ruing the fact that the opposition in the next parliament would be "a tribal one."[20] Whatever the reasons underlying BNF support among the Bangwaketse, its successes elsewhere throughout the country were clearly not underpinned by tribalism. That the BDP's rhetoric shifted so swiftly to emphasize the provision of basic services illustrates an awareness of this fact. As the following years would demonstrate, the pressures of electoral accountability created clear incentives for the government to prioritize policies that would expand the provision of basic services and infrastructure to the rural majority.

---

[16] Botswana Daily News, October 20, 1969.   [17] Botswana Daily News, October 20, 1969.
[18] Botswana Daily News, October 23, 1969.   [19] Botswana Daily News, October 23, 1969.
[20] Botswana Daily News, October 23, 1969.

6.4 Botswana 1970–74

After the elections of 1969, the Government's focus swung very much towards the promotion of rural development. As noted by Seretse Khama in the foreword to the National Development Plan 1970–75:

> Planning is choosing. There are so many things we should like to do for our people, to improve living standards…Do we improve hospitals in towns or concentrate on extending preventative medical services in rural areas?…We must, if our planning is to be successful, take social and political considerations into account. Above all we must be constantly aware of the needs and wishes of the people themselves…Pragmatism and principle alike dictate that our policies take fully into account the demands of social justice…The greatest challenge ahead of us is undoubtedly rural development…Progress in our countryside will be less obvious and dramatic than in the mining sector and in the capital, but it should not be assumed that we are neglecting rural development. In fact the reverse is the case.   (RB 1970)

For a few years it would appear that this new focus on rural development was largely rhetorical, but all this would change in the run-up to the next elections.

6.4.1   Development between 1970–73

The shift in rhetorical emphasis noted in the immediate aftermath of the 1969 elections permeated into the new National Development Plan, published in September of the following year. As in previous plans the government was careful to manage expectations, reiterating that budget constraints meant "there are therefore very few local funds to be spent on development" (RB 1970, 12). Nevertheless, despite the continued lack of resources, the government's change in emphasis was striking. Whereas in previous plans the development of rural areas had been pitched as a long-term goal, this one stated explicitly that, "During this Plan period Government intends to devote considerable resources to the task of rural development" (RB 1970, 13).

Perhaps because of the budgetary constraints, the strength of this new rhetorical commitment to short-term rural development was not fully matched by concrete proposals for achieving this end. A major element of the Plan was a program of agricultural development designed to "ensure that rural income levels rise as fast as possible" (RB 1970, 27). This program focused both on developing the lucrative but unequal livestock sector, and on expanding crop production with the aim of achieving national self-sufficiency in food. To the latter end, policy proposals involved increasing the amount of land under cultivation, increasing crop yields through improved farming standards, introducing cash crops, and developing irrigation farming.

Alongside these proposals for enhanced crop production, the Plan also proposed policies to further develop the livestock sector through improved animal husbandry and water management. Interestingly, these took a backseat to proposals for the development of arable farming, with the government taking pains in the Plan to acknowledge inequalities in the distribution of cattle wealth, whereby more than 50% of the national herd was owned by only about 10% of agricultural holders. These efforts may have reflected a recognition that with many wealthy cattle owners among its ranks the BDP risked being viewed as elitist, and needed to broaden its appeal to the rural majority. As a result, it was necessary to downplay policies designed to develop the livestock sector, including proposals for land tenure reform, that were surely motivated at least in part by self-interest on the part of government elites (Vengroff 1977, Picard 1980).[21]

Compared to agricultural policies the government's commitment to address the development of basic service provision was more limited. Despite Masire's announcement in the days following the 1969 election that the government's priority would be expanding access to education, the Plan made very little provision for this. No major commitments were made to significantly increase primary school places, and projections estimated an increase in enrollment numbers of about 14% over the Plan period (1970–75), which was below the estimated rate of population growth. In fact, contrary to Masire's post-election pledge, the government explicitly maintained its prior position that "investment in primary education should be directed during the Plan period mainly to the upgrading of standards rather than to increasing the quantity of education" (RB 1970, 99).

With regard to the expansion of medical services the Plan was somewhat bolder. The government set itself the target of reducing the number of people per doctor from 24,000 to 14,000 by 1975, while also committing to increase the number of registered nurses and midwives in the country. Moreover, in an implicit acknowledgment that health services were unequally concentrated in urban areas the Plan made provisions to expand and improve district hospitals, as opposed to the larger and more advanced hospitals located in the urban townships. It also promised that, "Future development of preventive services will be concentrated at village level and on maternal and child welfare" (RB 1970, 113).[22]

---

[21] It is important to acknowledge the self-interests of cattle-owning elites in Botswana, and the impact of these interests on policy-making during the period since independence, as has been highlighted by Picard (1987) and Holm and Molutsi (1992), among others. Rural interests are not homogenous in Botswana, just as they are not elsewhere in Africa, and not *all* rural policies are driven by electoral incentives. It is equally important to acknowledge, however, that policies designed to assist the livestock sector represented just a fraction of pro-rural policies implemented in Botswana during this period.

[22] It is important to acknowledge the structure of decentralization in Botswana, and the key role that local authorities were supposed to play in the development and provision of basic services. At

While the government's newfound rhetorical commitment to rural development was not matched by concrete policy proposals, the opposite was true of the
urban and industrial sectors. Lurking behind its expressed dedication to achieve
social justice by addressing the "greatest challenge" of rural development was a
quiet commitment to the successful creation of a mining sector. Just as in the
period prior to the 1969 elections, this strategy made sense given the potential
abundance of resources that might be had from lucrative mining operations. The
notable difference from the earlier period, however, came in how this strategy was
presented. As well as being grossly overshadowed by the emphasis on rural development, plans to develop the mining sector were framed as being the responsibility
of private companies. These companies would be responsible, in cooperation with
the government, for "a massive program of capital works over the next four years"
(RB 1970, 17). Rural development plans also overshadowed the fact that for the
Shashi Complex alone this "cooperation" was to cost the government more than
40% of its entire capital expenditure budget over the next four years.

At start of the 1970s therefore, and despite the lack of any significant change
in the country's economic fortunes, the BDP Government undertook a clear
rhetorical shift towards an emphasis on rural development. Given the unexpected
electoral losses in 1969, and Khama's own foreword to the 1970 Development Plan,
it is hard not to infer that this pragmatism was driven by political considerations.
Within the Plan itself, the extent of this shift appeared to remain largely rhetorical,
despite Khama's assurance that rural development was not being neglected. But
these assurances alone are illuminating; the election results had opened the BDP's
eyes to the incentives generated by electoral accountability in the context of a
significant rural majority.

But while these incentives may have resulted in a rhetorical shift, in the early
1970s with the next elections more than four years away they did little to alter
actual development spending. As Table 6.1 shows, the proportion of capital expenditure directed to rural areas actually fell during this period, although the absolute
amount remained fairly stable. This relative drop reflected the huge increase in
spending on urban areas, driven by the commencement of the Shashe Project. As
this project geared up and the construction of the new mining town at Selebwi-
Phikwe got underway, urban capital expenditures grew dramatically, more than
doubling to over P5 million in the first year, and peaking at over P25 million in
1972/3. Total public expenditure on the Shashe Project alone was in the region of
P55 million during this period (Colclough and McCarthy 1980, 91).

the local level, in 1970 the development expenditure of District Councils was dominated by education
spending, followed by spending on water resources and health services. The government highlighted
in the Plan that it had encouraged Councils not to over-emphasize education, and to spend more on
water and health. The Plan also highlighted the significant under-spend of central government grants
by local authorities, which it blamed on a lack of administrative capacity, and committed to a program
of reforms designed to address this deficiency in order to speed up the development process.

At the same time, with capacity stretched by this great burst of urban construction, development in other areas fell back, with only 60% of targeted expenditure on non-Shashe Project development being met between 1970 and 1973. This included the creation of 17,000 more secondary school places, and the construction of a technical training centre in Gaborone. But committed development in other areas went unrealized, with rural projects in particular experiencing greater delays than those in urban areas (Colclough and McCarthy 1980, 92). As is clear from the figures in Table 6.1, rural projects received less than 10% of total capital expenditure between 1970/1 and 1973/4, with fully 75% benefiting urban areas. And despite the strong commitment to agricultural development espoused in the National Development Plan, only 2% of capital expenditure went to the agricultural sector.

The latter part of 1972 saw some growth in effort on the part of the government to realize rural development, however small. In December 1972, for example, the government introduced subsidies for a number of rural bus routes throughout the country. Somewhat more substantially, in May 1972 the Ministry of Finance and Development Planning had begun working with the District Councils and Commissioners on a long-term plan to expand rural health facilities. By late November of that year the Ministry of Local Government and Lands had put together a proposal that envisaged the establishment of 161 new health posts and fifty-one clinics phased fairly evenly over the next five years, with thirty-five health posts and seven clinics proposed for construction in 1973–74.

These efforts reflected the view expressed in a meeting between the President and the Minister of Local Government and Lands on November 13, 1972 that "1973 should be a starting date for a concentrated effort to develop the Rural Areas". To some extent this view was met with action, with rural capital expenditure doubling in 1973/4, as can be seen in Table 6.1. This increase led to a slight uptick in the proportion of total capital expenditure allocated to rural relative to urban areas, although this remained well below the relative proportions of the late 1960s. One further important change that occurred at this time was the government's decision in January 1973 to halve primary school fees. Unsurprisingly, this led to a significant increase in enrollment, with the number of children enrolling in Standard 1 (the earliest year of primary school) up by 60% in 1973 compared to 1972. Lower rural incomes meant that the impact of this policy was felt more keenly by rural households than those in urban areas. Moreover, that this policy change occurred in the year before a scheduled election fits with the claim by Harding and Stasavage (2014) that electoral incentives have motivated the widespread abolition of primary school fees across Africa in recent years.

This pro-rural effort was given rhetorical force in the revised National Development Plan published in 1973, which prioritized rural development even more forcefully than the 1970 Plan, and articulated plans for its realization more clearly. The growing push for rural development at this time likely had two main drivers, the first of which was the achievement of self-reliance in the recurrent budget for the first time in 1972/3, largely as a result of increased revenues from the newly renegotiated Customs Union Agreement. These surpluses had been expected in the 1973 Plan, though it had not been anticipated that they would be realized quite so soon. Nevertheless, the availability of surplus funds increased the government's scope to act on its rhetorical commitments to rural development.

The second driver was political. As the 1974 elections began to loom on the horizon, the government became keen not just to push for rural development but to make sure that the rural majority knew about it. The strong pro-rural message of the 1973 Plan was to be spread via a "popularization" project. Developed in the latter part of 1972 by the Division of Extra Mural Services at the request of the Ministry of Local Government and Lands, and building off a pilot project run the previous year for the 1970 Plan, the popularization plan sought to "enable people to learn about the general direction of development and some of the projects government plans to implement." This was to be done via a series of weekly radio programs and study guides designed for as many as 1,000 "radio learning groups," with parts of the study guides to be reproduced in the national newspaper, the Daily News. Learning groups were to be arranged via Chiefs, and held within village kgotlas, with 2,000 radios provided to facilitate them (Parsons, Henderson, and Tlou 1995, 301).

The loosening of financial constraints in 1973 meant that the government had greater capacity to act, and the slight increase in rural expenditure at this time may be taken as a sign of the government's sincerity in its commitments to rural development. Still, the fact that urban capital expenditure continued to dwarf that directed to rural areas suggests somewhat less sincerity in the proclamations that rural development was the government's primary aim. The heightened rhetorical push for rural development as the next elections approached, and the government's desire to spread awareness of its pro-rural commitments at this time, are illuminating. Certainly action towards rural development would not have been possible without funds, but the nature and timing of this action had a clear political motivation. Real change would come the following year, as the elections drew ever closer.

6.4.2   The accelerated rural development program

In November 1973 the government initiated the Accelerated Rural Development Program (ARDP). Its impetus came right from the top; on November 9 the President's Permanent Secretary circulated a confidential paper to all Permanent Secretaries, the Commissioner of Police, the Director of Personnel, and the Attorney General, in advance of a meeting scheduled to take place ten days later. The paper stated that "His Excellency the President has instructed that a hard look be taken at the ability of the Government to carry out the targets laid down in the National Development Plan 1973–78". After noting the unexpected increase in the availability of funds, the paper went on to emphasize the importance of considering "the political factor." In short, the President's concern was that in the face of rising expectations, failure to achieve real development "at the grassroots level" could have serious political ramifications.

A central focus of the paper was the administrative and implementation challenges obstructing the realization of development projects, especially in rural areas. The key problem was the time required to implement rural development projects, which meant that it could be "many months before any visible improvements to implementation performance takes place." As a result, it was suggested that a small group of key rural development projects be given special priority, with the criteria being that they be "quickly implementable and have clear objectives attached to them." Underlying these criteria was the goal that "a visible demonstration of Government's development intentions in every village above a certain size can be soon achieved".

This paper set in motion a chain of events that would dominate the machinery of Botswana's government for the coming years. And the explicit political motivation at its core would remain central. At a cabinet meeting in the days following the meeting of Permanent Secretaries the decision was taken to launch the ARDP, a program designed to achieve the rapid and widespread implementation of a set of key rural development projects. Most revealingly, at the meeting on November 23 the President gave the Ministry of Finance and Development Planning one week to produce proposals for a set of rural development projects that would "be visible, on the ground, by a target date of 30 September 1974" (Chambers 1977, 9). It is not a coincidence that the next election was to be held in October 1974. As noted by Danevad (1995: 388), "the political motive behind this sudden increase in spending was obvious."

Acting on this sense of urgency, the Coordinator of Rural Development gave the various Ministries 48 hours to put concrete proposals on the table for consideration. In a confidential savingram on November 28 the Permanent Secretary to the Ministry of Local Government and Lands listed an ambitious set of "visible" rural building targets that it aimed to complete by September of the following year, which included 400 classrooms, 400 teachers' houses, 40 school stores, 40 health posts, 20 clinics, 63 government quarters, 60 council staff quarters, 4 council/government office blocks, 56 customary courts/offices, and 8 public market buildings. It also proposed the completion of a variety of other "visible" non-construction projects, such as the purchase of 20,000 school desks and 50 new council trucks. Along with proposals from the Ministries of Works and Communications, and of Mineral Resources and Water Affairs, these would form the bulk of the ARDP. As a result, "visibility came to mean mainly buildings, roads and water supplies" (Chambers 1977, 10).

Construction was divided between major (large) villages and small villages. With the exception of northern Kgalagadi, work in the major villages was contracted to private contractors, while that in small villages was undertaken either by Council works units or by local builders. Private contractors were generally reluctant to take on work in smaller villages in more remote areas, but their use in major villages freed up the capacity of Council works units to focus on small villages. One implication of the extensive use of private contractors in this way, however, was that they were often very expensive, leading to large cost overruns. Apart from the construction of small dams and livestock auction sale yards, all of the projects undertaken under the ARDP had been proposed in the National Development Plan. But as as result of the ARDP their implementation was vastly accelerated. This was particularly true of primary school facilities and stores, of Government and Council staff housing, and of roads in the major villages. There was also significant acceleration of projects to construct rural health facilities and drill boreholes.

Progress on the construction of primary school buildings in small villages was astonishing. By the start of August 1974, 61 new classrooms had been completed, with a further 122 in progress, of a planned total of 339. The number of new classrooms completed or under construction (183) therefore represented a 10% increase in the total number of classrooms in the entire country in less than a year. In addition, work on 21 (of 81 planned) toilet blocks, 9 (of 41) offices, 58 (of 264) teachers' houses, and 20 (of 78) stores was either completed or underway.[23] By the end of September the number of primary school stores completed or under construction had risen to 35. The rapid pace of the construction of rural health services in small villages was also remarkable. By the end of July work had begun on 7 (of 56) rural health posts, 7 (of 25) clinics, and 5 (of 31) nurses' houses. By the end of September the number of health posts either completed or under construction had increased to 19, with work underway on 11 nurses' houses and 5 maternity wards. Along with the construction of education facilities, there is little doubt that this would have represented a significant, and *visible*, expansion in terms of rural development.

Construction work in the major villages was slower to get started than in small villages, but progress was still hugely impressive. By the target date of September 1974, work on primary school and health facilities had started at 17 different major village sites (of 27 included in the program), and construction of Government and Council staff housing was underway at all sites, with two Government staff quarters already having been completed in Ghanzi. In addition, 30 Customary Court offices had been completed, with work on a further 11 in progress.

---

[23] Figures contained in a savingram from the Coordinator of Rural Development to all Permanent Secretaries, District Commissioners, and District Council Secretaries, November 15, 1974.

As well as buildings, significant headway was made on the construction of new roads. As discussed in Chapter 5, roads are a particularly visible element of development. This is likely to have been especially so in Botswana in the early 1970s, given the extremely limited extent of the existing road network—as noted in Section 6.2, there were only 12 kilometers of paved road at independence in 1966. The ARDP initiated the construction of a series of roads in rural areas and through major villages. As of late September 1974 17 kilometers of a new 62-kilometer road linking Molepolole and Letlhakeng had been graveled, and 18 kilometers of a new 38-kilometer road between Kanye and Mmathethe had been cleared. Although these roads were not due for completion until the middle of the following year, the clearing and graveling work would have been highly visible at this time in advance of the elections. In 7 of the 8 major villages substantial progress had been made on almost 40 kilometers of bitumen road and 30 kilometers of gravel road, with roads in 5 of the villages due for completion before the end of the year. Again, even if not completed, progress on these road projects would have been obvious at the time of the election, with earthmoving underway, gravel laid, and culverting in progress.

Developments in the provision of rural water supplies would have been equally visible. By the end of August 1974 138 boreholes had been drilled, at a rate of 25–30 per month, of which 80 were successful. By mid-September 4 new dams had been completed, with a further 2 due for completion by the end of the month. In addition, by late September construction of water supply projects involving the equipping of boreholes and installation of reticulation piping had been completed in 7 small villages and was underway in a further 6. At the same time in the major villages, more substantial water supply projects involving the provision of pumping equipment and storage tanks had been completed in Kanye, and were in progress in Ramotswa, Mahalapye, Moshupa, and Maun.

In addition to buildings, roads, and water supplies, the ARDP had resulted in a variety of other visible developments by September 1974. The District Councils had between them received 50 new vehicles. And in the major villages 4 livestock sale yards had been completed, with a further 3 under construction. Taken together, these achievements were little short of astonishing. In the space of only ten months the government had driven through a remarkable program of rural construction, in a way that would very likely have dramatically altered the landscape of rural Botswana. The distribution of these works seems to have been spread quite evenly around the country, in a manner that was broadly proportional to the distribution of the population.

Although it is hard to effectively measure the visibility of projects resulting from the ARDP, data from a rare survey undertaken at the time provide suggestive evidence that the impact of the development program was fairly widespread.[24] Across the sample as a whole, 29.5% responded positively to a question asking

---

[24] A survey of political knowledge and attitudes was undertaken in the final stages of the 1974 election campaign, with what was purported to be a broadly representative sample of 853 interviews. Details of the survey are reported in Parson (1977).

whether any new teachers' quarters, roads, latrines, water taps, boreholes, or health clinics had been built in or near their village since the rains ended that year. Although more than 70% of respondents were therefore not conscious of any such development works, this likely underestimates awareness of the ARDP, since it fails to ask about classroom construction, which was the largest component of the program in small villages up to that point. Notably, awareness of ARDP projects was substantially higher among respondents in major villages, where 48.8% said that new developments had taken place, than in small villages where the corresponding proportion was 25.2% (Parson 1976, 396).

Unsurprisingly, this rapid rural development program came at a high cost. As the figures in Table 6.1 show, rural capital expenditure increased almost fourfold between 1973/4 and 1974/5. Although total capital expenditure directed to urban areas was still greater than that spent on rural areas, the difference between the two reduced substantially at this time, such that in the run-up to the 1974 election the distribution of capital was almost equal across urban and rural areas. This represented a remarkable change from the previous four years, during which urban expenditure had far outstripped that directly benefiting the rural majority.

Although the rapid results of the ARDP were certainly impressive, the urgency of its implementation created serious inefficiencies and significant cost overruns. In order to achieve the target of visible outcomes on the ground by the end of September 1974, the government's approach was essentially that money was no object. A Council official reported being told, "Don't worry about the money. We will give it to you as you need it." (quoted in Chambers, 1977). The program of roads through major villages ended up costing almost 40% more than initially estimated, depite reductions in both quality and quantity. This was not simply the result of naive estimates; the cost per kilometer of the major village roads was almost 60% higher than the North–South road, which was completed at the same time and to a higher specification, but outside the remit of the ARDP (Chambers 1977, 9).

Similarly, construction costs for building works in the major villages increased to 54% higher than initial estimates, with the cost of construction per square meter estimated to have been roughly twice as much in major villages than in the smaller villages (Chambers 1977, 14). This highlights the additional expense of undertaking the program at such rapid pace, since contractors were employed in major villages in order to free up the capacity of Council works teams for construction in the smaller villages. In the absence of such urgency the use of large contractors in major villages could have therefore been avoided, and with it significant additional costs.

Questions were also raised about the value and appropriateness of the projects that were undertaken. A Council Works Superintendent stated at the time that, "These buildings are rather strange to us and I do not think that our works teams will be able to maintain them," while an inhabitant of Gaberone questioned "Who the hell wants a tarred road in a village anyway?" (quoted in Chambers, 1977).

Among some Batswana the ARDP was seen for what it was, as 'a building program rather than a development program.' This may have been a slightly uncharitable characterization of a program that undoubtedly led to significant advances in rural development throughout the country. Nevertheless, it highlights a legitimate debate over whether the ARDP represented the optimal approach to development at the time. Clearly it was better to have done it than not, and the urgency of the work had notable positive externalities, including the expansion of administrative capacity of both the central government and the District Councils. But it is equally clear that political motivations undermined the effectiveness of an unprecedented level of development expenditure.

It would be misleading to present Botswana's rapid program of rural development in the early 1970s as entirely cynical or opportunistic. Almost all of the projects undertaken under the auspices of the ARDP had been proposed in the National Development Plan, and unexpected circumstances meant that necessary funds were available earlier than anticipated. But the explicit target of achieving rural development outcomes that would be visible on the ground prior to the next elections, and the pursuance of this target no matter the cost, tells its own story.

6.4.3   The 1974 election

The election in October of 1974 saw the same set of parties competing once again. Due to the creation of a new constituency, thirty-two seats were to be contested. The BDP ran candidates in all thirty-two constituency contests, and between them the BPP, BNF, and BIP fielded twenty-eight. Following its losses in 1969, the BDP campaigned heavily in the Ngwaketse and Kgatla tribal areas (Colclough and McCarthy 1980, 43). The nature of this campaign clearly reflected an acknowledgment of the incentives generated by electoral accountability in the context of a large rural majority.

Campaign
The emphasis of the BDP's 1974 election manifesto could hardly have been more different than that of 1969. In short, this was a manifesto on rural development. From the outset it highlighted the government's recent achievements in improving living standards, expanding access to education, and rapidly increasing the pace of rural development. Unlike the previous manifesto, which had focused primarily on achieving financial independence through economic modernization, this time around an emphasis on social justice was placed front and center. And the manifesto made it quite clear that the achievement of social justice was to come through the continued pursuit of rural development.

The 1974 manifesto dedicated an entire chapter to the topic of rural development. In contrast to 1969, this contained an explicit focus on the provision of services to rural areas, including health clinics, schools, roads, water supplies, and bus services in order to improve the quality of rural life. It also contained a commitment to initiate a rural electrification project, such that "Bright lights will not therefore be confined to our modern connurbations" (BDP 1974, 24). Explicit promises were made to develop agriculture with a range of policies to assist both the livestock and arable sectors, as well as to expand employment opportunities in rural areas, in part by supporting rural industries with reduced rents for businesses in smaller villages. Importantly, with regards to agriculture the manifesto highlighted the government's recent move to establish a grain marketing board in order to control prices and improve marketing.

The Botswana Agricultural Marketing Board (BAMB) was established in early 1974, and acted quickly to purchase large quantities of sorghum through an emergency buying program in order to prop up rapidly decreasing producer prices. Purchases under the program represented about 8% of the total crop from an unusually good annual harvest. Importantly, with immediate cash payments and a minimum purchase of only a single bag, BAMB's policies were designed to benefit smaller farmers—fully 45% of the grain purchased during the emergency program in 1974 came from producers with less than ten bags for sale (Colclough and McCarthy 1980, 133). Not only was this election-year policy therefore clearly pro-rural but by design it sought to address problems of rural inequality that were a grievance for the rural masses.

Unsurprisingly the BDP's manifesto emphasized the achievements of the ARDP in an explicit effort to establish the credibility of its commitment to rural development. This commitment extended even to the goal of encouraging new rural retail outlets in order to "improve the living standards of the poorest consumers" (BDP 1974, 32). Its pledges in the area of health policy were overtly pro-rural, acknowledging that in recent years the development of health services had focused too heavily on urban areas, and promising that in future "Botswana's health services will cater for the majority especially in the rural areas" (BDP 1974, 39). A similar rural focus permeated its commitments on education, with effort taken to highlight the "great impetus" exerted to improving rural primary schools under the ARDP.

Urban development was not completely ignored in the manifesto. Promises were made to reduce urban inequalities and assist in the development of improved urban housing. But even here the manifesto was explicit that "rural development must be given clear priority," and that where choices had to be made urban development would not be possible if it meant diverting resources away from the rural areas (BDP 1974, 36–7). In perhaps the most notable shift, the manifesto rolled back on previous calls for rural residents to achieve development through self-help activities. Highlighting that "self-help activity has regrettably been largely confined to the rural areas," the manifesto made clear not only that the government would be providing basic necessities for the rural areas but also that "the next

BDP Government will expect more self-help efforts from our urban communities" (BDP 1974, 51). Rhetorically at least, the message could hardly have been clearer.

Interestingly, very little mention was made of the benefits that had been targeted to urbanites during this period, in particular through a generous public sector pay review introduced early in 1974. This large increase in public sector salaries was detrimental to the economy, leading to a significant decline in the savings ratio, but the decision was politically rather than economically motivated (Colclough and McCarthy 1980, 73). Despite its strong pro-rural message to the electoral majority, the BDP wished to quietly maintain and develop its support among the urban elites. This slight disconnect between rhetoric and policy was reflected by the balance of capital expenditure. Although much more evenly spread across urban and rural areas than in previous years, this still represented a significant urban skew when the distribution of the population was considered. Therefore while the government's pro-rural rhetoric and policy clearly demonstrated its responsiveness to electoral incentives, this did not come entirely at the expense of urban and elite interests (Danevad, 1995).

The BDP's same pro-rural message was expounded forcefully on the campaign trail. For more than two months prior to the election the BDP leadership toured the country, repeatedly highlighting its achievements in rural development. New health posts and primary schools were flagged up, as were new water resources, livestock facilities, roads, and even post offices.[25] At campaign meetings the President highlighted the significant sums of money allocated to particular areas, such as the 5,000 rand for a pipeline at Botshabelo village,[26] and the total of 1.1 million rand spent on projects in Kgalagado District.[27] In doing so, he sought to underpin his claim that the BDP "do not just talk about rural development and hope thereby to bring it about, we are determined to do something positive about it."[28]

The BDP campaign also sought to emphasize the government's recent policies designed to benefit the rural poor. This included the slashing of primary school fees, which was highlighted alongside a commitment to abolish fees altogether in the near future,[29] and the establishment of the BAMB to tackle problems of falling grain prices.[30] Through these repeated pronouncements on the campaign trail, and in a reflection of its manifesto, the BDP sought to make clear its commitment to prioritize rural development, emphasizing that in order to be "really meaningful," Botswana's development "should not be confined to the urban areas but should also be extended to the rural areas where the majority of our people live."[31]

As in 1969, in the final weeks of the campaign the BDP once again derided the opposition for being narrowly tribalist, and condemned campaigns based on tribal

---

[25] As reported in numerous Botswana Daily News articles between August and October 1974.
[26] Botswana Daily News, October 9, 1974.   [27] Botswana Daily News, September 11, 1974.
[28] Botswana Daily News, September 20, 1974.   [29] Botswana Daily News, August 2, 1974.
[30] Botswana Daily News, August 14, 1974.   [31] Botswana Daily News, September 30, 1974.

differences.[32] In what appears to have been an effort to undercut tribal sympathies and win back support lost in Ngwaketse District President Khama re-instated Seepapitso IV of the Bangwaketse, who had been suspended from performing the functions of the chief the previous year.[33] And in September 1974, despite arguing strongly that it was not done "to achieve any short-term political advantage,"[34] the decision to commence preparations for the issuance of a national currency was no doubt taken in part to bolster the BDP's credentials as the party of national unity and independence. But while the importance of national unity was a feature of the BDP campaign, the overarching message was rural development.

Results

In the event, this message was successful in boosting BDP support. The BDP's share of the votes returned to almost the level of 1965, rising to 77% from the 68% it had received in 1969. The BPP and BNF each retained two of the three seats they had won in 1969, and the BIP hung on to its solitary seat in Okavango. But the BDP was able to win back the Ngwaketse/Kgalagadi seat from the BNF and the Muchudi seat from the BPP, giving it twenty-seven seats in total.[35] The BDP was also able to return the Vice President Quett Masire to a constituency seat (he had sat in the parliament as a specially elected member for the previous term), although he ran in the Ngwaketse/Kgalagadi constituency rather than compete against Bathoen again. Although never seriously in doubt, the BDP's legislative dominance was therefore successfully reasserted by the 1974 elections.

This reassertion was nationwide, with the increase in BDP support being spread widely throughout the country. Fig. 6.4 shows the changes to the BDP's vote share between 1969 and 1974 by constituency. In only six of the thirty-two constituencies did the party win a smaller share of the vote than it had done in 1969, and in five of those the reduction was fairly marginal, equating to a drop of less than 4%. Moreover, in none of these constituencies was a BDP victory under threat—across the six it's lowest vote share was 75.6%, in Moshupa. Three of the constituencies where BDP support fell had been won unopposed in 1969, so the mere presence of an opposition party candidate on the ballot in these constituencies meant that some fall in the BDP's vote share was almost inevitable. One of these three, Moshupa, was the only constituency where the BDP suffered significant losses. While the incumbent BDP member of parliament E.S. Masisi had won the seat unopposed in 1969, in 1974 the BNF candidate G.A.T. Gare won 24% of the votes in the constituency. That Moshupa was previously uncontested by the BNF, and was located in Southern (formerly Ngwaketse) District where BNF support was strongest, means this outlying result was not hugely surprising.

---

[32] Botswana Daily News, October 21, 1974.   [33] Botswana Daily News, October 9, 1974.
[34] Botswana Daily News, September 9, 1974.
[35] The BDP-held Gaborone and Ramotswa constituency had been split in two, increasing the total number of parliamentary constituencies to thirty-two. Both of these were won by the BDP in 1974.

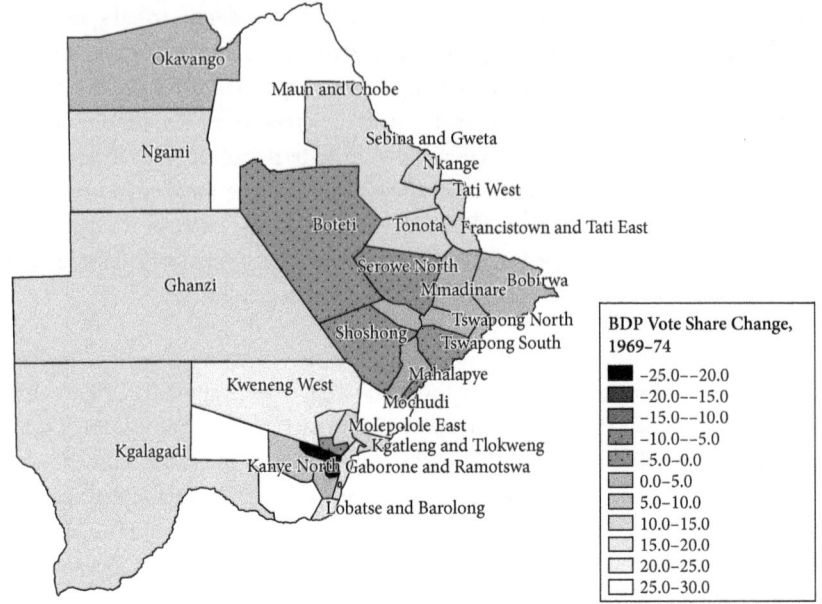

Fig. 6.4 Changes to BDP vote shares, 1969–74, by constituency

Note: Map drawn using boundaries set by 1972 Delimitation Commission.

Comparing Fig. 6.4 to Fig. 6.3, some of the BDP's greatest gains came in constituencies where it had lost most support in 1969. While this will of course have been partly mechanical, due to ceiling effects resulting from the fact that some of the greatest gains were to be had in these areas, it also demonstrates the party's strategic efforts to win back lost support by appealing to rural interests. Fig. 6.4 also demonstrates just how widespread the success of these appeals had been, and how large. In sixteen of the thirty-two constituencies the BDP experienced double-digit gains in its vote share, and in three of these constituencies it increased its share of the vote by more than 25%. The breadth of these gains was reflected again by the results of the concurrent elections for local councils, in more than 80% of which the BDP won seats previously held by opposition parties. Overall then, it is hard to view the 1974 elections as anything other than a resounding success for the BDP Government.

One small fly in this ointment was the continued reduction in turnout. Following the drop between 1965 and 1969, participation fell again from 54.9% in 1969 to only 31.2% in 1974. This was despite the fact that 84.5% of respondents surveyed in the run-up to the election had stated an intention to vote (Parson 1977). As in 1969, the fall in citizen participation may have been due in part to widespread misunderstanding of the electoral process, and in particular the requirement for voters to register in advance. But again, it may also have been driven by voter apathy. As the map in Fig. 6.5 shows, turnout rates varied across the country. That being said, beyond being slightly lower in the most sparsely populated areas of the country, it is hard to discern any obvious pattern in the distribution of this variation, at least in terms of levels of or changes in support for the BDP.

Although it is hard to isolate the factors that catalyzed this resurgence in BDP support, it seems likely that it was due in no small part to the government's efforts to court the support of the rural majority. Survey evidence suggests that these efforts had been successful, with two-thirds of respondents stating that the government had "helped [them] live more comfortably," and 87% of respondents with children stating that the reduction in primary school fees had helped them send their children to school (Parson 1976). These positive evaluations of the government's performance support the idea that efforts to improve living standards and access to basic services, and to ensure the population were aware of these efforts, were working.

As in 1969, in the immediate aftermath of the election the BDP again sought to paint what opposition support there was in tribalist terms, with the President claiming that the seats which went to the opposition were the result of people being given the false impression that the government wanted to do away with the chieftainship.[36] What did not occur this time around was any dramatic shift in government rhetoric; the BDP had successfully established itself as a champion of rural development, to great electoral benefit.

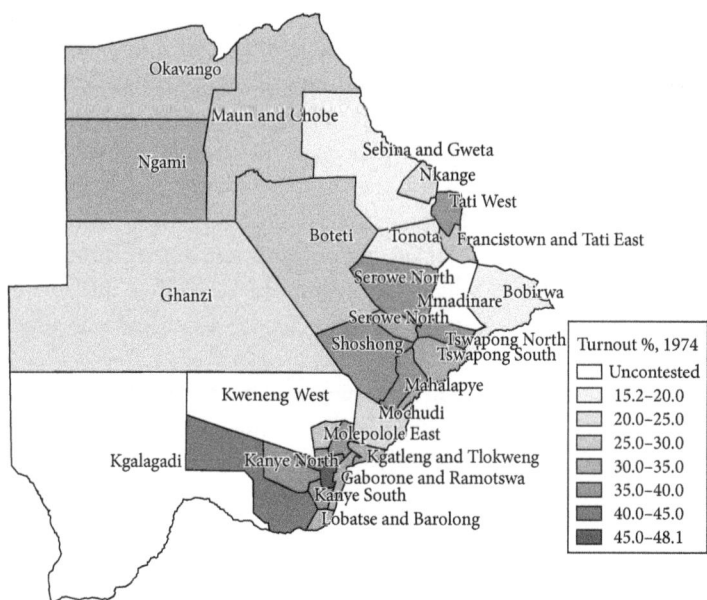

Fig. 6.5 Turnout %, 1974, by constituency

Note: Map drawn using boundaries set by 1972 Delimitation Commission.

---

[36] Botswana Daily News, October 29, 1974.

6.5 Conclusion

Electoral losses in 1969 taught Botswana's government an important lesson: when the vast majority of voters are rural, government policy needs to benefit rural interests. And perhaps even more importantly than that, government policy needs to be *seen* to be beneficial to rural interests. At independence Serestse Khama's government was very likely sincere in its commitment to develop Botswana's rural areas over the long term. And the loosening of financial constraints in the early 1970s no doubt facilitated the efforts to achieve this ahead of schedule. But the nature and timing of the shift in both rhetoric and policy illuminate the impact of electoral incentives at work. In a bid to avoid further losses and claw back past opposition gains, Botswana's government undertook a vast program of rural development with the explicit goal of ensuring results that were visible, on the ground, immediately prior to the coming election. The motivation could hardly have been clearer. The result was the rapid expansion of access to basic services via the construction of primary schools, classrooms, health clinics, roads, and water services. It also resulted in the slashing of primary school fees, and price subsidies to agricultural producers. While certainly beneficial to rural interests, these policies may not have been optimally welfare-enhancing. But they were visible. And so, through them, was the credibility of the government's rhetorical commitment to rural development.

Botswana is in many respects unique in Africa, though it appeared far less so at independence. One factor that set it apart at that time was a commitment to electoral competition that has become near pervasive throughout Africa since the 1990s. By looking closely at the nature of development and electoral competition during Botswana's first decade of independence, therefore, it is possible to observe the operation of the incentives for pro-rural development that are created by electoral incentives. The precise operation of such incentives likely varies over time and space, resulting in differing sets of priorities realized through a variety of different policy tools, of which the Botswanan case offers just one possible configuration. But this case is useful in that it clearly demonstrates the theoretical mechanism at work.

At the same time, and of equal importance, illuminating the operation of the mechanism in this case also conveys the particular benefit of controlling for potential donor pressure for rural development. The robust quantitative evidence presented in earlier chapters makes a compelling cross-national case in support of the book's argument about Africa's rural democracies. But despite the empirical rigor, it is hard to completely separate the effects of electoral incentives from other contemporaneous factors. This historical case achieves that goal, while also providing more nuanced insights into how the theoretical mechanism operates on the ground, in one flavor at least. From this case it is clearer still that, in the context of a rural majority, the incentives created by electoral competition can induce governments to pursue pro-rural policies.

7

Conclusion

Even prior to his election to the Ugandan parliament in 2017, the singer Bobi Wine was perhaps the most audible manifestation of widespread dissatisfaction across Africa's cities. As Uganda's self-styled "Ghetto President," Wine took up the cause of urban disillusionment through his lyrics, lambasting the government for the plight of the urban poor. In one memorable example, his 2014 song *Time Bomb* railed against high prices for services such as education and electricity, likening the raw deal handed to urbanites to struggling with the impossible task of carrying water in a basket. Needless to say, the Ghetto President was more popular in Kampala's slums than in State House, and in 2018 Wine was allegedly beaten viciously by soldiers for his troubles.[1]

Such violent repression of urban protest is sadly not unusual, as examples from Malawi in 2011, Nigeria in 2012, and Sudan in 2018–19 attest. Given the severity of the potential consequences, protesting is unlikely to be an option taken lightly, and its manifestations therefore reflect some of the more extreme degrees of urban dissatisfaction across Africa.[2] But as was demonstrated by the evidence presented in Chapter 3, this dissatisfaction is widespread. And although urban unhappiness no doubt has many causes, chief among them is frustration at the neglect of urban areas by African governments. This neglect, I argue, has its roots in democracy.

In this final chapter I revisit the book's argument and findings, reviewing what has been said, and what has been shown. I also consider the bounds to this argument, highlighting scope conditions, and the extent to which it may generalize beyond the continent. Having done so, I attempt to situate the argument and findings in the context of an ever-changing Africa. In a continent that has been experiencing historically unprecedented rates of urbanization, how should we expect political incentives, and subsequent policies, to evolve? How might pro-rural development affect the nature of urban–rural relations across Africa? How in turn might this influence the nature of electoral competition? And finally, how much cause do we have to be optimistic about democracy in Africa?

---

[1] 'People need hope': Ugandan Pop Star Beaten by Soldiers to Return Home. The Guardian (UK edition), September 19, 2018.

[2] For useful work on protests in Africa see Branch and Mampilly (2015) and Mueller (2018).

Rural Democracy: Elections and Development in Africa. Robin Harding, Oxford University Press (2020).
© Robin Harding.
DOI: 10.1093/oso/9780198851073.001.0001

7.1 Revisiting the Argument

We are frequently told that the re-introduction of multiparty elections across Africa has given rise to fraud, corruption, violence, vote-buying, ethnic mobilization, and conflict. What is less widely reported is that it has also led African governments to court votes through the provision of public goods and services. Although this cannot undo the negative consequences, it is important that this upside be added to the narrative. Meaningful multiparty electoral competition generates incentives for rulers to pursue a mixture of strategies, the particular make-up of which deserves further attention. My argument in this book is that insufficient focus has been directed to one of the ingredients that goes into this mix: the use of public policies to court the votes of a particular majority.

This is important for reasons beyond furthering our understanding of the electoral strategies pursued by African rulers. Convincing claims about the potential developmental benefits of democracy have centered on how structures of accountability resulting from mass electoral competition can induce rulers to broaden the public provision of goods and services. But these beneficial developmental effects are unlikely to be realized where elections are not used to effectively hold rulers accountable. Electoral strategies that involve cheating, clientelism, and ethnic mobilization all reduce the extent to which rulers are held to account for the provision of goods and services. By contrast, where rulers seek votes through public policies designed to provide goods and services, democracy is more likely to foster development.

The evidence provided in this book, particularly that in Chapter 4, demonstrates the positive impact that democracy can have on development. Across Africa the re-introduction of multiparty electoral competition has led to clear improvements in basic education and health outcomes. As the case of Botswana demonstrates, these benefits also extend to other policy areas, and their realization is not isolated to the post-Cold War period. But the argument that I put forward goes further than this, because it makes a claim about *who* benefits from democracy in Africa. Acknowledging that democracy creates both winners and losers, and that rulers seek the support of an electoral majority, the central claim here is that we should expect to see a rural bias in the beneficial impact of democracy across Africa. The reason for this is simple: because a majority of voters in most African countries live in rural areas, meaningful electoral competition creates incentives for governments to implement policies that primarily benefit rural interests.

The urban bias literature famously argued that authoritarian regimes in Africa prioritized urban interests due to the more credible threat of opposition and unrest in cities (Bates, 1981). But where political authority is determined via elections the discrepancies in individual power across urban and rural areas are reduced. In countries with low levels of urbanization, as is the case across much of Africa, this has generated incentives for rulers to prioritize rural interests when making policy. This is not to say that Africa's urban residents have necessarily suffered as a result of electoral competition, since urban unrest remains a risk to rulers. Faced with the need to win an electoral majority, however, rulers in predominantly rural countries seek to balance this risk against the powerful incentive to court rural votes.

It is worth noting at this point that acknowledging that governments in countries with rural majorities have an electoral incentive to prioritize rural interests tells us little about how and when they do so. Pitched necessarily at such a level of abstraction, the argument and analysis do not allow much scope for consideration of agency. As a result, the detailed discussion of Botswana in Chapter 6 provides valuable insights into the operation of agency within the argument. What this discussion makes very clear is that parties, candidates, and campaign rhetoric play a considerable role. Nevertheless, the way that this role is played is likely to vary in important ways across cases and contexts. Precisely what parties and candidates do, and how and when they do these things, are therefore big and important questions, which should be the focus of detailed future research.

As the evidence provided in Chapters 3 and 4 demonstrates, the incentives created by electoral competition in Africa have resulted in the benefits of democracy being felt most strongly in rural areas. The positive average effects of democracy on education and health outcomes is seen only in rural areas, and urbanites are significantly less likely than rural residents to approve of their incumbent's performance with regards to the key issues of creating jobs and improving the living standards of the poor. No doubt at least in part as a result of this, urbanites are also less likely to say that they would vote for incumbents, and less likely to express satisfaction with democracy, than are their rural counterparts. Democracy therefore appears to be working much better for rural Africans than for those in Africa's cities.

These average effects are both interesting and important, but they paint with a broad brush. The argument that in predominantly rural countries elections create incentives to pursue pro-rural policies implies an important conditionality, which helps explain cross-national variation. As the size of the rural majority decreases, so too will the electoral incentives to court rural votes. A growing urban population can more effectively demand recognition in policy-making, such that all of the differential urban–rural effects noted above will be conditional on the level of urbanization. And this is exactly what we see. Across Africa the extent of urban–rural differences in the impact of democracy on basic education and health outcomes dissipates with rising urbanization, as do the magnitudes of urban–rural differences in support for incumbents and satisfaction with democracy.

Evidence that the degree of democracy's rural bias is conditional on urbanization not only provides further support for the central argument but it also has significant implications for a rapidly urbanizing continent, as I discuss below. Before doing so, however, it is helpful to consider the necessary scope conditions that bound the argument, as well as the extent to which it may generalize both within and beyond Africa.

7.2 Generalizability and Scope Conditions

In making an argument about democracy I am inevitably playing with fire. The term is inherently contested, and one will face resistance no matter how it is approached. Nevertheless, the most flame-retardant path is one of transparency: I take democracy in a minimalist sense, as the selection of rulers through competitive elections. Furthermore, and following Przeworski (2018), I take competitive elections to be represented by a meaningful contestation for office, the outcome of which is not entirely predetermined. This conceptual approach may be disagreeable to some, but it provides a clear foundation on which the theoretical argument is built.

It is also a useful approach because it allows me to differentiate between elections in Africa that meet this minimum bound and those that, for a lack of meaningful contestation, do not. As is evidenced by the results in Chapter 4, such a meaningful level of competition appears to be a necessary scope condition for the argument. Although the analysis suggests that improvements to basic education and health outcomes do follow from the introduction of multiparty elections irrespective of their quality, the incentives required for rulers to pursue more demanding electoral strategies that would lead to the type of rural bias expected by the argument do not materialize until the electoral playing field is somewhat more level.

This is not all that surprising. Faced with fairly weak electoral constraints, rulers who are prepared to rig or coerce their way to victory may be expected to choose not to pay the higher costs of designing and implementing policies in order to more carefully construct an electoral majority. If this is the case, then we should not expect such weaker electoral constraints to induce a strategy of pro-rural development. Admittedly the stronger measure of democracy used in the analysis in Chapter 4 is fairly blunt, in that it requires simply that elections have led to the replacement of the chief executive. Again though, this measure has the benefit of transparency. In the cases where we can be more confident that our measure of "democracy" represents a meaningful contestation for office, its presence is sufficient to induce electoral strategies that result in policies of pro-rural development.

A further scope condition is the requirement that voters condition their support, at least in part, on the provision of goods and services. That they do so is a core assumption underlying the theoretical argument, because if it does not hold then there would be little reason to think that politicians will implement pro-rural policies in order to win rural votes. Using data on two different types of goods in Ghana (education and roads), the evidence presented in Chapter 5 provides some support for this assumption, thereby counteracting the prevailing view of electoral choice across Africa being dominated by clientelism and ethnic voting. While these factors may influence vote choice, they are not its only determining factors.

It is important to note that the argument does not require voters to *only* condition their support on the provision of goods and services but that they do so at least in part. Along with findings from existing cross-national work, the evidence from Ghana suggests that African voters are indeed evaluative in this way. Nevertheless, the extent of evaluative voting likely varies across countries, due to factors such as the political salience of ethnicity (which is itself likely to be endogenous to the choice of electoral strategies by political actors), and the extent and efficacy of clientelism. A further limiting factor to evaluative voting may well be the presence of strong liberation parties, such as South Africa's ANC, to whom many voters still feel a strong sense of loyalty and identification. It is possible that the support resulting from such loyalty trumps evaluations of policy performance, though we might well expect such dynamics to be waning with the passage of time. Whatever their nature, the pro-rural logic of democracy may operate with less strength where such factors reduce the evaluative character of voter choice. Whether or not this is true remains an empirical question that future work could usefully seek to address.

Within Africa then, the argument about rural democracy should apply wherever elections represent a meaningful contestation for executive office, and wherever voters condition their support at least in part on the provision of goods and services. And of course, given the effects of urbanization (both theorized and observed), any expectations that democracy will lead to pro-rural outcomes should be limited to countries with rural majorities. Moreover, the extent of any such rural bias will be conditional on, and decreasing in, the level of urbanization. These conditions likely apply to a large number of African countries. Looking outwards, at this point we might also wish to ask whether the argument applies beyond Africa, to countries in other parts of the world. To which instinctively the answer is, why not?

Nothing in the argument about rural democracy is Africa-specific, and therefore where the scope conditions discussed above hold, so too should the claim. Indeed, Varshney's (1995) work provided compelling evidence that the introduction and persistence of democracy in a predominantly rural India led to policies that were beneficial to rural interests. The reason why this argument is so pertinent to countries in Africa is not due to the argument itself but rather to the fact that these countries are so rural. Globally, more people live in cities than in rural areas, with the UN estimating the world's population to be 55% urban in 2018.[3] By continent, only in Africa does the rural population significantly

---

[3] Data from the United Nations: https://population.un.org/wup/Publications/, accessed January 2019.

outnumber urbanites.[4] That said, while the urban proportion of Asia's population in 2018 was approximately 50%, this headline figure masks considerable variation, and many countries in Asia remain predominantly rural (including Pakistan, and the Philippines). As in India then, there seems little reason to think that the argument would not be applicable to these countries, if the necessary scope conditions hold therein.[5]

7.3 Future Developments

> If Parliament cannot come to the ghetto, the ghetto will come to the Parliament.
>
> Bobi Wine, July 11, 2017[6]

As well as its applicability over space, it is also worth considering how the argument is likely to fare over time. Africa is changing, in some ways rapidly so. Of particular relevance to the issue at hand, rates of urbanization are higher in sub-Saharan Africa than anywhere else in the world. In light of this, here I consider the implications of rapid urbanization and the potential changes to urban–rural linkages that may result. In particular, how are political incentives, and subsequent policies, likely to evolve? How might pro-rural development affect the nature of urban–rural relations across Africa? How in turn might this influence the nature of electoral competition? As Bobi Wine suggests, will the interests of the urban poor prevail politically? And finally, how much reason do we have to be optimistic about democracy in Africa?

7.3.1 Urbanization

Although sub-Saharan Africa is still predominantly rural, this is changing quickly. In the three decades since 1990 the proportion of the continent's population living in urban areas increased by more than thirteen percentage points, and by 2035 the continent is projected to be majority urban.[7] Although levels of urbanization vary substantially across Africa, by 2035 almost a dozen more countries across the continent are projected to see their populations become predominantly urban. It seems fairly clear then, given the conditionality of this book's argument with respect to urbanization, that expectations of rural bias in policy formulation will

---

[4] In 2018 60% of the population of sub-Saharan Africa was rural.
[5] The same might also be said of the numerous island-states in the Caribbean and in Melanesia, where rural dwellers predominate.
[6] "When Ghetto Boss Excited Parliament," The Observer (Uganda), July 14, 2017.
[7] All data on urbanization is taken from the United Nations: https://population.un.org/wup/Publications/, accessed January 2019.

dissipate accordingly. One important question that follows is what this does to political incentives, and how electoral strategies will evolve as a result.

Although Bobi Wine may be bringing urban interests to the parliament in Uganda, these interests are unlikely to weigh too heavily on the minds of the leadership in a country whose population remains 75% rural. But the sentiment underlying Wine's declaration that "the ghetto will come to the Parliament" may foreshadow a certain inevitability about politics in Africa. Given the rate of urbanization across the continent, urban constituencies look set to gain increasing influence over policy-making. So what influence will the rising power of cities have on policy?

Following the logic of this book's argument, one fairly intuitive expectation would be that we will see greater attention paid to policies that are valued highly by urbanites. This might include cheaper food, and better and more affordable access to services such as electricity, sanitation, transportation, and post-primary education. In 2017 the government of Ghana, whose population had just a few years previously become predominantly urban, chose to abolish secondary school fees. Although this policy applied to all Ghanaians, urban and rural alike, its benefits have been felt primarily by urbanites who tend to live closer to secondary schools, and who are more likely to have completed the prerequisite primary schooling. Programs to ensure free secondary education are not limited to countries with urban majorities, and have been introduced in Kenya and Uganda, both of which remain predominantly rural. But it may well be the case that such policies are pursued more effectively in countries like Ghana, Gambia, and South Africa, where urbanites represent a majority.

We might also ask whether the rising political influence of urbanites may alter electoral strategies. Interestingly, and despite expectations to the contrary, Nathan (2019) offers compelling evidence that clientelism and ethnic voting persist in urban areas of Ghana. This suggests that increasing urbanization across Africa is unlikely to eradicate these particular responses to electoral competition. At the same time, pro-urban policies such as free secondary education highlight that the mix of electoral strategies will likely continue to include efforts to court voters through the provision of goods and services. Widespread protests against the dangerous state of roads in Accra, which erupted in late 2018, can be taken as evidence of urban Ghanaians clearly voicing their policy demands. As Africa becomes increasingly urban, we should not be surprised if policy-making across the continent follows suit.

7.3.2 Urban–rural linkages

The evidence presented in Chapter 3 suggests that the pursuance of pro-rural policies by Africa's rulers has left urbanites dissatisfied, because their interests are being neglected at the expense of the rural majority. In certain instances this discontent bubbles over, resulting in protest and sometimes violence, but for the most part it remains a largely peaceful grievance. This may be in part because urbanites have respect for the democratic process, even where its consequences are not in their favor. And it may also follow from rulers efforts to balance policy so as to reduce the risk of potentially destabilizing urban protest. In addition to these factors, however, it is also important to acknowledge the possible tempering effect of urban–rural linkages.

The rapid process of urbanization across Africa is being driven in part by migration from rural areas (Awumbila 2017). People are motivated to relocate to urban areas in search of both economic and social opportunities, often moving to find jobs, or to access education facilities. This is certainly not a new phenomenon in Africa, but its scale may be greater at present than at previous points in time. One consequence of migration-driven urban growth is the blurring of urban–rural distinctions. Rural–urban migrants retain rural links, rural identities, and rural interests, to an extent at least. And the inverse is also true; rural residents have personal and economic interests in urban issues, due to flows of migrants and remittances back and forth between cities and the countryside.

If such migration-led urbanization continues apace, the breadth and depth of urban–rural linkages will only increase, which may have important consequences for policy-making. One possibility is that such linkages will continue to limit what might otherwise be a growing likelihood of destabilizing urban opposition, as urban dissatisfaction with pro-rural policies is counterbalanced by urbanites' concern for rural interests. Although it is hard to predict exactly how governments will respond to these dynamics, one possibility is that it may reduce the need for policy-making to pander too much to the demands of any urban discontent.

The potential growth and strength of urban–rural linkages may also serve to prevent Africa's urban transition from leading to 'urban democracy' once urbanites are in the majority. Although the conditionality of the main argument might suggest that policy-making under democracy will become pro-urban once urbanites are in the numerical ascendancy, such an outcome could be offset by the retention of rural interests by rural–urban migrants. If this is the case, we should not necessarily expect continued migrant-driven urbanization to lead to rural neglect, or to urban–rural antagonism or conflict.

At the same time, however, it is important to acknowledge that urban population growth is also driven by natural increase (for example, through greater life expectancies or reduced mortality rates), and the re-designation of previously rural areas as new urban settlements, as well as migration from rural areas (Fox 2017). Although rural migrants contribute significantly to Africa's urban transition, it is also a function of longer life expectancies in urban compared to rural areas, and of the creeping expansion of increasingly sprawling urban agglomerations. In fact, these alternative drivers of urbanization are arguably more important in Africa than they were in Europe and East Asia, where labor opportunities from industrialization drew people in from the countryside.[8] Although rural–urban migration is no doubt significant, much of Africa's urban growth is taking place naturally, with the lack of employment opportunities in manufacturing rendering cities a less attractive destination for potential rural–urban migrants than might have been the case in other contexts.

Natural urban growth has somewhat different implications for urban–rural linkages. The growth of native urban populations, whether these consist of second-, third-, or fourth-generation immigrants, or those with even longer ties to urban locations, inevitably leads to a weakening of urban links to the countryside. As urban–rural linkages become more distant and further removed, so the acknowledgment of and concern for rural interests on the part of urbanites will lessen. If such concerns do in fact have any tempering effect on urban discontent, then natural urban growth may result in rising and more vocal levels of urban discontent at governments' pursuance of pro-rural policies. This in turn could be expected to influence the response of policy-makers seeking to fend off the potentially destabilizing effects of urban protests.

Urbanization is a complex and multi-causal process, the precise nature and consequences of which are specific to any given context. Although in general it seems reasonable to expect that the urban transition across Africa will offset electoral incentives to pursue pro-rural policy agendas, the precise ways in which this will play out should be the focus of future study. Understanding how policy-makers respond to the changing incentives resulting both from rapid urbanization and its consequent impact on urban–rural linkages will become increasingly important, especially as environmental challenges place ever greater burdens on scarce resources. The impact of these dynamics on the nature of electoral competition deserves further attention, both across and within Africa's varied democracies.

7.3.3 Challenges to democracy?

In one sense, the argument put forward in this book provides good reason to be optimistic about democracy in Africa. In contrast to the pessimism generated by the acknowledgment of how African elections are replete with fraud, clientelism, and mobilization along ethnic lines, this book has highlighted that democratic electoral competition also creates incentives for African rulers to court voters with policies that have beneficial developmental implications. These incentives have resulted in significant rural development across the continent, leading to real improvements in essential development outcomes such as infant mortality rates

---

[8] See "Vexed in the City," The Economist, November 8, 2018.

and access to primary education. This has happened, I argue, because African governments are responding to the accountability structures imposed by electoral competition. And therefore in this sense at least, democracy in Africa is working.

Nevertheless, and perhaps in part as a consequence of this, the dynamics of urbanization have the potential to present their own democratic challenges. If the pursuance of pro-rural policy agendas against a background of natural urban growth does exacerbate urban discontent, the result could be a rise in vocal and even violent protests, waves of which could challenge the stability and sustainability of democracy. As it stands, Africa's urbanites remain overwhelmingly supportive of democracy.[9] But it is all too easy to imagine the tide turning, especially in a context of rising concerns about the fragility of supposedly rock-solid democracies in the West.

As well as destabilizing protest, growing urban discontent also has the potential to unleash populist political forces, as the work by Resnick (2014) has highlighted. Such populism can, in certain flavors at least, be anti-democratic in nature. One useful response might be to consider the possibilities of better managing urban discontent through institutional design. The strength of African presidencies means that democracy across the continent is highly majoritarian. Alternative and perhaps more proportional institutional arrangements that provide greater inclusivity may have the potential to reduce tensions, should these arise. Although democracy in Africa may be working, it is still worth considering whether it can be made to work *better*.

Real though they may be, however, the risks posed by these potential challenges should not detract from the importance of acknowledging that mechanisms of democratic accountability appear to be working in Africa. Democratic elections are in essence a means to process the conflicts that inevitably arise between people with heterogeneous preferences (Przeworski 2018, 126). The architecture of democracy is varied, and its design in any given context should be carefully considered so as to most effectively manage potential conflict, and avoid political violence. But as well as representing a means to manage conflict, democracy has the potential to impact positively on development, by making rulers accountable to the mass electorate. If this potential is to be realized these accountability structures need to operate effectively. That they appear to be doing so in Africa, at least in part, should provide cause for optimism.

---

[9] In Round 6 of the Afrobarometer Survey Series carried out in 2014/15, more than three quarters of urbanites expressed support for democracy as the most preferable form of government.

Bibliography

Achen, Christopher. 1995. *Cross-Level Inference*. Chicago, Ill.: University of Chicago Press.

Al-Samarrai, S. 2005. "Financing Primary Education for All: Public Expenditure and Education Outcomes in Africa." *DFID Researching the Issues Series* 57.

Amporfu, Eugenia. 2013. "Equity of the Premium of the Ghanaian National Health Insurance Scheme and the Implications for Achieving Universal Coverage." *International Journal for Equity in Health* 12 (4):1–9.

Angrist, Joshua D. and Jorn-Steffen Pischke. 2009. *Mostly Harmless Econometrics*. Princeton, N.J.: Princeton University Press.

Arriola, Leonardo R. 2013. *Multiethnic Coalitions in Africa: Business Financing of Opposition Election Campaigns*. Cambridge: Cambridge University Press.

Avenstrup, R., X. Liang, and S. Nellemann. 2004. "Kenya, Lesotho, Malawi and Uganda: Universal Primary Education and Poverty Reduction." *A paper presented at the Scaling up Poverty Reduction Conference, Shanghai*, May 25–7, 2004.

Awumbila, Mariama. 2017. "Drivers of Migration and Urbanization in Africa: Key Trends and Issues." *United Nations Background Paper* UN/POP/EGM/2017/12.

Baldwin, Kate. 2016. *The Paradox of Traditional Chiefs in Democratic Africa*. New York: Cambridge University Press.

Bates, Robert H. 1993. "Urban Bias: A Fresh Look." *Journal of Development Studies* 29 (4):219–28.

Bates, Robert H. 1981. *Markets and States in Tropical Africa: The Political Basis of Agricultural Policies*. Berkeley: University of California Press.

Bates, Robert H. and Steven A. Block. 2013. "Revisiting African Agriculture: Institutional Change and Productivity Growth." *The Journal of Politics* 75 (2):372–84.

Bawumia, M. 1998. "Understanding the rural–urban voting patterns in the 1992 Ghanaian presidential election. A closer look at the distributional impact of Ghana's Structural Adjustment Programme." *The Journal of Modern African Studies* 36 (01):47–70.

BDP. 1969. *Botswana Democratic Party Election Manifesto 1969*. Gaberones, Botswana: Botswana Press.

BDP. 1974. *Botswana Democratic Party Election Manifesto 1974*. Gaberones, Botswana: Botswana Press.

Beck, T., G. Clarke, A. Groff, P. Keefer, and P. Walsh. 2001. "New Tools in Comparative Political Economy: The Database of Political Institutions." *The World Bank Economic Review* 15 (1):165–176.

Besley, Tim and Masayuki Kudamatsu. 2006. "Health and Democracy." *American Economic Review* 96 (2):313–18.

Bingham Powell, G. Jr., and Georg S. Vanberg. 2000. "Election Laws, Disproportionality and Median Correspondence: Implications for Two Visions of Democracy." *British Journal of Political Science* 30 (3):383–411.

Bleck, Jaimie and Nicolas van de Walle. 2018. *Electoral Politics in Africa since 1990: Continuity in Change*. New York: Cambridge University Press.

Blimpo, Moussa P., Robin Harding, and Leonard Wantchekon. 2013. "Public Investment in Rural Infrastructure: Some Political Economy Considerations." *Journal of African Economies* 22 (suppl_2):ii57–ii83.

Boone, Catherine. 2014. *Property and Political Order in Africa*. New York: Cambridge University Press.

Boone, Catherine and Michael Wahman. 2015. "Rural Bias in African Electoral Systems: Legacies of Unequal Representation in African Democracies." *Electoral Studies* 40:335–46.

Branch, Adam and Zachariah Mampilly. 2015. *Africa Uprising: Popular Protest and Political Change*. London: Zed Books.

Bratton, Michael. 2008. "Vote Buying and Violence in Nigerian Election Campaigns." *Electoral Studies* 27 (4):621–32.

Bratton, Michael, Ravi Bhavnani, and Tse-Hsin Chen. 2012. "Voting Intentions in Africa: Ethnic, Economic, or Partisan?" *Commonwealth and Comparative Politics* 50 (1):27–52.

Brown, D.S. and A.M. Mobarak. 2009. "The Transforming Power of Democracy: Regime Type and the Distribution of Electricity." *American Political Science Review* 103 (2):193–213.

Bueno de Mesquita, Bruce, Alastair Smith, Randolph M. Siverson, and James D. Morrow. 2005. *The Logic of Political Survival*, Cambridge: MIT Press.

Canache, Damarys, Jeffery J. Mondak, and Mitchell A. Seligson. 2001. "Meaning and Measurement in Cross-National Research on Satisfaction with Democracy." *Public Opinion Quarterly* 65 (4):506–28.

Carlitz, Ruth D. 2017. "Money Flows, Water Trickles: Understanding Patterns of Decentralized Water Provision in Tanzania." *World Development* 93:16–30.

Chambers, Robert. 1977. *Botswana's Accelerated Rural Development Programme 1973-6*. Gaberone, Botswana: The Government Printer.

Chandra, Kanchan. 2004. *Why Ethnic Parties Succeed: Patronage and Ethnic Head Counts in India*. Cambridge: Cambridge University Press.

Chazan, Naomi. 1999. *Politics and Society in Contemporary Africa*. Basingstoke: Lynne Rienner.

Cheeseman, Nic. 2015. *Democracy in Africa: Successes, Failures, and the Struggle for Political Reform*. Cambridge: Cambridge University Press.

Cheeseman, Nic and Brian Klaas. 2018. *How to Rig an Election*. New Haven: Yale University Press.

Cheibub, Jose A., Jennifer Gandhi, and James R. Vreeland. 2010. "Democracy and Dictatorship Revisited." *Public Choice* 143 (1–2):67–101.

Cheibub, Jose Antonio and Adam Przeworski. 1999. Democracy, Elections, and Accountability for Electoral Outcomes. In Adam Przeworski, Susan C. Stokes and Bernard Manin (eds.) Democracy, Accountability, and Representation. Cambridge: Cambridge University Press.

Chen, Jowei and Jonathan Rodden. 2013. "Unintentional Gerrymandering: Political Geography and Electoral Bias in Legislatures." *The Quarterly Journal of Political Science* 8 (3):138–269.

Clausen, Aage R. 1968. "Response Validity: Vote Report." *Public Opinion Quarterly* 32 (4):588–606.

Colclough, C. and S. McCarthy. 1980. *The Political Economy of Botswana: A Study of Growth and Distribution*. Oxford: Oxford University Press.

Collier, David and Steven Levitsky. 2009. *Conceptual Hierarchies in Comparative Research: The Case of Democracy*. In David Collier and John Gerring (eds.) Concepts and Methods in Social Science: The Tradition of Giovanni Sartori. London: Routledge.

Conry-Krutz, Jeffrey. 2009. "African Cities and Incumbent Hostility: Explaining Opposition Success in Urban Areas." Manuscript.

Cutler, David M. and Adriana Lleras-Muney. 2006. "Education and Health: Evaluating Theories and Evidence." *NBER Working Paper Series* (https://www.nber.org/papers/w12352).

Danevad, Andreas. 1995. "Responsiveness in Botswana Politics: Do Elections Matter?" *The Journal of Modern African Studies* 33 (3):381–402.

Darvas, Peter and Alexander Krauss. 2011. *Education in Ghana: Improving Equity, Efficiency and Accountability of Education Service Delivery.* Washington, D.C.: World Bank.

De Groote, H., G. Owuor, C. Doss, J. Ouma, L. Muhammad, and K. Danda. 2005. "The Maize Green Revolution in Kenya Revisited." *eJADE (electronic Journal of Agricultural and Development Economics)(FAO)* 2 (1):32–49.

de Kadt, Daniel and Horacio A. Larreguy. 2018. "Agents of the Regime? Traditional Leaders and Electoral Politics in South Africa." *Journal of Politics* 80 (2):382–99.

Eicher, Carl K. 2003. "Flashback: Fifty Years of Donor Aid to African Agriculture." *Working Paper.*

Elischer, Sebastian. 2013. *Political Parties in Africa: Ethnicity and Party Formation.* Cambridge: Cambridge University Press.

Fearon, James D., Kimuli Kasara, and David D. Laitin. 2007. "Ethnic Minority Rule and Civil War Onset." *American Political Science Review* 101 (1):187–93.

Ferree, Karen. 2004. "The Microfoundations of Ethnic Voting: Evidence from South Africa." *Afrobarometer Working Paper* (40).

Foster, Vivien and Nataliya Pushak. 2011. *Ghana's Infrastructure: A Continental Perspective.* Washington, D.C.: World Bank.

Fox, Roddy. 1996. "Bleak Future for Multi-Party Elections in Kenya." *The Journal of Modern African Studies* 34 (4):597–607.

Fox, Sean. 2017. "Mortality, Migration, and Rural Transformation in Sub-Saharan Africa's Urban Transition." *Journal of Demographic Economics* 83 (1):13–30.

Franck, Raphael and Ilia Rainer. 2012. "Does the Leader's Ethnicity Matter? Ethnic Favoritism, Education, and Health in Sub-Saharan Africa." *American Political Science Review* 106 (2):294–325.

Fridy, K.S. 2007. "The Elephant, Umbrella, and Quarrelling Cocks: Disaggregating Partisanship in Ghana's Fourth Republic." *African Affairs* 106 (423):281–305.

Gelman, Andrew and Jennifer Hill. 2007. *Data Analysis Using Regression and Multilevel/Hierarchical Models.* New York: Cambridge University Press.

Glickman, Harvey. 1995. *Ethnic Conflict and Democratization in Africa.* Atlanta, Georgia: African Studies Association.

Gyimah-Boadi, Emmanuel. 2001. "A Peaceful Turnover in Ghana." *Journal of Democracy* 12 (2):103–7.

Gyimah-Boadi, Emmanuel. 2009. "Another Step Ahead for Ghana." *Journal of Democracy* 20 (2):138–52.

Hainmueller, Jens, Jonathan Mummolo, and Yiqing Xu. 2016. "How Much Should We Trust Estimates from Multiplicative Interaction Models? Simple Tools to Improve Empirical Practice." Available at SSRN: http://ssrn.com/abstract=2739221 or http://dx.doi.org/10.2139/ssrn.2739221.

Harding, Robin. 2015. "Attribution and Accountability: Voting for Roads in Ghana." *World Politics* 67 (4):656–89.

Harding, Robin. 2020. "Who Is Democracy Good For? Elections, Rural Bias, and Health and Education Outcomes in Sub-Saharan Africa." *The Journal of Politics* 82 (1).

Harding, Robin and David Stasavage. 2014. "What Democracy Does (and Doesn't) do for Basic Services: School Fees, School Quality, and African Elections." *The Journal of Politics* 76 (1):229–45.

Hicken, Allen D. 2007. How Do Rules and Institutions Encourage Vote Buying? In Frederic C. Schaffer (ed.) Elections for Sale: The Causes and Consequences of Vote Buying. Boulder, Colo: Lynne Rienner.

Hjort, Jonas. 2010. "Pre-colonial Culture, Post-colonial Economic Success? The Tswana and the African Economic Miracle." *The Economic History Review* 63 (3):688–709.

Holm, John D. and Patrick P. Molutsi. 1992. "State-Society Relations in Botswana: Beginning Liberalization", in Goran Hyden and Michael Bratton (eds.), *Governance and Politics in Africa*. Boulder, Colo: Lynne Rienner.

Horowitz, Donald L. 2000. *Ethnic Groups in Conflict*. Berkeley: University of California Press.

Ichino, Nahomi and Noah L. Nathan. 2013. "Crossing the Line: Local Ethnic Geography and Voting in Ghana." *American Political Science Review* 107 (2):344–61.

Ishiyama, J. and K. Fox. 2006. "What Affects the Strength of Partisan Identity in Sub-Saharan Africa?" *Politics & Policy* 34 (4):748–73.

Ishiyama, John. 2012. "Explaining Ethnic Bloc Voting in Africa." *Democratization* 4 (1):761–88.

Jayne, T.S., Robert J. Myers, and James Nyoroc. 2007. "The effects of NCPB Marketing Policies on Maize Market Prices in Kenya." *Agricultural Economics* 38 (3):313–25.

Jensen, Peter Sandholt and Mogens K. Justesen. 2013. "Poverty and Vote-Buying: Survey-Based Evidence from Africa." *Electoral Studies* 33:220–232.

Kasara, Kimuli. 2007. "Tax Me If You Can: Ethnic Geography, Democracy, and the Taxation of Agriculture in Africa." *American Political Science Review* 101 (01):159–72.

Kasfir, Nelson. 1979. "Explaining Ethnic Political Participation." *World Politics* 31 (3): 365–88.

Kimenyi, M.S. and R.G. Romero. 2008. "Identity, Grievances, and Economic Determinants of Voting in the 2007 Kenyan Elections." Department of Economics Working Paper Series.

King, Gary, Ori Rosen and Martin A. Tanner. 2004. *Ecological Inference: New Methodological Strategies*. Cambridge: Cambridge University Press.

Koter, Dominika. 2016. *Beyond Ethnic Politics in Africa*. New York: Cambridge University Press.

Kramon, Eric. 2009. "Vote-buying and Political Behavior: Estimating and Explaining Vote-buying's Effect on Turnout in Kenya." *Afrobarometer Working Paper* (114).

Kramon, Eric. 2013. Vote Buying and Electoral Turnout in Kenya. In Michael Bratton (ed.) Voting and Democratic Citizenship in Africa. Boulder, Colo: Lynne Rienner.

Kramon, Eric and Daniel N. Posner. 2016. "Ethnic Favoritism in Primary Education in Kenya." *Quarterly Journal of Political Science* 11 (1):1–58.

Kroth, Verena, Valentino Larcinese, and Joachim Wehner. 2016. "A Better Life for All? Democratization and Electrification in Post-Apartheid South Africa." *The Journal of Politics* 78 (3):774–91.

Kudamatsu, Masayuki. 2012. "Has Democratization Reduced Infant Mortality in Sub-Saharan Africa? Evidence from Micro Data." *Journal of the European Economic Association* 10 (6):1294–317.

Kuenzi, Michelle and Gina M. S. Lambright. 2007. "Voter Turnout in Africa's Multiparty Regimes." *Comparative Political Studies* 40 (6):665–90.

Lehoucq, Fabrice E. 2007. When Does a Market for Votes Emerge? Historical and Theoretical Perspectives. In Frederic C. Schaffer (ed.) Elections for Sale: The Causes and Consequences of Vote Buying. Boulder, Colo: Lynne Rienner.

Leith, J. Clark. 2005. *Why Botswana Prospered*. Montreal: McGill-Queen's University Press.

Lemarchand, Rene. 1972. "Political Clientelism and Ethnicity in Tropical Africa: Competing Solidarities and Nation-Building." *American Political Science Review* 66 (1):68–90.

Lemarchand, Rene. 1988. "The State, the Parallel Economy and the Changing Structure of Patronage Systems." In Donald Rothchild and Naomi Chazan (eds.) *The Precarious Balance: State and Society in Africa*. Boulder, Colo.: Westview Press.

Lewis, Peter. 1998. "Political Transition and the Dilemma of Civil Society in Africa." In Peter Lewis (ed.) *Africa: Dilemmas of Development and Change*. Boulder, Colo.: Westview Press.

Lindberg, Staffan I. 2010. "What Accountability Pressures Do MPs in Africa Face and How Do They Respond? Evidence from Ghana." *The Journal of Modern African Studies* 43 (1):117–42.

Lindberg, Staffan I. and Minion K.C. Morrison. 2005. "Exploring Voter Alignments in Africa: Core and Swing Voters in Ghana." *The Journal of Modern African Studies* 43 (4):1–22.

Lipton, M. 1977. *Why Poor People Stay Poor: Urban Bias in World Development*. Cambridge, Mass: Harvard University Press.

Marae, Gerard. 1993. *Ethnicity and Politics in South Africa*. London: Zed Books.

Min, Brian. 2015. *Power and the Vote: Elections and Electricity in the Developing World*. Cambridge: Cambridge University Press.

Mozaffar, Shaheen. 1995. *Ethnic Conflict and Democratization in Africa*. Atlanta, Georgia: African Studies Association.

Mozaffar, Shaheen, James Scarritt, and Glen Galaich. 2003. "Electoral Institutions, Ethnopolitical Cleavages and Party Systems in Africa's Emerging Democracies." *American Political Science Review* 97 (3):220–32.

Mueller, Lisa. 2018. *Political Protest in Contemporary Africa*. New York: Cambridge University Press.

Nathan, Noah L. 2019. *Electoral Politics and Africa's Urban Transition: Class and Ethnicity in Ghana*. Cambridge: Cambridge University Press.

Norris, P. and R. Mattes. 2003. "Does Ethnicity Determine Support for the incumbent Party?" Tech. rep., KSG Working Paper Series.

Nugent, P. 1999. "Living in the Past: Urban, Rural and Ethnic Themes in the 1992 and 1996 Elections in Ghana." *The Journal of Modern African Studies* 37 (02): 287–319.

Omolo, Ken. 2002. "Political Ethnicity in the Democratisation Process." *African Studies* 61 (2):209–21.

Oquaye, Mike. 2006. *Keynote Address: Reflections on Elections in 2004*. In Kwame Boafo-Arthur (ed.) *Voting for Democracy in Ghana: The 2004 Elections in Perspective.*, Accra Ghana: Freedom Publications.

Oucho, John O. 2002. *Undercurrents of Ethnic Conflict in Kenya*. Leiden: Brill.

Parson, Jack. 1976. *Aspects of Political Culture in Botswana: Results of an Exploratory Survey*. Gaberones, Botswana: mimeo.

Parson, Jack. 1977. "Political Culture in Rural Botswana: A Survey Result." *The Journal of Modern African Studies* 15 (4):639–50.

Parsons, Neil, Willie Henderson, and Thomas Tlou. 1995. *Seretse Khama 1921–1980*. South Africa: Macmillan Boleswa.

Picard, Louis A. 1980. "Bureaucrats, Cattle, and Public Policy: Land Tenure Changes in Botswana." *Comparative Political Studies* 13 (3):313–56.

Picard, Louis A. 1987. *The Politics of Development in Botswana: A Model for Success?* Boulder, Colo: Lynne Reinner.

Posner, Daniel N. 2004. "The Political Salience of Cultural Difference: Why Chewas and Tumbukas Are Allies in Zambia and Adversaries in Malawi." *The American Political Science Review* 98 (4):529–45.

Posner, Daniel N. 2005. *Institutions and Ethnic Politics in Africa*. Cambridge: Cambridge University Press.

Posner, Daniel N. and David Simon. 2002. "Economic Conditions and Incumbent Support in Africa's New Democracies: Evidence from Zambia." *Comparative Political Studies* 35 (3):313–36.

Przeworski, Adam. 1999. Minimalist Conception of Democracy: A Defence. In Ian Shapiro and Casiano Hacker-Cordon (eds.) Democracy's Value. Cambridge: Cambridge University Press.

Przeworski, Adam. 2018. *Why Bother With Elections?* Cambridge: Polity Press.

Rabinowitz, Beth S. 2018. *Coups, Rivals and the Modern State: Why Rural Coalitions Matter in Sub-Saharan Africa*. New York: Cambridge University Press.

RB. 1966. *Republic of Botswana Transitional Plan for Social and Economic Development*. Gaberones, Botswana: Government Printer.

RB. 1968. *Republic of Botswana National Development Plan 1968–73*. Gaberones, Botswana: Government Printer.

RB. 1970. *Republic of Botswana National Development Plan 1970–75*. Gaberones, Botswana: Government Printer.

Reinikka, Ritva and Jakob Svensson. 2004. "Local Capture: Evidence from a Central Government Transfer Program in Uganda." *Quarterly Journal of Economics* 119 (2):679–705.

Resnick, Danielle. 2012. "Opposition Parties and the Urban Poor in African Democracies." *Comparative Political Studies* 45 (11):1351–78.

Resnick, Danielle. 2014. *Urban Poverty and Party Populism in African Democracies*. New York: Cambridge University Press.

Robinson, James A., Daron Acemoglu, and Simon Johnson. 2003. *An African Success Story: Botswana*. In Dani Rodrik (ed.) In Search of Prosperity: Analytic Narratives on Economic Growth. Princeton: Princeton University Press.

Ross, Michael. 2006. "Is Democracy Good for the Poor?" *American Journal of Political Science* 50 (4):860–74.

Rubinoff, Arthur G. 1997. "Review of Democracy, Development and the Countryside: Urban-Rural Struggles in India by Ashutosh Varshney." *The Journal of Asian Studies* 56 (1):244–6.

Salih, M.A. Mohamed, ed. 2003. *African Political Parties: Evolution, Institutionalisation, and Governance*. London: Pluto Press.

Samuels, David and Richard Snyder. 2001. "The Value of a Vote: Malapportionment in Comparative Perspective." *British Journal of Political Science* 31 (4):651–71.

Sances, Michael W. 2017. "Attribution Errors in Federalist Systems: When Voters Punish the President for Local Tax Increases." *Journal of Politics* 79 (4):1286–301.

Schedler, Andreas. 2002. "The Menu of Manipulation." *Journal of Democracy* 13 (2):36–50.

Scott, James C. 1969. "Corruption, Machine Politics, and Political Change." *American Political Science Review* 63 (4):1142–58.

Stasavage, D. 2005a. "Democracy and Education Spending in Africa." *American Journal of Political Science* 49 (2):343–58.

Stasavage, David. 2005b. "The Role of Democracy in Uganda's Move to Universal Primary Education." *The Journal of Modern African Studies* 43 (1):53–73.

Steffensen, Jesper. 2006. *Study on Improving Basic Education Through a More Transparent, Equitable and Better Financial and Performance Management*. Copenhagen, Denmark: Nordic Consulting Group.

Throup, David W. and Charles Hornsby. 1998. *Multi-Party Politics in Kenya*. Oxford: James Curry.

van de Walle, Nicolas. 2001. *African Economies and the Politics of Permanent Crisis, 1979–1999*. Cambridge: Cambridge University Press.

van de Walle, Nicolas. 2003. "Presidentialism and Clientelism in Africa's Emerging Party Systems." *The Journal of Modern African Studies* 41 (02):297–321.

van de Walle, Nicolas. 2007. "Meet the New Boss, Same as the Old Boss? The Evolution of Political Clientelism in Africa." In Herbert Kitschelt and Steven Wilkinson (eds.) *Patrons, Clients and Policies*. Cambridge: Cambridge University Press.

Varshney, A. 1995. *Democracy, Development, and the Countryside: Urban-Rural Struggles in India*. Cambridge: Cambridge University Press.

Vengroff, Richard. 1977. *Botswana: Rural Development in the Shadow of Apartheid*. Cranbury, NJ: Fairleigh Dickinson University Press.

Vicente, Pedro and Leonard Wantchekon. 2010. "Clientelism and Vote Buying: Lessons from Field Experiments in West Africa." *Oxford Review of Economic Policy* 25 (2): 292–305.

Vicente, Pedro C. 2014. "Is Vote-buying Effective? Evidence from a Field Experiment in West Africa." *Economic Journal* 124 (574):F356–87.

Wantchekon, Leonard. 2003. "Clientelism and Voting Behavior: Evidence from a Field Experiment in Benin." *World Politics* 55 (3):399–422.

Weghorst, Keith R. and Staffan I. Lindberg. 2011. "Effective Opposition Strategies: Collective Goods or Clientelism?" *Democratization* 18 (5):1193–214.

Youde, J. 2005. "Economics and Government Popularity in Ghana." *Electoral Studies* 24 (1):1–16.

Young, Daniel. 2009a. "Is Clientelism at Work in African Elections? A Study of Voting Behavior in Kenya and Zambia." *Afrobarometer Working Paper* (114).

Young, Daniel. 2009b. "Support You Can Count On? Ethnicity, Partisanship, and Retrospective Voting in Africa." *Afrobarometer Working Paper* (115).

Index

Locators in italic indicate a figure or table; those followed by 'n' indicate chapter note numbers